T5-CVD-877

R0014727779

CHICAGO PUBLIC LIBRARY
HAROLD WASHINGTON LIBRARY CENTER

R0014727779

X

CURRICULUM LEADERS: IMPROVING THEIR INFLUENCE

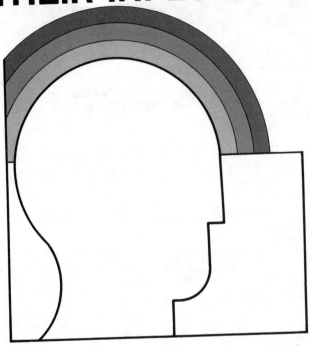

A Report from the ASCD Working Group on the Role, Function, and Preparation of the Curriculum Worker

by   Donald J. Christensen, Chairperson

Eugene Bartoo

Maenelle Dempsey

Lucy Dyer

Veronica Kollar

Charles A. Speiker

Allan Sturges

Edited by Charles A. Speiker

Preface by
Philip L. Hosford

Association for Supervision and Curriculum Development
1701 K Street, N.W. Suite 1100
Washington, D.C. 20006

REF
LB
1570
•A178
1976

cop. 1

Copyright © 1976 by the Association for Supervision and Curriculum Development

All rights reserved. No part of this publication may be reproduced or transmitted in any form or by any means, electronic or mechanical, including photocopy, recording, or any information storage and retrieval system, without permission in writing from the publisher.

The materials printed herein are the expressions of the writers and are not necessarily a statement of policy of the Association.

Stock Number: 611-76084
Library of Congress Catalog Card Number: 76-27590
ISBN 0-87120-081-3

Contents

iii

Preface

PHILIP L. HOSFORD

CURRICULUM changes. Instructional procedures change. They always have and always will. Frequently, those responsible for changes in curriculum and instruction are accused of negligence because of the slowness of change. Less often, they are berated for changes too hastily made. These extremes are diminishing, however, as the professional role and preparation of curriculum leaders become better defined.

Quality in curriculum leadership is currently provided by people competent in both supervision and curriculum development. ASCD is composed of just such people. We have consistently supported efforts to refine and professionalize the role of the curriculum leader and this book represents our latest effort in this cause.

Here, the history of our concern is traced from the ASCD 1946 Yearbook, *Leadership Through Supervision,* through the ASCD 1965 Yearbook, *Role of the Supervisor and Curriculum Director in a Climate of Change.* Results of current surveys indicating who we are and what we have been doing are reported. National interest in improving the preparation and certification of curriculum leaders is documented. Minimum standards are recommended for experience, preparation, and certification of the curriculum leader. The annotated bibliography is an integral part of the book and a valuable contribution to our field.

More important to me, however, is the sense obtained from reading the manuscript—a sense of where we have been and where we are going as curriculum leaders. If curriculum is the set of experiences planned to influence learners toward desired goals, and instruction is the *process* of influencing learners toward those goals, then the similarity of competencies for improving instruction and developing curriculum becomes clear. For example, continuous

urriculum development is essential if the supervisor is to be
helpful to teachers and learners. Similarly, supervisory skills are
ssential in the conduct of modern curriculum development efforts.
One function devoid of the other seems entirely inappropriate in a
democratic education undertaking.

We now know that how we teach is at least as important as
he selection of what we teach. The planned curriculum can be
mproved through continuous curriculum development facilitated
by skillful supervision. The silent curriculum created in the process
of instruction can be improved through supervision and continuous
curriculum development. Supervisory and curriculum development skills are both necessary to facilitate change at the most
appropriate time. Such a combination of knowledge and skills may
evolve as the formal minimum requirement for all of us desiring
to be known as curriculum leaders.

This book should accelerate that evolution.

PHILIP L. HOSFORD, *President 1976–77*
Association for Supervision
and Curriculum Development

THANKS IS EXTENDED to the chief state school officers and university
professors for their cooperation in the preparation of the chapter
on certification. Also, thanks is extended to the ASCD professors of
curriculum who critiqued the bibliography; to the 500 curriculum
workers who participated in the curriculum worker survey; and to
the ASCD units, boards, and individuals who submitted possible
competencies.

Special thanks is extended to Gerald Firth, Gary Griffin, Ben
Harris, Richard Kimpston, Donald Myers, and Edmund Short for
special treatment of the bibliography; to Socius, a social research
firm based in Minnesota, for assisting in the preparation of the
curriculum worker surveys; and to Myra Taub for her diligence in
managing the necessary mailings and in typing the several drafts
of the manuscript.

Final editing of the manuscript and publication of this booklet
were the responsibility of Robert R. Leeper, Associate Director and
Editor, ASCD publications. The production was handled by Elsa
Angell with the assistance of Teola T. Jones and Polly Larson, with
Nancy Olson as Production Manager. The cover and design of this
booklet are by Michael J. Davis.

Foreword

CHARLES A. SPEIKER

A TRULY UPLIFTING EXPERIENCE for me since joining the ASCD staff has been the privilege of participating in and learning from the Working Group on the Role, Function, and Preparation of the Curriculum Worker. Members of this group have unselfishly attended to the charges given them by the Board of Directors of ASCD. They have also demonstrated their ability to blend their systematic and creative qualities in accomplishing the needed tasks and activities.

Initially, the group was commissioned to investigate the current thoughts and practices surrounding the certification of the curriculum worker. As evidenced by the papers contained in this monograph, the group's perspective has broadened to include attention to the role, function, and preparation of the curriculum leader.

Eugene Bartoo presents a historical review and performs a conceptual house cleaning. His paper is intended as the beginning of a framework for guiding further analysis and for issuing recommendations by the working group. The theoretical concerns contained in the Bartoo article suggest that greater attention should be given to the use of terminology and its clarification; and, that the development of any preparation program goes beyond the mere collection of what has been done or what is being done. It would be a flaw to argue that because something *is* being done it *ought* to be done. Similarly, it would be flawed argument to state that merely because certain opinions and perceptions suggest that something ought to be done, that that suggestion be implemented without a theoretical reference. A total overhaul of preparation programs based on sound principles and concepts including those tenets from the field of psychology could be proposed as a result of this paper and its implications.

Allan Sturges presents data to challenge our current practices.

1

After data are in hand on what state certification officials think about and are doing about curriculum leader certification, and after opinions from professors about the preparation and certification of the curriculum leader are gathered, then what? It may be that we must go back to the word "certification" and determine the *whys* and *whats* of certification. What are the assumptions behind the practice of certifying? Did certification develop from a now out-dated control theory? Does certification still continue to serve in preparing the curriculum leader? What expertise was brought to bear when certification requirements were developed? Has anyone shown a connection between certification and ability to perform satisfactorily on the job? Is there a service to the curriculum leader beyond a ritual entrance and sanctioning ceremony? This chapter on certification will stimulate additional questions and investigation as well as clarify the present situation. A preliminary report of this study was included in the March 1975 issue of *Educational Leadership.*[1]

Chapter 3 by Allan Sturges and Veronica Kollar likewise provides a stimulus for numerous questions. The collection of "Competencies for Curriculum Workers" in its raw state alone (967 statements) provides material for further study. Moreover, the same questioning strategy that could be used in the certification issue could be used in the area of competencies. Certification need not imply "competence to do a job satisfactorily." Also, possessing certain competencies does not necessarily imply that a satisfactory job will be done. It could also be said that very few "competencies" are even stated in the raw data, depending on the definition of "competency" used. It may be that a great many professors are equating "behavioral or performance objectives" with "competency." It may be that one could only generate a *competency* based on certain theoretical formulations (which may have no relation to existing courses) and related to the actual functions, duties, tasks, activities, or needs of a particular district. One might call this approach a delicate combination of the notions "reality preparation" and "reality research and theory building." Then, to test the worth of a preparation program, one would possibly interview graduates on the job: finding out what they do, how they do it, and whether or not their preparation was of assistance. At the very least the results of the Sturges-Kollar efforts provide a ground for the generation of recommendations in Chapter 5.

[1] A. W. Sturges. "Certification of Curriculum Workers: Where Do We Stand?" *Educational Leadership* 32 (6): 398-400; March 1975.

An initial attempt at "reality research" was conducted by Donald J. Christensen, whose findings are presented in Chapter 4. These data, coupled with follow-up data collection activities and answers to some of the pertinent questions, could form the basis of a "sanctionable" program of preparation—sanctioned perhaps by a select group of professionals, external to a certification system. This is but one possible image of the future.

Chapter 5 is an attempt to answer the question, "So what?" After a yearlong study, members of the group decided that their recommendations were needed as to the role, function, preparation, and certification of the curriculum leader.

A review of the literature was initiated. This included the use of several descriptors, among which were: "curriculum," "curriculum research," and "curriculum development." The search of the literature of education included use of such sources as the ERIC file, dissertation abstracts, and general literary sources. The "Annotated Bibliography" in this document was prepared by Maenelle Dempsey with assistance from Lucy Dyer, a graduate student in Curriculum and Instruction at Georgia State University, Atlanta.

The annotated bibliography, in the writer's opinion, would have deserved to be published on its own merit. A comprehensively current search has apparently escaped the grasp of students interested in this area. This bibliography is sufficient in size and scope to be manageable and useful.

For the present, the monumental task of determining the current state of certification and preparation of the curriculum leader seems to be launched. Certainly, rigorous study and development will continue to be *relevant* rather than be lost to pessimism, skepticism, or faddism. This monograph represents the necessary first step toward the task of systematically understanding, studying, and improving the role, function, and preparation of the Curriculum Leader.

Introduction: The efforts of a working group

DONALD J. CHRISTENSEN, CHAIRPERSON

In 1973, AN ASCD COMMITTEE began to study the preparation and certification of curriculum workers. The Executive Council recognized a need for continuing the investigation and in May 1974 established a working group to examine further the status of curriculum leaders' certification. Five persons were invited to serve on this working group. The committee was convened by Charles A. Speiker, Associate Director of ASCD, in October of that year in Columbus, Ohio.

At that two-day session a plan to assess the curriculum leaders' certification was formulated. That plan noted a rationale which asserted that before elements of certification could be recommended, there must be an understanding of what curriculum is, what curriculum leaders ought to do, what curriculum leaders presently do, a basis for curriculum and curriculum planning in educational philosophy, and an indication of the status of certification as it presently exists.

To address this plan, members of the committee agreed to undertake separate investigations which focused on:

1. The role, function, training, and attitudes of curriculum leaders

2. State department certification practices, and professors' views on the certification of curriculum leaders

3. Institutes', associations', and individuals' views on competencies of curriculum leaders

4. Research that addressed the preparation of curriculum leaders.

4

The total thrust of this project was a collective effort formulated by the working group. The format of the problem, the nuances of shaping the task, and its direction and focus were arrived at through group process. In addition to the October 1974 meeting, the working group met in December 1974 in Washington, D.C., at the ASCD offices, and in March 1975 during the Annual ASCD Conference in New Orleans.

Finally, in October of 1975, the group met in Alexandria, Virginia, to draw to a close their yearlong effort through the drafting of an initial set of recommendations and a position paper on the role of the curriculum leader.

It is to be noted that parts of this document were prepared by individual members of the working group, to address the task jointly identified by the total group. Accordingly, this document is a collection of individually prepared papers. The authors of these papers recognize the limitations of their studies. This complex field has been discussed, described, and studied for many years, and definitive answers are not easy to come by. However, review of the papers seemed to indicate a thread of concern and agreement. For example, note the similarities as to what the practitioners have said regarding competencies and those listed by professors and others. Furthermore, agreement seemed to be present in the need for certification and in research reported in the annotated bibliography. The data accumulated by the members of the working group were examined in relation to each topic, not collectively. Thus, the combined data are a fertile field for extended analysis of the preparation and role of the curriculum leader at the various levels of service to schools.

Editor's note: Midway through the working group's activities a distinction between curriculum worker and curriculum leader was noted. The term "curriculum worker" applied to most educators—whether central office administrator, teacher, or principal. The term "curriculum leader" applied to that person with primary responsibility for the planning, coordination, and/or management of curriculum activity in a district. It is the concept of the "curriculum leader" that occupied most of the working group's efforts.

Who is the curriculum worker?

EUGENE BARTOO

One wonders how the indefinite, advising-without-authority role of the curriculum specialists managed to prevail as long and as satisfactorily as it did before anyone requested objective evidence of its effectiveness. Had not the academicians, the youth of America, the minority group parents, and the teachers demanded a greater voice in matters of curriculum and instruction, things might have continued indefinitely as they were. But the often disruptive demands of these groups could not be ignored or talked away. Action had to be taken. The role of the administrator as the "official leader" was quite clear (Hein, 1973, p. 376).

~⌀

The schools can no longer safely assume (in the age of the managers) that curriculum leadership is one and the same with school administration; curriculum design integrity and continuing professional leadership in academic affairs demand clear role differentiation beyond any existing precedents, actual or theoretical (Wilson, 1971, p. 71).

~⌀

THE QUESTION IN THE TITLE seems quite simple on the surface. It is certainly germane to the discussion about certification since one presumes that the group to be certified ought to be identified. The question, however, is not simple, but quite complex as can be seen if the question were to be reworded to disclose the reason for asking the question: Is the concept "curriculum worker" sufficiently well defined as to allow the differentiation of curriculum workers from non-curriculum workers?

6

More particularly, the *concept* "curriculum worker" is to be thought of as the *category* "curriculum worker." The concept refers to a classification or grouping of persons on the basis of some sort of rationale. In answering the above question, we seek clarification of a type of concept referred to as a category. This specification is helpful in interpreting various constructions of the curriculum worker concept because it forces the consideration of those logical demands made when one is operating categorically.[1]

There are two ways to define a category. One way is to identify the criteria to be used in determining membership in the category. The other way is to list all the members of the category, or enough of them to make the criteria for membership clear. Either way is sufficient for the purpose of definition. This process seems appropriate for the task of determining whether the curriculum worker category is sufficiently well defined.

The methodology suggested here is that of concept elucidation. The source of information upon which such elucidation is performed is, of course, the literature about the curriculum worker. A strict adherence to the methodology would dictate that only works which contain the term "curriculum worker" should be presented. To do so, however, would limit the analysis so severely that the tacit meaning of the concept would be destroyed. That tacit meaning involves notions that (a) the curriculum worker is the major practitioner in a field of activity and knowledge, (b) the term curriculum worker is a kind of catch-all phrase referring to those practitioners who have also been labeled with several other descriptors, and (c) the category of curriculum worker is not necessarily separate from or identical with the category of, say, curriculum specialist. The argument here is that to only hunt for the specific term curriculum worker is to make the category mistake (Ryle, 1949).

Yearbooks of ASCD

The one organization in the United States that has a history of literature dealing with descriptions of and prescriptions for

---

[1] The logic of categories owes most of its explication to Russell and Whitehead's *Principia Mathematica*. An interesting and widely quoted application of this logic is: Gilbert Ryle. *The Concept of Mind*. New York: Barnes & Noble, 1949. The curriculum field in particular is now finding some of its language scrutinized from this framework; for example: L. B. Daniels. "What Is the Language of the Practical?" *Curriculum Theory Network* 4 (4): 237-61; 1975.

curriculum workers is the Association for Supervision and Curriculum Development (ASCD). That organization has also prompted and promoted the work of the group compiling these working papers.[2]

The last major publication dealing specifically with the curriculum worker concept was ASCD's 1965 Yearbook (ASCD, 1965). Although the title lists the supervisor and the curriculum director as the actors to whom the imminent roles pertain, Carlson, as Chairman of the Committee that planned the publication, reported:

. . . the Committee decided that for the purposes of this Yearbook, since the titles "supervisor" and "curriculum director" often are used interchangeably as to function, the terms might be used in the broadest sense to indicate persons who, either through working with supervisors, principals, or others at a central office level, contribute to the improvement of teaching and/or the implementation and development of curriculum. . . .
As the Yearbook developed, the use of terminology as agreed upon by the Committee was maintained with one exception: additional terms of curriculum worker—curriculum specialists, consultants, curriculum leaders, and instructional leaders—all have been used in the same sense as supervisor and curriculum director (pp. 2-3).

The description, then, of curriculum worker was made by citing the criterion of *function*, that is, "persons who . . . contribute to the improvement of teaching and/or the implementation and development of curriculum." The term curriculum worker was used only once in the Carlson chapter and the verbal conjunction of supervisor and curriculum director was maintained. The positions of the writers of the other chapters of the Yearbook served to support and embellish the criterion of function presented by the Committee.[3]

Van Til's chapter of the Yearbook added a criterion to the definition. Written over a decade ago, the chapter was produced in the midst of national curriculum reform in the subject matter areas. In this chapter Van Til warned of the dangers of ignoring the specialized wisdom that the "professional educator" could bring

[2] The writer wishes to acknowledge the help of the other members of the Working Group on the Role, Function, and Preparation of the Curriculum Leader sponsored by ASCD: Donald Christensen, Maenelle Dempsey, Veronica Kollar, and Allan Sturges. The writer would also like to thank Lucy Dyer, Richard Derr, and Robert Harnack who read earlier drafts of this paper and made many extensive and helpful comments.

[3] It may be important to recognize that the Yearbook Committee membership is not the same as the group of writers who produced the Yearbook, although it can be assumed that the two groups did not work in total isolation.

o the reform effort; a warning that was not generally heeded. While paying respect to the various education specialists, including supervisors and curriculum directors, he wrote of the "role of the *generalist*" as one who "must bear the responsibility for the long and comprehensive view of the curriculum" (pp. 26-27). This criterion was reiterated in the Shafer and Mackenzie chapter (p. 69).

Two more criteria were added to the definition of curriculum worker by Babcock. He resolved the awkward, or perhaps redundant, use of the phrase "supervisor and curriculum director" by referring to such a person as a "curriculum leader" and later as the "curriculum supervisor" or the "supervisor of curriculum" (p. 58). One important criterion added is that of *leadership*. He also stated that the curriculum leader is part of the administrative structure of the school and argued that such a leader should occupy a *staff position*, as opposed to a line position (the second criterion, p. 61).

The other chapters amplify the four criteria of definition presented. Shafer and Mackenzie elaborated on the special functions of the curriculum worker. Klohr itemized some potentially fruitful areas for further work in the theory and research about and for the curriculum worker.

Before investigating other descriptions of the curriculum worker concept it is important to take a second look at the seemingly redundant use of the terms "supervisor" and "curriculum director." One would think that if they are used interchangeably, then they could be dropped for a single term, or that one or the other alone could be used. Each of these options has been taken on occasion by other writers with no apparent loss of meaning. However, the 1965 Yearbook retained the two terms in the title. A partial understanding of this curiosity lies in the genesis and history of ASCD.

ASCD was born in March of 1943 at the Chicago meeting of the National Education Association (NEA). ASCD had been, until 1975, affiliated with the NEA, as had most other professional educator groups. The ASCD department was conceived through the marriage of the Department of Supervisors and Directors of Instruction, founded by the NEA in 1921, to the Society for Curriculum Study, an organization of about the same age as the Department of Supervisors. As the *Journal of Addresses and Proceedings* documents (NEA, 1942):

The Department of Supervisors, founded in 1921 as the Conferenc on Educational Method, has long been concerned with the improvement o instruction. Within the last several years supervision has been inter preted as embracing teacher growth in three large areas, namely, th area of wholesome emotional and mental development, the area of socio economic understanding and adjustment, and the area of professiona competence. The Society for Curriculum Study, organized in 1924 t promote progressive curriculum revision, has more recently emphasize the guidance of teachers in effective personal and professional growth An inevitable result of this similarity of purposes has been increase overlapping of membership (p. 313).

Educational Leadership, the journal of ASCD, presented it first issue in October of 1943, carrying as subheading the titles o the two parent journals: *Educational Method* of the Department of Supervisors and the *Curriculum Journal* of the Society for Cur riculum Study. *Educational Leadership* purported to serve a myriad of constituencies and the membership in the fledgling organizatior was listed as including supervisors, principals, professors of educa tion, curriculum specialists, teachers, and superintendents of schools.

A check back through the ancestry of the 1965 Yearbook is revealing as regards the curriculum worker concept *vis à vis* the supervisor and the curriculum director. ASCD's first Yearbook dealing with persons or the role and function of persons who later seemed to be referred to as curriculum workers was issued in 1946. The title, *Leadership Through Supervision*, is indicative of the nature of the contents—supervision. As will be seen in a later section of this paper, concepts of supervision had changed over the past century and this Yearbook was seminal in that it collected an emerging point of view. As Wilhelms summarized:

. . . the supervisor is an organizer of opportunity, and that good supervision is the facilitation of opportunities. Opportunity for whom? For teachers,.primarily. . . . Opportunity for what? . . .
1. Opportunity for teachers to learn what they need and want to learn
2. Opportunity for teachers to play their full part in policymaking (p. 119).

The policymaking to which Wilhelms referred was identified as "the real results of the whole school's efforts—the philosophy of purpose, the mode of treatment of the student, the content of the curriculum, and the tools used in the task" (p. 121). Wilhelms saw supervision's greatest function as "the institutionalizing of this casual policymaking" (p. 121).

It seems clear from this glimpse at the 1946 Yearbook that the supervisor, if not a curriculum builder, was certainly a curriculum leader. However, most of the book was an attempt at a role description rather than a function description.[4]

The next Yearbook of the curriculum worker lineage was issued in 1951 by ASCD and was entitled *Action for Curriculum Improvement*. The Yearbook purported to offer "the forward looking principles and practices of curriculum improvement now being developed in American schools" (p. v). It can be contrasted with the 1946 Yearbook. While the former was an attempt at role description, the latter was an attempt at a function description. And the persons identified as carrying out the function were "the teacher, the administrator, the supervisor, the specialist" (p. 42). While the book dealt very little with the specialist (although the interpretation seemed to be that of subject matter and materiel expert) there was extended discussion of the teacher's importance in curriculum building; the supervisor's role as "resource person, coordinator, service agent, and consultant" (p. 164) and "divorced from administrative functions" (p. 85); the necessity of an administrator in the central curriculum staff with the "authority and responsibility for education program leadership on all levels included within the particular [school] system" (p. 125).

Leadership for Improving Instruction (1960) was the closest ancestor to the 1965 effort in the curriculum worker lineage. It was the first to use explicitly the term "curriculum worker." Overall, the publication attempted the application of a body of social and behavioral science research to the concept of leadership. The kinds of leaders addressed, according to chairman Hass, were teachers, principals, superintendents, guidance counselors, guidance specialists, supervisors, curriculum specialists, instructional consultants, directors of instruction, and curriculum consultants (pp. 1-4).

Part of Mackenzie's chapter specifically used the term curriculum worker (pp. 67-87). A reading reveals that Mackenzie separated the curriculum worker from the principal, the teacher, the superintendent, the guidance worker, the department head, the business director, and the research director. Cited as examples of titles of curriculum workers were "helping teachers, supervisors,

---

[4] Role is used to mean the *expectations* held as to the behavior of persons in a particular grouping. Function is used to mean *types of activity* to be engaged by the role performer. Function seems to be subsumed in role. The theater metaphor is apt and the example of the hero (role) rescuing-the-victim-in-distress (function) may help to clarify the difference.

coordinators, and directors of instruction" (p. 69). A problem with the role of the curriculum worker (identified as a "major organizational role") was its ambiguity, even more so than those roles of principal and teacher (p. 75).

The Johnson and Wilson chapter took a tangential stance. Listed among those "official leaders [who] work to spearhead action for the improvement of instruction" (p. 108) were two positions closest to Mackenzie's curriculum worker: the instructional consultant considered as being parceled into the three categories of building consultant, the high school department chairperson, and the consultant from the central office (pp. 113-16) ; and the assistant superintendent for instruction or director of instruction (pp. 117-19). No mention was made of the term curriculum worker and the term supervisor was apparently subsumed in the instructional consultant grouping.

This brings us back, then, to the verbal conjunction maintained in the 1965 Yearbook between the supervisor and the curriculum director. In a sense, the conjunction is an acknowledgment of the two areas of effort, the improvement of instruction and the development of curriculum that were now being viewed as one. However, the conjunction was not simply verbal. The four yearbooks, when viewed as a progression, exemplify some concerns in relation to the task of defining the curriculum worker concept.

The definition of the curriculum worker category could not be made by listing a sufficient number of members. Confusion was apparent over the inclusion of certain administrators such as the assistant superintendent for curriculum and instruction. Although titles were recognized as not being important, it was difficult, nevertheless, to identify the audience to which the model actors' roles were being presented without the use of real titles. It was clear that the supervisor permeated the category: necessary for membership, but not sufficient.

The definition of the curriculum worker category was made through the specification of criteria. The 1965 ASCD Yearbook presented four such criteria, each having roots in earlier publications of the association. Each of the criteria has certain problems when applied individually and in concert to the universe of education workers. The criteria are *status leadership, staff position* (as opposed to line), *generalist* (as opposed to educational specialist), and the *function* of the improvement of instruction and/or the development of curriculum.

In the following sections the intention is to elaborate upon each of the criteria in order to help clarify their meaning. This elaboration is to be primarily historical. However, elaboration alone is not sufficient. The confusions, problems, controversy, and perhaps contradiction in the identification of the role of the curriculum worker coalesce around each of the criteria. Therefore, a particular aspect of the confusion, problem, controversy, or contradiction is also to be presented. If curriculum leadership is to be enhanced through role specification, then the problems inherent in the application of these criteria must be solved.

Status Leadership

Although it is generally recognized that many different kinds of education workers contribute to curriculum work, the curriculum worker has been conceived as the leader of this work. Of all the criteria, this criterion seems to have the greatest acceptance; it is the least issue laden.

The notion of the curriculum worker as a status leader is rooted in the two histories of supervision and curriculum development. A definitive history of educational supervision has not been published. However, two textbooks on supervision have sketched an outline of the changing viewpoints of supervision and both show the connection between supervision and administration (Gwynn, 1961; and Lucio and McNeil, 1969). Supervision originally was thought of as inspection and was carried out by the superintendent of schools. As the size of schools increased and as new subjects were added to the curriculum, persons entitled supervisor were employed to aid in the inspection task. In the early 1900's, the industrial efficiency movement captured the thinking of educational leaders causing the task of supervision to shift to the determination of the standards of good teaching (Callahan, 1962). The efforts of the Committee on the Economy of Time of the Department of Superintendence of the NEA during this period were the impetus for two important yearbooks of the National Society for the Study of Education (NSSE).[5] The first was a kind of textbook on supervision done by Franklin Bobbitt (1913) and the second was a presentation of what were known to be the principles of

---

[5] See especially Chapter 6 of Daniel Tanner and Laurel Tanner. *Curriculum Development: Theory Into Practice.* New York: Macmillan Publishing Co., Inc., 1975, for documentation of the Superintendents' Committee and its centrality in the early creation of the connections between supervision and curriculum making.

curriculum making up to that time, the Twenty-Sixth Yearbook (NSSE, 1926).[6] Each of the books signaled the emergence of fields of supervision and curriculum development.

The curriculum worker as a leader has in effect eliminated the teacher from consideration as a curriculum worker by virtue of the status portion of the leadership criterion. While much literature on education workers suggests various leadership roles for each actor by recognizing that there are emergent leaders as well as status leaders, the basic building block of organizations is a dualism: there are leaders and there are non-leaders. This, of course, is a labor-management dualism and an important manifestation of this dualism is collective bargaining. ASCD's 1965 Yearbook was written at the early stages of the collective bargaining movement by teachers, and the writers did not seem to be aware of the ramifications of the movement. The teachers' position regarding who makes up its bargaining group or sphere of interest has been consistent: curriculum workers were not teachers and hence were adversaries. One by one, status leader groups were removed or withdrew from the NEA.

There is a curious paradox in the collective bargaining process. Negotiation is an adversarial process and to the teachers, the adversary includes the curriculum worker. The adversary is to be challenged and overcome (the strategy of the negotiation); at the same time the adversary is to be maintained (the only way for further negotiations to occur). The negotiation process challenges the Weberian concept of authority. The leader has the authority of position and, theoretically, the authority of competence.[7] By being a status leader, the curriculum worker is forced to assume the authority of competence (at something) and, at the same time, defend that competence from attack.

An example of one aspect of competence that creates an existential contradiction for the curriculum worker concerns the deter-

[6] Cremin has identified this book as a sign of the beginning of curriculum as a field of study and practice in: Lawrence Cremin. "Curriculum-making in the United States." *Teachers College Record* 73: 207-20; December 1971. Walker has also recently reviewed this Yearbook for the purpose of examining the roots of the curriculum field in: Decker Walker. "The Curriculum Field in Formation: A Review of the Twenty-Sixth Yearbook of the National Society for the Study of Education." *Curriculum Theory Network* 4 (4): 263-80; 1975.

[7] See: Norman J. Boyan. "The Emergent Role of the Teacher in the Authority Structure of the School." In: Fred D. Carver and Thomas J. Sergiovanni, editors. *Organization and Human Behavior: Focus on Schools.* New York: McGraw-Hill Book Company, 1969, for a discussion of these two uses of the concept of authority.

mination of "good" instruction. The authority for the improvement of instruction has been the primary function of the supervisor. During the scientific management days of Bobbitt, instruction was to be improved through the development of the standards of good teaching. Because those standards could not be determined, that era came to an end (Callahan, 1962). A recent review of research indicates that there is still no scientific basis for the identification of the kinds of teaching that produce certain kinds of learning (Macdonald and Clark, 1973). Now, merit pay, a concept predicated on the determination of good teaching, is often the counter proposal of boards of education to the demand for higher pay by teachers, while the supervisory staff is often asked to construct the proposed package for the board. This places the supervisor in the untenable position of advocating an empirically unsupportable package. One suggested remedy was to create "a strong collegial supervisory structure, unequivocally based on the authority of the competence of senior colleagues" (Boyan, 1969, p. 207). This remedy does nothing with the definition of teacher competence, but simply shifts the *assumed* ability to determine teacher merit to another group.

Staff Position

This criterion of curriculum worker category membership is closely linked to the previously discussed criterion of status leadership. Both criteria are stated in organizational role language, that is, they refer to a generalized organizational structure of schooling and they suggest certain "expectations held by members of a social system . . . for the behavior of incumbents of particular institutional positions. . . ." [8]

The criterion of staff position is contingent upon the criterion of leadership. The argument in support of this contingency is rather straightforward. If the criterion of status leadership is accepted then the concern focuses upon the appropriate structure and style of leadership. As regards structure, most older organizational thinking was patterned after the military and the classes of line and staff exhausted the possible positions. Both of the classes refer to the authority for decision making; line positions have the authority and staff positions advise and suggest. Since

---

[8] This is part of a formal definition of the concept of role offered by Sanford W. Reitman in: "Role Strain and the American Teacher." *School Review* 79 (3): 545.

the conception of the supervisor and the curriculum specialist as types of consultants is well rooted in tradition, the choice of staff is understood. As regards style, there has been an almost religious fanaticism in this country in support of a non-authoritarian, non-autocratic style of leadership. While that style may fit any particular type of leadership position, it seems most appropriate for the staff position.

While Callahan (1962) has explained the influence of the industrial efficiency movement on the thinking and actions of administrators and supervisors for the first two decades of the 20th century, no one has given a similar analysis of the "human relations movement" upon supervision, the model for supervision that succeeded the industrial efficiency model. Scrupski has held that the advent of the human relations model for supervision coincided with the zenith of the progressive education movement (Scrupski, 1975). This explanation seems partially warranted for three reasons:

1. Supervisory thought can be viewed by using the metaphor "the supervisor as a teacher of teachers." Supervisors would, then, tend to view their tasks using a mind set similar to the one used when they were teachers;

2. Many of the supervisors of the 1930's and 1940's must have been educated earlier as teachers under a heavy exposure to progressive pedagogical techniques; and,

3. Democratic human relations was one of the slogans used as a descriptor for the proper behavior for a progressive educator.[9]

It was the growth of the human relations model for supervision that bridged the chronological gap between the demise of the scientific management approach to supervision advocated by Bobbitt (1913) and the birth of ASCD. Clearly, the supervisor of the human relations type would not only have found "line command" over the improvement of instruction a historically ineffective stance, but an inappropriate one as well.

Thus far, little has been said of the history of the curriculum director. The Twenty-Sixth Yearbook of the NSSE was identified

---

[9] The growth and influence of human relations as a managerial ideology was not confined to the schools. As is most often the case, the situation in the schools reflected the situation in society at large. Perrow has traced the underpinnings and the growth of the human relations movement in industrial management thinking. This growth involved a changing conception of labor in response to the union movement; the work of the organizational theorists Chester Barnard and Elton Mayo; and the substantial and controversial empirical support by Roethlisberger and Dickson (the "Hawthorne effect" studies). See: Charles Perrow. *Complex Organizations: A Critical Essay.* Glenview, Illinois: Scott, Foresman and Company, 1972. Chapters 2 and 3.

earlier in this paper as signaling the beginning of curriculum as a field. As Walker has pointed out, the Yearbook suggested two major professional roles: that of the "specialist in curriculum making" and that of the "professor of curriculum" (Walker, 1975b, pp. 14-17). However, Walker's interpretation of the recommendation to create "a separate and autonomous Department of Curriculum-Construction" in the schools, placing the curriculum maker "within the regular school district administrative hierarchy—above the teachers and below the superintendent" is a bit overdrawn (Walker, 1975b, p. 16). Such an interpretation may account for the establishment of the assistant superintendent of curriculum and instruction, a "line" position. It does not explain, however, the increased reliance by large school districts upon the use of outside curriculum specialists (who were many of these same professors of curriculum).

Lawler has described the changing function of the outside curriculum consultant of the 1920's from that of an authority on course of study revision to that of an organizer of groups of teachers to identify and solve instructional problems. The work of the Curriculum Associates of the Eight-Year Study was held as exemplary while Lawler's own study was a case history of the work of the curriculum consultants of the Horace Mann-Lincoln Institute of School Experimentation (Lawler, 1958).

Curriculum consultants generally believe that their role in working for the improvement of instruction is (a) to work with school staffs as resource persons for both curriculum content and process; (b) to act as group members in the search for data and exploration of ideas relative to program planning and maintenance (p. 27).

Furthermore, these outside curriculum consultants viewed the leadership responsibilities of the curriculum worker (Lawler's own term) employees at the schools to include:

1. Providing resource assistance;
2. Participating in problem definition;
3. Freeing the group [or teachers] to carry on curriculum study;
4. Providing coordination;
5. Aiding the principal;
6. Providing released-time for teachers;
7. Facilitating continuity in personnel;
8. Providing and clearing lines of communication (p. 131).

The points of Lawler's work relevant to the staff position of curriculum worker are three: (a) Although Lawler's book deals with outside consultants, the role and function of the consultants were viewed as a model for the curriculum worker[10] ; (b) That this role and function demanded involvement of the school staff in curriculum study instead of an earlier stance by the consultant as an expert-assessor-of-course-of-study-revision working alone; (c) Where the consultants worked with the school curriculum staff, that staff's responsibilities were loaded with non-line-of-command types of action verbs: "freeing," "aiding," and, of course, "facilitating."

We see, then, that both the supervisor and the curriculum director were urged to occupy a persuasive, but not authoritative, stance toward curriculum work. Moreover, this stance was urged for both types of functionaries during the 1930's, 40's, and 50's era.

The concepts of line and staff positions reflect a military model of organizational decision making. That model may not be appropriate for schools and, indeed, it is no longer applied in most modern organizations. Drucker's treatment of management employs the shift of organizational development from determining who is responsible for the work of other people, that is, the command mode, to determining the responsibility for contribution. "Function rather than power has to be the distinctive criterion and the organizing principle" (Drucker, 1973, p. 394). Since it is commonly agreed that the improvement of instruction and the development of curriculum is everyone's responsibility, the focus upon function in the schooling organization creates an identity problem for the curriculum leader. If curriculum development is everyone's responsibility then it is no one person's special responsibility.

This leads us, now, to a discussion of specialism and its relationship to the curriculum leader—the generalist.

Generalist vs. Specialist

The term "generalist" is often juxtaposed with the term "specialist" to imply opposite meanings.[11] Indeed, this juxtaposition is necessary for the dialectic used in order to understand the meaning

[10] It is interesting to note that the Executive Director of the Horace Mann-Lincoln Institute of School Experimentation during the time of Lawler's study was Gordon Mackenzie; the same Mackenzie of the 1951, 1960, and 1965 ASCD Yearbooks.

[11] Quite obviously a crude conception of specialists would negate the necessity of considering a conception of generalist in that any group that has some reason to be grouped is "special." From philosopher-kings to pediatric neurologists, all are specialists. In this sense, the curriculum worker as a generalist is a description of a specialist.

of generalist as it is applied as a criterion toward the task of identifying the curriculum worker. In the Shafer and Mackenzie chapter of the 1965 ASCD Yearbook in which the criterion was identified, both "generalist" and "specialist" were used to delineate types of curriculum workers by referring to the scope of their varied responsibilities. This application of the generalist vs. specialist criterion was apparently derived from an "overarching theory of leadership" in order to "interrelate administrative as well as instructional roles." The generalists were central office administrators who would "assume certain broad functions" while the specialists were consultative, or supervisory personnel who would be "confined to functions peculiar to [their] subject matter area or specialty" (ASCD, 1965, p. 69).

The sense of the meaning of the terms as used here needed elaboration, for the criterion addressed was crucial. However, Shafer and Mackenzie did not follow up their allusion to the generalist-specialist binomial as it related to function. Confusion results when function is the variable offered to determine the boundary between the specialist curriculum worker and the generalist curriculum worker, while span of authority was used as that variable in the stated examples. That is, the difference between the generalist and the specialist is either the number of people under command or the range of subject matter over which there is authority. It is quite possible, as a counter example, that the supervisor of mathematics and the curriculum director function in identical ways; for example, make decisions about scope, sequence, balance, goals, teaching, and evaluating.

Another treatment of the generalist-specialist dichotomy as applied to the curriculum worker was offered by Caswell (1966). Here the sense of specialist was that of subject matter expert and the sense of generalist was of one concerned with the general education of students. In fact, Caswell's generalist was the curriculum worker (his term). He held that the generalist's unique contribution was the "development and consistent implementation of general objectives," "the achievement of a desirable sequence or continuity in the experience of the student," and the "task of developing a reasoned balance of emphasis upon various areas of study" (pp. 214-15).

Schwab's efforts provide yet another source in distinguishing between generalist and specialist as applied to the curriculum worker (Schwab, 1970, 1971, and 1973). The first aspect relates to Schwab's argument that the curriculum field is "moribund" due to its "reliance on theory." This reliance has taken two forms: (a) Theories are adopted from outside the field of education in order to deduce proper school procedures as well as the attempted construction of an inclusive theory of curriculum. (b) The demands of theory are incompatible with the practical demands of curriculum problems (Schwab, 1970). One could argue that if specialism connotes reliance upon identifiable theory for perspective and guidance, then curriculum work is not specialistic.

A second aspect generated by Schwab in the discussion of the specialist-generalist binomial is the generic nature of curriculum problems within schooling. This point reiterates the non-specialistic nature of curriculum work while at the same time it places bounds upon the universe of curriculum work. Theory, by necessity, delimits problems too severely while the method of the practical (deliberation) operates on a satisfiably broad, but nevertheless, identifiable subject matter; that is, schooling problems.[12] Curriculum work is generalist work, yet there are many deliberative actors doing the work who are specialists.

The third point is that the language of the practical places curriculum deliberation within the realm of participation by the specialist. It does not exclude by virtue of specialism many deliberative actors (Daniels, 1975, p. 238). This is not to suggest that the non-specialistic nature of curriculum deliberation is mundane. There are other models of deliberation which demand preparation and training in order to participate, for example, in law and in theology.

Schwab's three articles focused upon the nature of curriculum work and not upon the curriculum worker. Schwab proclaimed that the nature of curriculum work was non-theoretical; it was non-specialistic. Yet it must be done by many different kinds of specialists. One such specialist was identified as a curriculum specialist (Schwab, 1973). On the face of it, the position that there is no isomorphism between curriculum work and the curriculum worker is within the tradition of the curriculum field. "Curriculum planning is a cooperative enterprise" was a slogan that permeated the curriculum literature (for example, Krug, 1957, *passim*). However, Cremin's influential review of curriculum making argued that the establishment of a separate curriculum field and the professionalization of practitioners within that field created such an isomorphism.

[12] This point is made in: Ian Westbury. "The Character of a Curriculum for a 'Practical' Curriculum." *Curriculum Theory Network* 10: 30; Fall 1972.

What it also did, willy-nilly, was to demarcate the analysis and development of the curriculum as the special preserve of a definable group of specialists working within the schools and trained within the education faculty of the university. The consequences of this staking out were prodigious with respect to who would "make" curricula from that time forward and to assumptions under which curriculum-making would proceed (Cremin, 1971).

Cremin's thesis was that the curriculum reform movements of the 1960's were using the same "paradigm of curriculum-making that had prevailed for three-quarters of a century" (p. 216) while purporting to wrest the reins of control from the curriculum profession in order to heal an ailing educational system. The thesis was inaccurate. It is true that the reform movement did intend to "take the responsibility for curriculum-making out of the hands of such curriculum specialists" (Woodring, 1964, p. 6). And it is true, that the paradigm for the new curriculum making was the same paradigm used at the initiation of the curriculum field—a paradigm predicated on a notion of curriculum making as course of study revision.

However, the paradigm for curriculum making had changed since the days of William Torrey Harris and Franklin Bobbitt and the Twenty-Sixth Yearbook of the NSSE. It was the changed paradigm that was the one under attack by the 60's reformers because the changed paradigm was viewed as that of belittling the importance of the subject matter disciplines. This changed paradigm, however, never intended to belittle subject matter; nor did it intend to exclude, or reduce in importance any one of the hallowed triad of learners, society, and subject matter; nor make any one of the three more prominent than the others (Herrick, 1965). The changed paradigm, however, was not well articulated (presumably a job for curriculum theory) nor well verified (only partially accomplished by the Eight-Year Study). The curriculum reform movement stopped any further development of the paradigm by returning curriculum development to materiel production.[13]

Schwab's efforts can be viewed against the experiences of the 1960's and indeed as emanating from those experiences since he was involved in the development of science materials. His efforts can also be viewed as an attempt to add to the development of the paradigm of curriculum making as interrupted by the reform

[13] A much more satisfying account than Cremin's of the purposes behind the 60's curriculum reform movement will be found in: Joel Spring. *The Sorting Machine: National Educational Policy Since 1945.* New York: David McKay Company, Inc., 1976.

movement. A reading of "The Practical 3" places his thought comfortably close to the curriculum planning groups that were proposed prior to World War II. While he identifies the need for a "curriculum specialist," the prescribed functions of that specialist clearly require a breadth of knowledge indicative of a generalist. In the "Arts of Eclectic," the course presumably described for curriculum workers would give quite powerful, but non-specialistic, tools for instructional analysis. Further analysis of the implications of Schwab's work for the functions of the curriculum worker will await another paper. At present, it is clear that "the practical," "the method of deliberation," and "the arts of the eclectic" offer generic elements of some power for development of the curriculum field and its practitioners.

The implication of those elements is not revolutionary in the sense identified by Kuhn (1962). As has been stated earlier, Schwab's efforts are well within the pre-1960 tradition of the curriculum field. The functions of Schwab's curriculum specialist are similar, in kind, to the functions of Caswell's generalist. The major function of that specialist is to allow curriculum planning to be balanced, that is, that each "agent of translation" [14] has equal effect. The knowledge of the curriculum specialist is of types and kinds of curriculum material. The skill of the curriculum specialist is that of coordination. The problem with the Schwab prescription is the distance in time, perhaps in geography, and certainly in effect from the classroom action. The implementation of the product of the planning group is presumably by persons other than members of the group itself. One suspects that such implementation is to be made efficacious by supervisors. This top-down process of curriculum revision is not new. Yet, while the provision of persons who can give support as needed is a welcome relief to standard practice, this continues to project largely a worker role for the teacher.

We now proceed to the final criterion as presented by the 1965 ASCD Yearbook, that of *function*. This is the most important of the four criteria. It follows quite naturally from the previous criterion. If the curriculum worker's role is non-specialistic because of the generic nature of the field, then what are the functions of this role?

[14] In Schwab (1973) the agents identified were subject matter, learners, milieux (community), and teachers. These agents are necessary and sufficient and are to be manifested by persons who have specialized knowledge of each of these agents or areas and who serve on the curriculum-making group as deliberators.

Function

Function, its final criterion, was needed by the 1965 ASCD Yearbook Committee in order to distinguish the category of curriculum worker from the other categories of education workers who might also be "status leaders," occupying "staff positions," and considered "generalists." "Persons who . . . contribute to the improvement of teaching and/or the implementation and development of curriculum" (p. 2) was the criterion identified and it seems to relate to the functions of curriculum workers.

There are really two matters of paramount concern with this criterion. The first is the necessity to delineate the division of labor among education workers and to describe the role set of the curriculum worker. The second is the similarity of the functions of improving instruction and developing curriculum. Both issues must be resolved more adequately than the 1965 Yearbook prescribed and more adequately than they are presently prescribed.

The delineation of the division of labor and role set are concepts of "role theory" from the field of sociology. Essentially, division of labor "refers to the particular complement of specializations for a given domain of behavior and for a specific set of persons." Role set "refers to the complement of specializations characteristic of each behaver" and should occur after the devision of labor has been established (Biddle and Thomas, 1966, p. 40). Klohr recognized this need for the delineation of specialties in order to prevent "role diffusion" and suggested some ways to further the clarification of those specialties (ASCD, 1965, pp. 145-50).

An identification of the various particularized specializations is beyond the scope of this paper.[15] However, it is possible here to shed some light upon the general areas of the improvement of instruction and the development of curriculum. In relation to the concepts of division of labor and role set, the light to be shed concerns two questions:

1. Does the function "the improvement of instruction" and the function "the development of curriculum" place a boundary on the complement of specialization for the curriculum worker? (division of labor)

2. Are both functions the complement of specializations characteristic of each curriculum worker? (role set)

---

[15] See: Allan Sturges and Veronica Kollar, "Competencies for Curriculum Workers," Chapter 3 in this booklet, for a collection of competencies of the curriculum worker as produced by various individuals around the country.

The answer to the first question does not necessarily determine the answer to the second. The ASCD 1965 Yearbook answered the first question affirmatively, but apparently hedged on the answer to the second. That hedging is manifested in some later writings on the curriculum worker and it may be the essence of the curriculum worker certification problem.

If one can accept, for purposes of this paper, that most of the literature on supervision presents various points of view regarding prescription for the improvement of instruction, then this literature should indicate whether curriculum development is seen as part of the role set of the supervisor. A couple of examples would be sufficient to demonstrate that such views exist. These examples must not be obscure. The purpose of this exercise is to focus on what undergirds the issue of curriculum worker certification.

The first example was the supervisory model referred to as "clinical supervision" (Goldhammer, 1969; and Cogan, 1973).[16] The model emphasized supervisor-teacher interaction through techniques of counseling. Of primary importance was the personal growth of the teacher and the assumption that personal growth of the learner would follow.

Our minds struggle for images of a supervision whose principal effect is to expand the sense of gratification experienced by students and teachers and supervisors, gratification in being and gratification in the work they do (Goldhammer, 1969, p. 8).

While Goldhammer rejected curriculum concerns (pp. 3-11, passim), Cogan left curriculum development a possibility through lesson planning, the second phase of his cycle of clinical supervision. However, lesson planning was viewed as the end of a continuum whose origin was some "national charter of education" (p. 106). In a sense, clinical supervision was the high water mark of the human relations type of supervision.

The second example is the emergent work of Sergiovanni and his phrase "human resources supervision" (Sergiovanni, 1975). This type of supervision was viewed as "beyond human relations" in the sense that human relations supervision was based on McGregor's Theory X applied in a "soft" manner whereas human resources supervision is based, more carefully, upon McGregor's Theory Y. Major concerns of the supervisor center around such

---

[16] Although there are differences between each writer's view of clinical supervision, both tests are to be considered as "the model." Both men were involved in the Harvard-Newton Summer Program from which the notion of clinical supervision was developed.

concepts as "motivation," "job enrichment," "hygiene factors" (external rewards or motivators), and "commitment." The Sergiovanni example regards curriculum development in quite a different way than clinical supervision. Where the former rejected curriculum development, the latter splits curriculum. On the one hand, the supervisor must create an environment of job enrichment by giving teachers great decision-making power with regard to curriculum materials and content (pp. 23-24), while on the other hand a basic assumption of the human resources model is

. . . to create an environment in which teachers can contribute their full range of talents *to the accomplishment of school goals* [emphasis mine] (p. 12).

Sergiovanni's work comes out of management theory and makes supervision a managerial responsibility.

Let us now turn around the types of examples sought and present an instance of prescription for the development of curriculum without the concomitant concern for the improvement of instruction.

The example is Joyce's set of propositions for the improvement of the curriculum field (Joyce, 1971).

By focusing on a certain kind of educational institution (the school) and by focusing on functionaries (teachers) whose roles have developed within constraints of that institution, the curriculum field has forced itself to operate within parameters so restrictive that it has been unable to develop strong, validated theory and it has been impotent to improve education (p. 314).

Joyce's consistent view is that curriculum development is a kind of engineering process that precedes institution building. This view coincided with the rise of alternative schooling and the concern for deschooling.

There is a great deal of prescriptive curriculum worker literature that takes neither of the positions outlined earlier; that is, of ignoring either the improvement of instruction or the development of curriculum (for example, Harnack, 1968; Lewis and Miel, 1972; Lucio and McNeil, 1969; Taba, 1962; Tanner and Tanner, 1975). This type of literature is well within the tradition established by the ASCD yearbooks. However, much of that literature has not been able to move beyond the 1965 position: a position recognizing that the two functions of the improvement of instruction and the development of curriculum are similar, perhaps identical. The Tanner and Tanner effort is a case in point. While insisting that curriculum and instruction create an artificial dualism, the prescribed functions for the supervisor are the same as those listed in the Shafer and Mackenzie chapter of the ASCD 1965 Yearbook (Tanner and Tanner, 1975, chapter 13).

There is some value to an argument that could be seen through this sketch:

1. The ASCD 1965 Yearbook represented the high water mark for the attempts to integrate supervision and curriculum development. The Yearbook was written during the frenzy of curriculum and schooling reform through massive spending by the federal government. Thus the volume could be viewed as an attempt to maintain the tradition of the curriculum field.

2. Prior to World War II, as has been outlined, supervision and curriculum development were separate functions with separate practitioners and both areas were moving together.

3. After 1965, both supervision and curriculum development began to move apart again. Curriculum development was spurred by the growing body of "program development" literature studying and reporting upon the "projects" of regional and national scope. Implementation and dissemination became the processes of local curriculum development. Supervision was spurred by the reactive necessities of confrontation through collective bargaining and the active possibilities of the "human potential movement."

4. This moving apart was given some conceptual basis with the analyses of "curriculum" and "instruction" as "preactive" and "active" planning (Macdonald, 1965), or "intended learning outcomes" (Johnson, 1967) and "implementation," respectively.

5. The result, then, could be seen by conceiving of curriculum development as the adoption and management of a series, or set of projects, or programs, and by conceiving of the improvement of instruction as the twofold effort of matching types of teachers to program demands and the improvement of techniques. Both constructions are the province of administration with the power to direct the efforts. The boundaries of authority are determined through negotiated agreements.

Final Comment

This paper has intended to collect the criteria that have been used in the definition of the category of curriculum worker. Some effort has been made to indicate the historical roots of each criterion and some contemporary manifestations of the confusion or contradiction in each of the criteria. This paper has not intended to provide new criteria, but has assumed that if new criteria emerge, they will be related to, or would have grown out of, the extant 1965 statement.

As one views the curriculum worker rather than curriculum work, the type of discourse, of necessity, is limited by organizational considerations. Looking at the worker rather than the work is to consider a functionary. This constraint causes the loss of some of the richness of curriculum as a field of study.

The relationship between the study of curriculum and the practice of curriculum or curriculum work was not explored. Although contemporary thought seems to support the stance that the type of work and competence needed should control the type of study and knowledge presented, this vocational emphasis upon study is not universally accepted, or appealing. The meaning in the study of curriculum *is not wholly* contingent upon the existence of schools. The disposition to act that results from such study is not necessarily predicated upon the existence of only certain kinds of arenas for that action.[17]

Sources

Association for Supervision and Curriculum Development. *Leadership Through Supervision*. 1946 Yearbook. Washington, D.C.: the Association, 1946.

Association for Supervision and Curriculum Development. *Action for Curriculum Improvement*. 1951 Yearbook. Washington, D.C.: the Association, 1951.

Association for Supervision and Curriculum Development. *Leadership for Improving Instruction*. 1960 Yearbook. Washington, D.C.: the Association, 1960.

Association for Supervision and Curriculum Development. *Role of the Supervisor and Curriculum Director in a Climate of Change*. 1965 Yearbook. Washington, D.C.: the Association, 1965.

Bruce J. Biddle and Edwin J. Thomas. *Role Theory: Concepts and Research*. New York: John Wiley & Sons, Inc., 1966.

Franklin Bobbitt. *The Supervision of City Schools*. The Twelfth Yearbook of the National Society for the Study of Education, Part I. Bloomington, Illinois: Public School Publishing Co., 1913.

[17] Curriculum as an academic field of study can be encountered without direct and constant reflection upon schools. This activity is similar to theory building as an enterprise that can be pursued without immediate and direct consequence to schools.

Norman J. Boyan. "The Emergent Role of the Teacher in the Authority Structure of the School." Fred D. Carver and Thomas J. Sergiovanni, editors. *Organization and Human Behavior: Focus on Schools.* New York: McGraw-Hill Book Company, 1969.

Raymond E. Callahan. *Education and the Cult of Efficiency.* Chicago: University of Chicago Press, 1962.

Hollis L. Caswell. "The Generalist—His Unique Contribution." *Educational Leadership* 24 (3): 213-15; December 1966.

Morris L. Cogan. *Clinical Supervision.* Boston: Houghton Mifflin Company, 1973.

Lawrence A. Cremin. "Curriculum Making in the United States." *Teachers College Record* 73: 207-20; December 1971.

L. B. Daniels. "What Is the Language of the Practical?" *Curriculum Theory Network* 4 (4): 237-61; 1975.

Peter Drucker. *Management: Tasks, Responsibilities, Practices.* New York: Harper & Row Publishers, 1973.

Robert Goldhammer. *Clinical Supervision: Special Methods for the Supervision of Teachers.* New York: Holt, Rinehart and Winston, Inc., 1969.

J. Minor Gwynn. *Theory and Practice of Supervision.* New York: Dodd, Mead & Company, 1961.

Robert J. Harnack. *The Teacher: Decision Maker and Curriculum Planner.* Scranton, Pennsylvania: International Textbook Company, 1968.

Margaret G. Hein. "Planning and Organizing for Improved Instruction." William J. Ellena, editor. *Curriculum Handbook for School Executives.* Arlington, Virginia: American Association for School Administrators, 1973. Copright © AASA.

Virgil E. Herrick. *Strategies of Curriculum Development.* Dan W. Anderson, James B. Macdonald, and Frank B. May, editors. Columbus, Ohio: Charles E. Merrill Books, Inc., 1965.

Mauritz Johnson, Jr. "Definitions and Models in Curriculum Theory." *Educational Theory* 17: 127-40; April 1967.

Bruce R. Joyce. "The Curriculum Worker of the Future." Robert M. McClure, editor. *The Curriculum: Retrospect and Prospect.* The Seventieth Yearbook of the National Society for the Study of Education, Part I. Chicago: the Society, 1971.

Edward Krug. *Curriculum Planning.* Revised edition. New York: Harper & Brothers, 1950.

Thomas S. Kuhn. *The Structure of Scientific Revolutions.* Second edition. Volume II, Number 2 of the *International Encyclopedia of Unified Science.* Otto Neurath, Rudolf Carnap, and Charles Morris, editors. Chicago: The University of Chicago Press, 1962.

Marcella R. Lawler. *Curriculum Consultants at Work.* New York: Teachers College Press, Columbia University, 1958.

Arthur J. Lewis and Alice Miel. *Supervision for Improved Instruction: New Challenges, New Responses.* Belmont, California: Wadsworth Publishing Company, Inc., 1972.

William H. Lucio and John D. McNeil. *Supervision: A Synthesis of Thought and Action.* Second edition. New York: McGraw-Hill Book Company, 1969.

James B. Macdonald. "Educational Models for Instruction." In: James B. Macdonald and Robert R. Leeper, editors. *Theories of Instruction.* Washington, D.C.: Association for Supervision and Curriculum Development, 1965.

James B. Macdonald and Dwight F. Clark. "Critical Value Questions and the Analysis of Objectives and Curricula." In: Robert M. W. Travers, editor. *Second Handbook of Research on Teaching.* Chicago: Rand McNally & Company, 1973.

National Education Association. *Journal of Addresses and Proceedings.* San Francisco, California, 1942.

National Society for the Study of Education. *The Foundations and Technique of Curriculum Construction.* Part I and Part II. The Twenty-Sixth Yearbook of the Society. Bloomington, Illinois: Public School Publishing Company, 1926.

Charles Perrow. *Complex Organizations: A Critical Essay.* Glenview, Illinois: Scott, Foresman and Company, 1972.

Sanford W. Reitman. "Role Strain and the American Teacher." *School Review* 79 (3): 543-56; August 1971.

Gilbert Ryle. *The Concept of Mind.* New York: Barnes & Noble, 1949.

Joseph H. Schwab. *The Practical: A Language for Curriculum.* Auxiliary Series, Schools for the 70's. Washington, D.C.: National Education Association, 1970.

Joseph H. Schwab. "The Practical: Arts of Eclectic." *School Review* 79 (4): 493-542; August 1971.

Joseph H. Schwab. "The Practical 3: Translation into Curriculum." *School Review* 81 (4): 501-22; August 1973.

Adam Scrupski. "Education Management: Promise and Failure." In: Nobus Kenneth Schimahara and Adam Scrupski, editors. *Social Forces and Schooling: An Anthropological and Sociological Perspective.* New York: David McKay Company, Inc., 1975.

Thomas J. Sergiovanni. "Human Resource Supervision." In: Thomas J. Sergiovanni, editor. *Professional Supervision for Professional Teachers.* Washington, D.C.: Association for Supervision and Curriculum Development, 1975.

Hilda Taba. *Curriculum Development: Theory and Practice.* New York: Harcourt, Brace & World, Inc., 1962.

Daniel Tanner and Laurel Tanner. *Curriculum Development: Theory into Practice.* New York: Macmillan Publishing Company, 1975.

Decker F. Walker. "The Curriculum Field in Formation: A Review of the Twenty-Sixth Yearbook of the National Society for the Study of Education." *Curriculum Theory Network* 4 (4): 263-80; 1975a.

Decker F. Walker. "Straining To Lift Ourselves." *Curriculum Theory Network* 5 (1): 3-25; 1975b.

Ian Westbury. "The Character of a Curriculum for a 'Practical' Curriculum." *Curriculum Theory Network* 11: 25-36; Fall 1972.

L. Craig Wilson. *The Open Access Curriculum.* Boston: Allyn & Bacon, 1971.

Paul Woodring. "Introduction." In: Robert W. Heath, editor. *New Curricula.* New York: Harper & Row, Publishers, 1964.

2 Certification: state requirements and selected professors' attitudes

ALLAN STURGES

PROBABLY ONE OF THE MOST CONFUSING POSITIONS in education to describe has been that of the curriculum worker. This is well documented in the previous paper. No common title or job description existed; little was known of the specific ways in which the worker should be prepared. And, there was limited information to indicate whether there was any national interest in the question of certification for the curriculum worker. Because of this, a working group was commissioned by ASCD to explore these questions.

Information included in this paper was derived from two surveys. One survey attempted to identify present certification procedures as reported by the certification officer in each state department of education. A similar survey instrument was directed to professors in selected universities whose faculties prepare curriculum workers (leaders).

Results of States' Survey

A questionnaire was sent to a certification officer in each state department of education. After the completed questionnaire were received from the majority of the state officers, a brief summary of their responses was returned to the appropriate officer for verification. The same summary form was sent to those officers who did not respond to the original questionnaire. Responses to the abbreviated summary of questions were received from certification officers in 50 states. These responses are reported in Table 1.

Of the 50 respondents, 34 indicated that curriculum workers should be certified; two responded that curriculum workers should not be certified; the remaining 14 did not respond to the question.

31

Table 1. Responses to Eight Questions Concerning Certification of Curriculum Directors, by State

(Based on Responses Received in 1974)

States	Questions								Explanations
	A Certification required?	B Minimum degree level	C Years of classroom teaching required	D Years of administrative experience required	E Years of supervisory experience required	F Amount of field experiences required	G Amount of intern experiences required	H Should curriculum directors be certified?	
Alabama	Yes[1]	M	2-5	—	—	—	—	Yes	[1] as supervisors of instruction
Alaska	Yes	M[1]	3	—	—	—	1 sem.	Yes	[1] approved programs
Arizona	Yes[1]	M[2]	3	—	—	—	—	—	[1] as supervisor [2] 45 hrs.
Arkansas	Yes	M[1]	2-5	—	—	—	—	Yes	[1] master's plus 15 semester hrs.
California	Yes	M[1]	5	1	—	—	1 yr.	Yes	[1] in academic area under revision
Colorado	Yes	S[1]	2-5	No	No	—	Vary	Yes	[1] approved program
Connecticut	Yes	M[1]	5	No	No	—	—	Yes	[1] master's plus 15 semester hrs.
Delaware	Yes	M[1]	3	No	No	No	No	—	[1] master's plus 30 semester hrs.
Florida	Yes	M[1]	5	No	No	No	No	Yes	[1] rank 2; rank 1 requires doctorate
Georgia	Yes	M[1]	3	Acceptable Experience		No	No	Yes	[1] for "AS-5" certificate
Hawaii	Yes	D	2	5 yrs.[1]	—	No	1 sem.	Yes	[1] 10 yrs. experience, with 5 yrs. in school administration
Idaho	No	—	—	—	—	—	—	—	
Illinois	Yes	M	2	No	No	—	No	Yes	

Indiana	Yes	S	3-5	No	No	—	1 sem.	—	
Iowa	No	—	—	—	—	—	—	—	
Kansas	Yes	M¹	3²	—	—	—	1 sem.	Yes	¹ 48 graduate hrs. ² as certified personnel
Kentucky	Yes	M¹	2-5	No	No	—	—	Yes	¹ master's plus 15 semester hrs.—approved program
Louisiana	No	M¹	5	No	No	—	—	—	¹ for supervisors
Maine	Yes	30 credits beyond B	3	0	0	Part of program	Part of program	Yes	
Maryland	Yes	M¹	2-5	No	No	—	—	Yes	¹ master's plus 15 semester hrs.
Massachusetts	Yes	M	0	No	No	—	—	Yes	
Michigan	No¹	—	—	—	—	—	—	Yes	¹ school districts determine requirements beyond teaching certification
Minnesota	Yes	M¹	3 yrs.	No	No	—	—	Yes	¹ 45 quarter hrs. beyond master's or specialist's for school administration
Mississippi	Yes	M	2-5	No	No	—	No	Yes	
Missouri	No	—	—	—	—	—	—	—	asst. to supt. requires master's degree and appropriate training
Montana	Yes	M	2-5	Yes	No	No	—	No	approved program and recommended by university
Nebraska	Yes	S¹	3	No	No	—²	Yes³	Yes	¹ approved program; ² determined by institution, approved by state; ³ "over extended period"

Table 1 (continued)

States	Questions								Explanations
	A Certification required?	B Minimum degree level	C Years of classroom teaching required	D Years of administrative experience required	E Years of supervisory experience required	F Amount of field experiences required	G Amount of intern experiences required	H Should curriculum directors be certified?	
Nevada	Yes	M	3	—	—	—	—	Yes	
New Hampshire	No	—	—	—	—	—	—	—	
New Jersey	Yes	M	3	No	No	—	—	Yes	
New Mexico	No	—	—	—	—	—	—	Yes	
New York	Yes	S	(2-5 years)		—	—	Yes	Yes	
North Carolina	Yes	M[1]	0	No	No	—	1 sem.	Yes	[1] approved program and recommendation from university competencies met
North Dakota	No	—	—	—	—	—	—	No	
Ohio	Yes	M	3	Yes	1[1]	—	1 sem.	Yes	[1] as member central office administration
Oklahoma	No[1]	M	2-5	No	No	—	—	Yes	[1] not as curr. directors but if asst. supt., then these requirements
Oregon	No[1]	M[2]	3	No	2-5	(Yes)	—	Yes	[1] as supervisors, not curr. directors; [2] 10 semester hrs. beyond master's

Pennsylvania	No	—	—	—	—	—	—	as member of administration team supervisor requires master's in field + 5 yrs. exp. + supv. program
Rhode Island	Yes	M[1]	2-5	No	Yes	—	No	[1] semester hrs. or 36 semester hrs. beyond BA
South Carolina	No	—	—	—	—	—	—	certified in areas of supervision
South Dakota	No	—	—	—	—	—	—	
Tennessee	No	—	—	—	—	—	—	
Texas	Yes	M[1]	3	No	No	1 sem.[2]	Yes	[1] 15 semester hrs. beyond master's; [2] for administrator; none for supervisor
Utah	Yes	M[1]	2-5	No	No	—	Yes	[1] professional certification required in 6 yrs.; requires specialist's degree or doctorate
Vermont	No	—	—	—	—	—	—	
Virginia	No	—	—	—	—	—	Yes	as supervisors
Washington	No	—	—	—	—	—	Yes	adm. and for teacher certificates now held by these people
West Virginia	Yes	M	3	No	—	2	Yes	new standards fall 1974 titled "General Supervisor of Instruction"
Wisconsin	Yes	M[1]	3	No	No	1 sem.	Yes	[1] approved programs; univ. recommends
Wyoming	Yes	M	0-2	No	No	—	Yes	as "Assistant Supt."

Key to abbreviations under Question B: B = bachelor's degree; M = master's degree; S = specialist's degree; D = doctorate.

Thirty-two states indicated that certification was currently required for curriculum workers. Although the survey was concerned with the curriculum worker, some respondents stated that certification was required but attached a footnote indicating that their response was to the position of "supervisor" or "coordinator."

Of the 32 states indicating that certification was required, the level of preparation varied in almost every instance. The required degree ranged from the bachelor's degree to the doctorate. One state required a bachelor's; 18 states required the master's; eight states required 15 semester hours beyond the master's; four required the specialist's; and, one required the doctorate.

The 32 states which had certification requirements indicated that classroom teaching experience was also required. Eleven states indicated that between two and five years teaching experience was required; 14 states required three years experience; and, three required five years experience.

Other types of experience were not as common a requirement for certification. Six of the 32 states required experience in administration, and five required experience in supervision. Twelve of the 32 states indicated that an internship was required as part of the preparation program; eight of the 12 indicated that the internship was for one semester.

Thirty-two state officers indicated that certification was issued through the state department of education, while eight states indicated that school districts and/or preparing universities could determine the requirements.

The content of the programs varied according to the number of hours required in curriculum (from two to twelve semester hours) for the master's and (from six to 30 for the specialist's) and in administration (from 12 to 15 for the master's and from six to 30 for the specialist's). Content required outside professional education courses ranged from 4 percent to 30 percent in the social sciences, from 10 percent to 30 percent in the behavioral sciences, and from 4 percent to 30 percent in the humanities.

Thirty-two respondents indicated specific courses that should be included in a curriculum worker's program. The most frequently recommended courses were recorded in Table 2.

In addition to courses in Table 2, 21 courses were listed in curriculum, administration, media, guidance, and educational psychology. These courses received recommendations by less than 20 percent of the respondents.

Course	Number of Respondents	Percent of Respondents
Elementary Curriculum	15	45
Secondary Curriculum	14	42
Curriculum Construction	13	39
Curriculum Development	13	39
Curriculum Design	10	30
Theories of Curriculum	9	27
Theories of Instruction	7	21
Principles of Supervision	16	48
Elementary Supervision	10	30
Secondary Supervision	8	24
Human Relations	8	24
Principles of Administration	12	36
Leadership	7	21
Measurement and Evaluation	11	33
Research Design	10	30

Table 2. Courses That Are Required for Curriculum Directors as Reported by Certification Officers (32 Respondents)

Several certification officers submitted statements that described their personal opinions on the question of certification. Typical comments included:

"Programs should be minimally stated but at the same time should provide for the development of identified skills and knowledge and the educational growth of the individual. Often programs which are stated in minimal requirements are approved and completed at the same level."

"Permit the college advisor plenty of leeway to 'tailor make' a program that best meets the needs of a particular applicant for admission to the program."

"Certification requirements [should be] minimally stated so that universities have flexibility in designing [the] program with collaboration from public schools, state departments, professionals in the field."

"A competency-based field-centered program for teacher education which requires that graduates of same demonstrate that they have/possess the desired and appropriate knowledges, skills, attitudes, and behaviors to enable children to learn is critical. The program should be primarily field-based and the program's objectives should be derived from the roles and responsibilities of the professional position for which the graduate is being prepared. The manner in which the individual gains the aforementioned competencies is not nearly so crucial as is the person's ability to utilize them."

"Method is just as important as content. Formal courses usually contain lecture, theory, and principles; field work provides [the] opportunity to demonstrate competency in applying knowledge through performance in leadership and interacting."

Summary of Findings—State Departments

Based on reported information, 32 states have certification programs for curriculum workers. Frequently, certification was listed as part of the administrative staff, with requirements not dissimilar to those required of a superintendent. Thirty-three state certification directors recommended that curriculum workers be certified.

Typically, a curriculum worker would have a minimum of a master's degree and be certificated as a teacher with at least three years experience. The program would emphasize content in the areas of curriculum and supervision, followed closely by content in administration and in measurement/evaluation/research design. The program would combine field-related experiences, probably in the form of an internship, with university-based classes. Both method of instruction and content would be considered equally important. The program would probably not be specifically stated but would provide maximum freedom for the preparing institution to provide an appropriate program for each student, and to provide the school district the opportunity to employ the person most appropriately prepared for the district's needs.

Results of Universities Survey

The survey instrument was also sent to the 78 universities which are listed as having doctoral programs for curriculum workers approved by the National Council for the Accreditation of Teacher Education (NCATE). Professors from 50 universities responded to the questions. Forty-six percent recommended that certification remain the responsibility of the state department of education; 20 percent recommended that universities should certify; and, 2 percent (one respondent) recommended that certification should be the responsibility of the state ASCD. Thirty-two percent did not respond to the question.

Sixteen percent of the professors recommended the master's degree as the minimum degree level for curriculum workers, 32 percent recommended the specialist's certificate, and 6 percent recommended the doctorate. Fifty-two percent recommended from two to five years classroom teaching experience; and, 22 percent recommended over five years teaching experience should be required.

The most frequently recommended courses to be included in the preparatory program for curriculum workers are illustrated in Table 3.

Course	Number Responding	Percent
Elementary Curriculum	24	48
Secondary Curriculum	22	44
Curriculum Development	20	40
Curriculum Construction	15	30
Curriculum Design	14	28
Theories of Curriculum	14	28
Theories of Instruction	12	24
Instructional Systems	9	18
Principles of Supervision	28	56
Principles of Administration	25	50
Educational Psychology	24	48
Learning Theories	13	26
Measurement and Evaluation	18	36
Statistics	13	26
Research and Design	11	22

Table 3. Courses That Are Required for Curriculum Directors as Reported by University Professors (50 Respondents)

An additional fifteen courses in administration, media, guidance, and educational psychology received recommendations by less than 20 percent of the respondents.

The professors indicated a wide range in the types of required content outside professional education courses for curriculum workers. In the social sciences, the amount ranged from 10 percent to 40 percent of the total program; in the behavioral sciences and the humanities the range was from 5 percent to 30 percent. Only 12 universities responded to these questions. Several also indicated that specific content was determined on an individual basis.

Forty-three of the 50 professors recommended certification for curriculum workers; only one professor specifically said "no"; six professors did not respond.

Several professors submitted statements of personal opinions on the question of certification. Typical comments included:

"I'm not convinced that certification, as we know it, is effective."

"People in this position are expected to hold an administrator's certificate and a supervisor's certificate."

Four professors specified a concern for the certification of curriculum workers and indicated current studies and attempts to develop a blend of competency-based and traditional programs.

Summary of Findings—Professors

The majority of the professors responding to the questionnaire agreed that curriculum workers should be certificated. There was also general agreement that certification should remain the responsibility of the state department of education, although approved university programs for curriculum workers may be a viable route for certification. There was general agreement on both the content and appropriate experience.

To synthesize responses, professors recommended that a "typical" curriculum worker would have a specialist's certificate, from two to five years classroom teaching experience, and would have course work in elementary and secondary curriculum, curriculum development, principles of administration, principles of supervision, and probably some preparation in evaluation.

There were several questions raised in the results of the survey. For example, there was an inference in the responses that a single definition of the title "curriculum worker" did not exist. Several respondents indicated certification was available under the title "supervisor," "assistant superintendent," or a similar term. There seemed to be a wide range of qualifications expected for curriculum workers. For example, note the degree spread from the bachelor's to the doctoral degree. These responses were from certification officers and professors.

Summary of Findings

There was close agreement between certification officers and university professors in most areas in which information was

Question	State Department	Professor
1. Who should certify?	State Department	State Department
2. Degree level?	Master's plus	Certificate of Specialization
3. Classroom experience?	2-5 years	2-5 years
4. Content of program?	Curriculum, Supervision, Administration, Evaluation	Curriculum, Supervision, Administration, Evaluation
5. Nature of program?	Flexible	Flexible

Table 4. Summary of Responses to Questions by
50 State Certification Officers and 50 University Professors

requested. An indication of areas of agreement and disagreement is shown in Table 4.

Conclusions

This study indicated general agreement for certification of curriculum workers by state departments of education. There also seemed to be agreement that the specific content of the program should be the province of universities, with appropriate input from school districts.

Because of the nature of the position of curriculum worker, the diversity of each school district's unique needs made difficult any final agreement on specific responsibilities of the position. The significance of this issue is emphasized in Chapter 4 by Donald Christensen.

Perhaps influenced by tradition, as well as for management reasons, the position of curriculum worker was usually considered an administrative position, thus requiring rather specific preparation in administration. However, there seems to be agreement that the curriculum worker's preparation should concentrate on the areas of curriculum, with support areas in supervision, administration, and evaluation.

Finally it should be noted that any hard-and-fast conclusions could not be drawn concerning the extent of *actual* agreement between the views of certification directors and of professors. The extenuating circumstances of local political pressure, lack of precise definition, and the unclear nature of curricular issues suggested the need for further study and development.

3 Competencies for curriculum workers

ALLAN STURGES AND VERONICA KOLLAR

FOR SOME TIME, interest has been exhibited in the development of a competency-based preparatory program for curriculum workers. Although literature has referred to the need for such a program, little is known as to the present state of the art.

The ASCD Working Group on the Role, Function, and Preparation of the Curriculum Worker agreed that part of its report to ASCD members would be a status study of current attempts to indicate those competencies that have been identified as appropriate for curriculum workers. This report is based on the findings in the survey.

A letter was mailed to universities and schools requesting information on the competency-based preparation of curriculum workers. A total of 29 individuals responded to the letter. Eighteen responses contained information regarding competency-based programs for curriculum workers. Two of the 18 respondents represented state ASCD groups, seven represented groups of faculty members at universities, one was received from a county board of education. Of the 18 responses providing information, two represented USOE funded projects and one represented Title III funding. See Table 1 for a listing of types of responses.

Reports were received in a variety of ways, ranging from notes to letters to copies of reports that had been distributed or published.

Of the 29 responses to the letter, eighteen submitted information indicating considerable progress had been made in identifying competencies appropriate to and necessary for curriculum workers. A wide range of information was reported, from a position paper to a list of 192 competencies grouped in seven areas. There also was a wide range in the specificity with which the competencies

42

From individual professors	8
From representatives of university faculty groups	7
From state ASCD groups	2
From county school board	1
*Other	11
TOTAL	29

Table 1. Types of Responses Received

* Responses indicating letter was being forwarded to another party, indicating no information was available, etc.

were stated. Table 2 contains summary data on respondents and the areas/number of competencies.

Thirteen of the respondents provided information indicating that considerable research and discussion had been conducted in preparing a list of competencies. These 13 respondents grouped the competencies within areas. These ranged from 12 areas for one respondent to four areas for four respondents.

When these areas were compared, it was found that the inclusion of competencies in curriculum was listed most frequently. Competencies in community relations and in-service were next most frequent, followed by competencies in organization, evaluation, instruction, research, and communication.

As indicated earlier, several different groups responded to the letter that asked for information. A selection of four different types of responses is presented to illustrate the ways in which competencies were identified. These four types that follow include a state ASCD group, a group of university professors, a funded research activity, and research directed primarily through the initiative of a single professor.

1. State ASCD Group

The New York ASCD identified 178 competencies that were grouped in four areas (coordination of curriculum planning and development, definition and application of curriculum theory, designing and applying curriculum research, and providing for the in-service needs of the staff).

The Committee on Professionalization for the NYASCD was formed in 1967. In 1973 the Committee published recommendations for the preparation of curriculum workers in *Impact* (Volume 9, Number 1, pp. 18-22).

Groups	Descriptions
Minnesota ASCD	Certification requirements; 4 areas
New York ASCD	4 areas and 178 competencies
Thomas County School Board	6 areas and 82 competencies for principals
University of Texas	7 areas and 27 competencies for funded special education
University of Pittsburgh	4 areas and 3 levels in each area
University of Minnesota	5 competencies for planning educational change
University of Missouri	5 areas, 5 contexts, and 33 competencies for funded special education
University of Maryland	12 areas and 82 competencies
SUNY—Buffalo	4 areas and 178 competencies based on NYASCD
SUNY—Albany	Tasks for superintendent and consultant

Individuals (Professors)	
Hunkins, University of Washington	Position paper, 8 areas
Myers, Oklahoma State University	17 competencies
McCleary, University of Utah	7 goals and 70 competencies for principals
Bishop, University of Georgia	6 areas and 49 competencies
Phillips, Kent State University	4 areas and approximately 17 competencies
Olson, Temple University	6 competencies
Schunte, University of Wyoming	3 competencies
Ahrens, University of Florida	7 areas and 192 competencies

Table 2. Description of Received Information

2. *Group of University Professors*

A faculty committee at the University of Maryland developed a system through which curriculum workers gained levels of competence, depending on the position for which they were being prepared. There was a level of common learning for everyone, specialized learning for those preparing for positions such as curriculum generalists or media specialists, and further specialization in areas such as curriculum professors, public school administrators, supervisors, educational technologists, or instructional materials.

The program listed 82 competencies grouped in 12 areas, with examples of ways to obtain experience for meeting the competencies.

The report provided the diagram shown in Table 3 to illustrate the levels of learning.

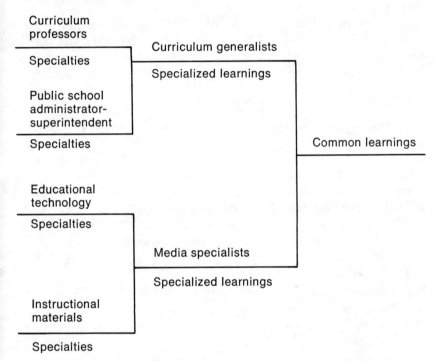

Table 3. Levels of Learning for Curriculum Workers

3. *Funded Research Activity*

The University of Missouri-Columbia, through a USOE grant to develop a training program for special education curriculum specialists, developed a 5″ x 5″ matrix of "Context" (curriculum, instruction, materials and media, communication processes, support systems) and "Functions" (evaluating, developing, training, advising, support systems). Interviews and a review of the literature identified 400 competencies. These were reduced to 100 by field testing and combining items. Seven hundred and twenty educators in 11 states were asked to rate the competencies, to develop the 5″ x 5″ matrix, and to prepare materials to assist students in acquiring the competencies.

4. *Research Directed Primarily by a Professor*

Professor L. E. McCleary, University of Utah, developed a preparatory program for principals that included 70 competencies grouped in seven areas (climate, public relations, staff personnel, instruction, programs and planning, student personnel, management).

A system model was prepared for the development of a competency-based curriculum. A survey of the literature assisted in identifying and grouping competencies. These data permitted their ranking by using the mean as the "index of importance."

ASCD Working Group Method

The list of competencies that was provided by the respondents was coded and typed on 3" x 5" cards. The coding system identified the person(s) who prepared the competency, the category under which it was listed, and the order in which it was listed under the category. This coding and placing all competencies on cards permitted further examination for duplication, differences, etc., while not losing the identity of the person(s) preparing them.

First, all competencies that were reported under a similar heading were combined. This produced stacks of cards under the following headings:

Curriculum
In-service
Community relations
Evaluation
Organization
Instruction
Research
Communication
Other

Because respondents grouped the competencies in a variety of categories (from four to 13 categories) there were some competencies that could, on inspection, be placed in a more specific category. Thus, the decision was made to review each competency and attempt to place it in the category that best described its area of concern.

From this sorting, competencies were grouped into the categories in Table 4.

Two additional categories ("Reporting" and "Working with Groups") were developed but later discarded, and these competen-

Category	Number of Competencies Listed
Curriculum	103
Instruction	62
Organization	34
In-service	215
Administration	145
Leadership	107
Evaluation	118
Research	96
Community relations	31
Communications	56
TOTAL	967

Table 4. Categories In Which Competencies Were Grouped

cies were combined with the categories of "Administration" and "Instruction" respectively.

This grouping included such a range of competencies in each category that additional readings were considered necessary. For example, competencies in the category "Curriculum" ranged from knowledge of theories, philosophies, and social forces to skills in developing a curriculum.

Category	Subcategory	No. of Competencies and (Subtotals)
Curriculum	Theory	18
	Philosophy	9
	Goals	19
	Objectives	20
	Construction	27 (103)
Instruction	Basic information (theory of instruction, etc.)	30
	Applications to instructional improvement	22
	Methods of Implementation	10 (62)
Organization	Knowledge and skills (systems, flow charts)	17
	Processes	11
	Attitudes toward organization	6 (34)
In-service	Personal characteristics to facilitate in-service	53
	Administrative responsibilities in in-service	38
	Skills and applications	106
	Development of leaders	12
	Materials in in-service	6 (215)

Category	Subcategory	No. of Competencies and (Subtotals)	
Administration	Management skills	28	
	Financial and budgetary responsibilities	21	
	Facilities	10	
	Personnel (instructional and non-instructional)	24	
	Materials	14	
	Student accounting and services	10	
	Instructional programs	17	
	(6) (12) (3)		
	Reporting (board, parents, for feedback)	21	(145)
Leadership	Personal attributes	43	
	Change processes	38	
	Resources identification (human/material)	18	
	Leadership with/for students	8	(107)
Evaluation	Knowledge and skills in evaluation	67	
	Application of evaluation (programs, objectives)	29	
	Application of evaluation (personnel)	12	(118)
Research	Knowledge and skills	29	
	Applications in working with staff	9	
	Problem identification	14	
	Design, constraints	26	
	Collection and analysis of data	12	
	Identifying conclusions, reporting, using results	6	(96)
Community relations	Community expectations and needs	2	
	Community involvement in programs	19	
	Involvement of curriculum worker in community	2	
	Community contacts, information dissemination	8	(31)
Communications	Theories and basic knowledge needed	22	
	Applied skills necessary to communicate	25	
	Activities in communication	9	(56)
		967	(967)

Table 5. Categories, Subcategories, and Number of Competencies

Repeated reading and sorting of the competencies resulted in subcategories within each category. The categories and subcategories are shown in Table 5.

Competencies under each of the 44 subcategories were examined for possible duplication. However, because of differences in phrasing it was not possible accurately to identify identical competencies. Under each category, however, an attempt was made to sequence the competencies in order of complexity and/or topic.

Summary

Of the 29 responses to a request for information on competencies for curriculum workers, 18 respondents submitted lists of competencies that had been identified in various ways. These competencies were usually grouped under categories such as "Curriculum," "In-service," and "Community Relations."

Because not all respondents used the same categories for grouping the competencies that were submitted, there were some competencies that could be placed under a more specific category. Thus, the 967 competencies were coded for identification and grouped by those categories that seemed most appropriate. Additional readings of the cards permitted further subgrouping under each category.

Several respondents indicated levels of expertise appropriate for various careers as curriculum workers. For example, one respondent indicated his submitted competencies were for principals, another indicated some were basic to several positions, and others for specific positions such as curriculum professors. In most instances, the various levels of expertise were inferred by the kind of knowledge expected and the types of applications.

To illustrate the various categories and position referents, the diagram shown in Table 6 was developed.

If each cell contained the competencies identified by the appropriate category and grouped by the subcategories, the illustration would be a rather complete summary of the survey.

The total list of competencies gave a very detailed description of actual and proposed preparation programs for curriculum workers, as viewed by respondents. Considerable effort was expended by several experts in identifying these competencies; and, there was general agreement regarding the necessary areas of competence. Yet, variance seemed to be in the degree of specificity with which the competencies were described and the level of learning expected of the student.

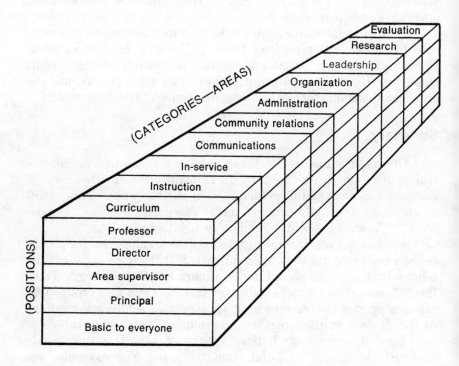

Table 6. Illustration of the Various Categories and Position Referents

Based on information in this study, there seemed to be or actually was:

1. Agreement that curriculum workers should be competent in curriculum, instruction, in-service, leadership, organization, administration, research, evaluation, communications, and community relations;

2. Information available on levels of competency for various specialties within the general heading of "curriculum workers";

3. A number of competencies available that were appropriate for curriculum workers; and,

4. Information that illustrated ways in which these competencies could be reached.

The accurate description of responsibilities of curriculum workers has not been available to this date. If the compiled list accurately reflected the necessary competencies of curriculum workers at several levels, perhaps there could be an opportunity to develop more systematic preparatory and certification programs and more adequately describe the curriculum workers' responsibilities to school patrons, board members, and colleagues in other areas of education. These competencies could eventually provide valuable information to a number of educators, particularly to professors who are charged with the preparation of curriculum workers.

4 The curriculum worker today

DONALD J. CHRISTENSEN

WHO IS THE CURRICULUM WORKER TODAY? What are the tasks, concerns, satisfactions, and career lines of the curriculum worker? Where does the curriculum worker's role fit in the scheme of things within the educational milieu? What does the curriculum worker expect in the future? These were a few of the questions that prompted the development and delivery of a questionnaire to a sample of curriculum workers across the United States.

The survey attempted several things. It was an effort to identify details such as curriculum workers' tenure in education, tenure in curriculum worker roles, degrees, job titles, and where curriculum worker positions fit within the school district organization. The survey attempted to capture curriculum workers' perceptions of competencies and confidence necessary to fill their curriculum worker role, and to assess curriculum workers' perception of their role among board of education, administrators, teachers, and the community. Furthermore, curriculum workers were asked to speculate upon achievements, problems, and their general observation of the role as they saw it.

Five hundred curriculum workers presently holding curriculum leader positions in public school districts were randomly selected from the membership of ASCD. Fifty percent of those receiving survey forms completed and returned them after the first mailing. A second mailing produced an additional 15 percent return of completed survey forms. The third mailing brought responses from 13 percent (67) of the sample. In total, 392 survey forms were completed and returned. Survey forms were mailed under a cover letter from Gordon Cawelti, Executive Director of ASCD. See appendix for a copy of the instrument used (pp. 85-86).

A preliminary summary of 100 completed surveys was prepared for the report to the membership at a Special Session during the national ASCD Annual Conference in New Orleans in March 1975. Subsequent to the Annual Conference, the entire 392 survey forms were analyzed.

The first 20 items were objective and required straightforward summarizing. The four remaining items required a substantial amount of analysis in order to bring some useful summary to many and varied responses.

Findings

The summarized data are reported for each of the 24 items on the questionnaire.

Position Title

Curriculum workers exist with a variety of titles. Respondents indicated 17 titles other than superintendent. The most frequently named title for curriculum worker, indicated by 22 per cent of the respondents, was director or coordinator with some specialty such as elementary or secondary education. In all, 35 percent of the respondents indicated the title of director or coordinator. The next most frequently named title was assistant superintendent. Assistant superintendent combined with assistant superintendent for curriculum and instruction accounted for 29 percent of the respondents. Other titles included consultant, specialist, supervisor, or chairperson.

Years in Present Position

A small portion (16 percent) of respondents stated that they had been in that position for more than 10 years. About one-fourth (24 percent) of the respondents indicated they had been in curriculum positions from six to ten years. Hence, well over half (60 percent) of curriculum workers reported being in curriculum workers' positions five years or less. The modal response was two years. Fourteen percent indicated being in the position for two years, and 12 percent indicated 1 year.

History of the Position

Not only was tenure in the position recent, but also the length of time the position existed was recent. About one-third (34 percent) of curriculum worker positions had existed ten years or longer and 40 percent of the curriculum workers' positions had existed for five years or less.

Areas of Responsibility

A majority (60 percent) of curriculum workers reported having responsibility for all curriculum areas and grade levels in the school district. The remainder (40 percent) were distributed in seven other areas, noting most frequently curriculum responsibilities in secondary (15 percent) or elementary (12 percent) grade levels. Table 1 was prepared to describe the data more completely.

Percent of Respondents		Curriculum Area
1.	9%	Secondary (grades 7-9, 6-12, 7-12)
2.	6%	Secondary (10-12)
3.	12%	Elementary (K-5, K-6, K-7, 1-6)
4.	1%	Preschool (includes K and elementary)
5.	4%	K-8 and 1-8
6.		Limited Subject Area
	1%	Secondary
	1%	Elementary
	4%	K-12
7.	2%	Other arrangements
	40%	Total of varied areas of curriculum responsibilities

Table 1. Areas of Curriculum Responsibilities Excluding K-12 and all Grade Levels

Task Description of Position

In field testing the instrument, 12 areas emerged as the most frequently mentioned descriptors of curriculum workers' tasks. These descriptors and their frequency are summarized in Table 2. Other task descriptors were so infrequently mentioned as to be negligible.

On the questionnaire, curriculum workers indicated those tasks named by these descriptors that required their attention. The most frequently mentioned area was in-service programs, mentioned by 94 percent of respondents. In nearly equal frequency were program evaluation and staff meetings. The most infrequently mentioned area requiring attention from the curriculum director was the area of teacher negotiations. About one in five curriculum workers was involved in this emerging aspect of educational management. The

Curriculum Task Descriptor	Percent of Respondents Indicating Involvement in Curriculum Task Area
Budget	69%
Community relations	71%
Developing standards	75%
Federal programs	62%
In-service programs	94%
Program evaluation	90%
Staff meetings	83%
Teacher evaluations	59%
Teacher negotiations	21%
Teacher supervision	67%
Testing	59%
Other categories	34%

Table 2. Summary of Curriculum Worker Task Areas

grouping of areas for curriculum workers' tasks seemed to fall into five distinct categories, by frequency of mention:

1. In-service programs (94 percent), program evaluation (90 percent), and staff meetings (83 percent)

2. Developing standards (75 percent)

3. Budget (70 percent), community relations (71 percent), and teacher supervision (67 percent)

4. Federal programs (62 percent), summer programs (63 percent), teacher evaluation (60 percent), and testing (60 percent)

5. Negotiations (22 percent).

Title of Supervisor

The majority (55 percent) of curriculum workers reported directly to the superintendent. Eighteen percent of the respondents reported to an assistant superintendent and 12 percent reported to a director. The remaining 15 percent of the respondents named various other persons in the school organization.

Tenure in the District

Many curriculum workers were relatively new to the educational scene. About one-fourth (23 percent) reported that they were in their particular district less than five years. Forty percent said that they were in the district 10 years or less. The remaining (60 percent) distributed evenly over a range from 11 years to over 30 years in the district.

Years as Professional Educator

Forty-two percent of curriculum workers indicated that they were in professional education from 20 to 29 years. Nearly the same number (38 percent) were in the profession for up to 19 years. Thirty-three percent were in education for 10 to 19 years. Twenty percent of the respondents were in the profession beyond 30 years.

Future Position

A majority (57 percent) of curriculum workers expressed no aspiration to other positions in education. Among those who indicated an aspiration to other positions, there was a variety of responses. Eighteen percent aspired to the superintendency. Five percent aspired to higher education. Other infrequently mentioned aspirations included principal, consultant, or coordinator.

Previous Positions

Teaching, administration, and supervision were generally the most common educational positions previously held by curriculum workers. About two-thirds of curriculum workers taught up to ten years; 30 percent taught for about five years; and, 36 percent taught for six to ten years. All respondents indicated that they had classroom teaching and administrative experience. A small proportion had taught for 15 years or more. About half (47 percent) had up to ten years administrative experience and the remainder had up to 20 years experience. About half the respondents did not indicate the years of experience in supervision. Of those who reported experience in supervision, about one-fourth had less than five years supervision and the others distributed evenly over 20 years. Fifteen percent had less than five years in any kind of other experience.

The respondents also reported their most recent previous position. Curriculum workers reported entry to the position from a variety of educational positions. About one-fourth indicated teaching (23 percent). The next most frequently mentioned categories were that of principal (21 percent) and director or coordinator (15 percent). Other areas included supervisor, consultant, counselor, and certain academic areas.

Current Certification

Responses to the question on certification were so varied as to defy simple summarization. Responses included various descriptors for teacher, principal, supervisory, general administration, special administration, superintendency, and various combinations in those certified categories. Clearly no uniformity of certification requirement existed across the nation.

Preparation, Schooling

The doctorate, Ph.D., or Ed.D. was held by 28 percent of the curriculum workers. Approximately two-thirds (62 percent) had a master's; 6 percent had a bachelor's; and, 4 percent indicated other degrees. Among those holding the doctorate, most earned the degree recently. Fifteen percent of the respondents earned their doctorate in the 1970's; 9 percent earned the doctorate in the 1960's; and, about 3 percent earned it in the 1950's or earlier. Twenty-seven percent of the respondents received their MA in the 1960's, 21 percent in the 1950's, and 6 percent in the 1970's. Twelve percent of the respondents held the doctorate in administration and curriculum; 9 percent held the doctorate in administration; and, about 4 percent held a doctorate in subject specialization. The field for the master's degree was similarly divided. Eleven percent were in administration and curriculum; 29 percent were in administration; and, 4 percent were in psychology and guidance. Seventeen percent had an MA in a subject area of specialization.

Perceptions on Competence, Confidence, and Others' Perceptions

The survey included seven items dealing with the curriculum workers' perceptions of competencies, confidence, and the curriculum worker's role generally. Respondents were asked to rate these items along a seven point ranking scale; 1 very low and 7 very high. Eighty percent of responses regarding competency and confidence were either 5, 6, or 7. That is to say, respondents felt quite competent and confident to address the demands of curriculum work. Curriculum workers expressed their perception of the importance of the curriculum worker's role more cautiously than they did that of their competency and confidence. Approximately one-third (35 percent) rated the community as seeing the curriculum worker's role as important (either 5, 6, or 7). About two-thirds of the respondents suggested that the Board of Education, teachers, and superintendent perceived the curriculum worker's role as important, rating those items as 5, 6, or 7.

Curriculum Decisions

Participants were asked to report their most successful curriculum decision in the past 12 months. About three-fourths of the respondents in the survey answered this item. Twenty-three percent did not respond. Those who did respond indicated that successful curriculum decisions seemed to be in three areas: those dealing with persons, that is the staff or the community; those dealing with the specific subject matter in the schools' curriculum; and activities that would be of a general curriculum nature not including either of these other two categories. About two out of every five curriculum workers (37 percent) saw their most successful curriculum decision as directly involving content areas. Examples of responses included such phrases as "extended vocational curriculum," "new elective programs—senior high English," "implement S.C.I.S. program," "changing science," "establish career education," "initiate algebra I," "elementary physical education," "including reading courses in English curriculum," "develop values in education," and the like.

About one in five curriculum workers (19 percent) cited activities dealing with staff and community as areas for the most successful curriculum decision. Such things were cited as "involve all teachers in curriculum development," "curriculum council development," "an entirely new system of reporting to parents," "in-service training for teachers," and the like. Activities in the general category showed quite a variety of responses which included: "developing a unified management system," "initiate middle school concept," "revise all curriculum into 60 day periods," "develop mini-unit guides," and "change from norm-referenced to criterion-referenced objectives."

Critical Problems

Curriculum workers were asked to comment on what were perceived as the most critical curriculum problems during the next five years. A small portion of respondents (16 percent) gave no answer. Responses seemed to fall into six general categories as follows:

1. Matters of a general educational nature dealing with views on educational procedures, policies, goals, or mission

2. Issues related to the social order

3. Specific educational or content areas

4. Issues related to finances and enrollment

5. Relationship with teachers, administration, and the public generally

6. Evaluation.

The most frequently mentioned area dealt with general educational policy or mission (Category 1). Over one-fourth of the respondents (27 percent) cited concerns in this area as having the gravest implications in the future. Such things were referred to as "matching curriculum to personal learning style," "converting from traditional to contemporary," "changing the teacher's role to one of learning facilitator," "conservatism," and, often mentioned was the area of "alternatives." Other topics included: how content or elements of the curriculum were established, and "moving from discipline-dominated to an issue-oriented curriculum." Numerous comments were made about changing toward an "open curriculum." A new curriculum to address "values," "open space education," was named. Yet, other topics included "individualizing instruction on a developmental continuum," "psycholinguistic philosophy," "awareness education," "relating learning theory to instruction," and "return to perceived traditionalism in education."

Category 2, involving nearly one-fourth (23 percent) of respondents dealt with social issues including general trends in society. Social problems involved about 10 percent of responses, including desegregation, integration, racism, changing communities, and migration of differing cultural groups in the community.

Category 3, cited most frequently by 16 percent of respondents, dealt with specific educational needs in content areas. Those areas included reading and language arts, vocational offerings, textbook selection, consumer education, career education, metric system, mathematics, and the like.

Category 4 included references by 13 percent of respondents. They mentioned declining enrollments and financially related problems.

In Category 5, comments dealt with people relationships, such as staff, administration, parents, teachers, and the public generally. Such items were cited as: "involving the community and staff in curriculum review," "determining who makes curriculum decisions," and "parental support for education." In this category, several references were noted about negotiations as inhibiting interaction with the community and interfering with curriculum planning. The last category dealt with evaluation. Six percent of respondents indicated that evaluation was an essential problem, naming either evaluation of teacher performance, curriculum, or instruction.

Deterrents to Progress

Curriculum workers were asked to describe that which detracted from the tasks and functions of the curriculum worker. By far the most frequent (57 percent) response dealt with organizational matters including such things as a "great number of meetings," "irrelevant meetings," "lack of administrative support," "unnecessary and great quantities of paper work" in the form of "forms, reports, and the like be prepared," "inadequate staff or other kinds of resources to carry out curriculum work," and other assigned tasks reported as unrelated to curriculum planning.

The other area that received notable response (16 percent) dealt with matters that were classified as the attitudes and the behavior of other people relating to the educational scene. Examples of things cited were the "attitude of the community toward education," "limits in decision-making latitude," "employer relations due to contracts," and "pressures" from various groups in the community. (One curriculum worker cited himself as the greatest distraction!) One respondent added that "most administrators are not capable of dealing with philosophy, psychology, and program development, consequently they are survival oriented." Another response noted the "political and social aspects" of the school system and the "power of hierarchy." A portion (20 percent) cited no distraction.

General Comments

The final item on the survey asked simply for "other comments about curriculum." A very few respondents (29 percent) commented, covering a variety of areas. Some responses dealt with concern over funding, concern that the curriculum worker's role in curriculum planning generally was not understood by teachers and administrators, and that the need for curriculum planning was not recognized. There was concern that schools addressed incorrect and inappropriate issues. Schools were not directed toward greater humanizing activities, and activities concerned with the overall development of children. Schools needed to humanize. There were comments by some (about 4 percent) noting satisfaction with the job, that the job was rewarding and that it was an exciting role.

A noticeable similarity in all comments on this item called for leadership in curriculum planning. Representative of responses calling for leadership are "we need a state ASCD"; "ASCD needs to take the lead in curriculum planning"; "things need to be prioritized"; "curriculum is like the weather, they all talk about it but what commitment do we have to improving it"; "we need a simpler system for reporting, evaluating, and using data concerning where we are and to determine where we hope to arrive"; "who looks at the total curriculum for the child?"; "we must have realistic goals and provide leadership"; "curriculum hucksters within and outside the profession"; "there is a great need to organize curriculum"; "we need leadership badly"; and, "we have no curriculum development program." Other comments illustrate the diversity of response: "it's great"; "one hell of a big job"; "curriculum is not as important as staff development and the implementation of curriculum"; "rural community education in mid-America is very ingrown and out-of-step with the world 100 miles away"; and, "curriculum is an exciting field, I love the challenge."

In summary, curriculum workers were veteran educators, recently entering the curriculum worker role. Furthermore, a clear majority of curriculum workers saw their position as a career position and did not aspire to further heights in the traditional education hierarchy. Curriculum workers were experienced teachers and administrators. The major proportion of curriculum workers hold graduate degrees, but only a small proportion hold the doctorate (Ph.D. or Ed.D.). Most curriculum workers rated their confidence and competency high.

Curriculum workers cited accomplishment in specific content areas (reading, mathematics, language arts) as their greatest accomplishment over the past year. However, when looking to problems and issues of the future, some curriculum workers saw the greatest problems in social and financial issues. A greater number of workers viewed problems in educational orientation or policy involving what education should be, and cited a general lack of leadership in curriculum planning. Generally curriculum workers were oriented to a wide perspective dealing with the role and mission of education, but circumstances forced curriculum workers to cite as their greatest achievements those dealing with specific content areas.

Curriculum workers perceived that boards of education, teachers, and administrators generally understood the importance of curriculum planning but that communities did not understand this function. If this perception were accurate, there would be small wonder why community pressure often exists for the curriculum workers' termination when enrollments and revenues decline.

Within the organization of school districts the curriculum worker's role was relatively new. A number of curriculum workers recently received the doctorate in curriculum planning or administration. It seemed likely that the curriculum worker was most vulnerable when a district faces cutbacks due to lack of leadership and public support, newness of the role, and recent entry of people into the position.

Undoubtedly, a most telling finding of this survey involved the status of certification among curriculum workers. At best, the situation was chaotic. There was no uniform certification among curriculum workers. Furthermore, there was no suggestion of even the slightest evidence of commonality insomuch as the name applied to curriculum worker certification. Curriculum workers appeared to labor under certification classes as numerous as the states and educational agencies themselves.

The curriculum workers' role, and the organizational dimensions of that role were unclear. A major effort needs to be launched to address this matter. Suggestions for further action include:

1. Exerting leadership in the definition and clarification of curriculum planning as an imperative to quality educational programs

2. Articulating the curriculum workers' role in curriculum planning

3. Forwarding uniform standards for training and certification of curriculum workers.

Summary and recommendations

EUGENE BARTOO, CHARLES A. SPEIKER,
ALLAN STURGES

THIS FINAL SECTION contains a summary of the previous research and thinking on the topics: the field of curriculum, curriculum practice, and certification. Each summary contains a status statement and is followed by an argued case or what ought to be. Each argued case is followed by a set of recommendations. The difference between the argued case and the set of recommendations is one of immediacy of action requested. The recommendations are calling for near future activity. The argued case describes a more far-reaching idealized state.

Curriculum Field

Current Status

The curriculum field is much maligned. The sources of the criticism come from inside as well as outside the field. The objects of the criticism range from the methodology of the field to the quality of the work of the field. Every area of endeavor suffers criticism and indeed self-criticism is often taken to be evidence of the vigor and conscience of that area. The amount and type of criticism can also be symptomatic of fundamental malaise. The point, however, is not to determine whether the curriculum field is terminally ill, but to indicate the areas of criticism most relevant to the professionalization of the curriculum leader.

One such area concerns the identity of the field. Many attempts have been made to establish the boundaries of the field using many different forms of inquiry. For example, boundaries have been established as logical consequences of certain definitions of "curric-

63

ulum," "instruction," and "learning." Surveys have been made of what curriculum people do, or should do, of what is written in curriculum texts, and of what types and kinds of curriculum courses are taught. The level of disagreement between and among the outcomes of such studies makes it very difficult to reach an acceptable understanding of the means of entry to the field, to establish canons of appropriate (good) activity in the field, to create vehicles of communication among workers in the field.

Another area concerns the effectiveness of the field. In the case of curriculum, effectiveness is used in the sense of its influence upon educational settings. The field has acted in ways similar to other fields. People have tried to gain more influence by the use of political means to gain power, the explication of competencies to demonstrate expertise, and the use of metaphors (for example, chemical) to argue for an ingredient that can be supplied (for example, curriculum worker as catalyst). The lack of influence of a field has direct consequences affecting the number of seekers of the knowledge of the field which determines the number of teachers, researchers, and practitioners in the field.

The Argued Case

The argued case is quite direct: if the curriculum leader is needed, then the leader ought to be a product of the curriculum field.

There must, however, be good reason for the above. The good reason involves both the identity of the field and the effectiveness of the field. The identity of the field determines what knowledge (in the broadest sense) the potential curriculum leader obtains and the effectiveness of the field determines how that knowledge is enhanced. The curriculum field cannot create the need for the curriculum leader, but can only react to the need.

It is suggested that the curriculum field become more agreeably defined *from the perspective of the curriculum leader*. The necessary accompanying suggestion is that the curriculum field be more effective *in its influence upon educational settings*. Each suggestion is dependent upon the other. The latter helps determine the relevance of the former and the former helps direct the object of the latter. Both suggestions do not exhaust the activities of the field. Alternative definitions of the field can and should be explored and non-utilitarian activities can and should take place.

Recommendations

There are several possibilities within each of the areas of field definition and effectiveness; only a couple are made here. The following recommendations and those in the other sections of this chapter would go far toward professionalizing the curriculum leader.

As regards field definition:

Determine the organizational implications of the various alternative definitions of "curriculum—instruction—administration—teaching."

As regards field effectiveness:

The field can be more informed of curriculum practice by encouraging and rewarding the participation of university persons in the curriculum deliberation of schools and encouraging and rewarding the participation of existent curriculum leaders in the education of future curriculum leaders.

The field should seek to establish standards of scholarship. Those standards also can recognize and relate to an applied function of curriculum scholarship.

Field of Curriculum Practice

Current Status

Chance or lack of conscious and deliberate activity on the part of curriculum leaders seems generally to characterize much of the curriculum activity in public schools. Most curriculum leaders are recent arrivals to positions that have been newly created or activated. These leaders often lack any formal preparation in the field of curriculum and likewise expend large amounts of energy in matters other than curriculum or directly curriculum-related activities. Most curriculum leaders are not quite convinced of the importance of the curriculum position and many times feel as though little control over their own position and its designated activities exists.

When curriculum work and position descriptions are analyzed and compared to the total district expenditure of resources (time, money, board meeting activities) there is little doubt that the role of the curriculum leader and the concomitant contribution to the education of the American child is suspect at best.

When curriculum leaders are asked to further clarify obstacles to or problems within their activity, they respond with concerns that are instructional or administrative in nature. However, most leaders are asking for a clarification of the role of the curriculum leader, minimal standards of preparation and training, and public sanctioning, that is, certification or a similar technique.

The Argued Case

It is assumed that to ensure that appropriate (conscious, deliberative, and significant) curriculum activity occurs in schools, the participants in the schooling enterprise ought to be aware of the importance of curriculum activity. Community members, boards, administrators, teachers, students, and support personnel ought to be able to articulate the importance of the curriculum activity and manifest this articulated importance in the activities and decicions made in the school system.

Curriculum leaders should initiate and maintain all curriculum activity from an informed position, accepting the preparation statements in the following section as guides to personal and professional growth. In addition, curriculum leaders should have in their possession an articulated position on their unique contribution to the education of children, and an accompanying description of functions, tasks, and activities that assist in the actualizing of the unique place of curriculum activity and the curriculum leader in schools.

In an attempt to guarantee that the aforementioned items are attended to, superintendents and boards of education at the state and local levels should establish guidelines for the development of an awareness of the curriculum activity in the individual schools. Further, each school district ought to have one person who has explicit responsibility for the planning, management, or coordination of curriculum activity whether this person is a superintendent in a small school, a building principal, or a teacher with a part-time assignment. The least that ought to be reasonably expected of school districts is that sustained, informed leadership guides curriculum activity.

Recommendations

Within the next calendar year, the following documents should be disseminated to every board president and superintendent at the state and local level and every aspiring or current curriculum leader:

1. A statement of the importance of the contribution of curriculum activity in schools;

2. A statement of the need to have curriculum activity follow from informed leadership;

3. A compilation of model job descriptions that follow from sound rationales and alternative management patterns.

Finally, every curriculum leader should attend at least one nationally approved training laboratory on the topic of curriculum leader skills if an honest self-evaluation so indicates.

Certification

Current Status

Although all schools have someone who is responsible for the curriculum, seldom is the person credentialed in curriculum. Smaller school boards usually assign the curricular responsibilities to the superintendent who assigns appropriate tasks to building principals. Larger systems have an assistant superintendent (or someone with a similar title) but the person is rarely prepared in curriculum. The usual route to certification is through existing certification requirements in administration. Specific courses and experiences in curriculum are not consistent among universities, nor is there a component of experience/field activities that are coupled to the program. In effect, most of the present curriculum leaders in schools were prepared as administrators, not as curriculum leaders.

There are few programs through universities that are specifically designed for the curriculum leader. Although there are several universities that list accredited programs in this area, most of the programs are primarily in administration.

There can be little doubt of the national interest in improving the preparation of curriculum leaders. The interest in certification was expressed from existing curriculum leaders (who deplored the minimal preparation they received in curriculum), from certification officers, and from university professors. An informal network for information exchange seems to exist through which various groups of specialists are sharing ideas in assisting the development of special advanced programs for curriculum leaders.

The Argued Case

To have a strong profession, the curriculum leader's advanced preparation should include completion of the doctoral degree with heavy emphasis in curriculum. This program should enable (through required internships, etc.) the future leader to work toward solutions of existing problems and to provide leadership.

Preparatory programs should receive the approval of a national group of experts identified by a professional organization such as ASCD. The members of this approval/accrediting team should be recognized experts in the field, and the team should include both practitioners and professors. The development of appropriate criteria by this national group would assure minimal standards of excellence, while encouraging universities to exceed the minimal standards. This group would also assure that in their preparation all graduates of the program would have the assistance of practitioners.

Each profession has the responsibility to audit the preparation and conduct of its members. There can be little argument that the person who is responsible for the content that is learned by thousands of students must be responsible also to the employing body, such as the school board. It would also seem apparent that colleagues in the profession should audit the quality of conduct. An ethics committee at the national level would meet this concern.

Preparation in a profession or trade includes licensing. Licensing of curriculum leaders is one of the very few positions in education that does not require completion of a program that concentrates in the area in which the practitioner will work. It seems long overdue that the curriculum leader should be required to possess certification indicating that minimal standards in his or her area of expertise have been met.

Recommendations

Preparation is a combination of knowledge and implementation skills. A minimal program is necessary for entrance into any profession; continuing preparation and practice are mandatory for continued growth.

For the curriculum leader in each school system, the preparation should include formal course work and opportunities to practice required abilities to implement various areas of curriculum, instruction, and administration. Based on the findings of the committee, a curriculum leader would have:

1. EXPERIENCE
    a. Minimum of two years classroom teaching experience
    b. Minimum of one year leadership experience (such as depart-

ment chairperson, elementary or secondary principal, internship, supervisor)

2. PREPARATION
    a. Certification as a teacher
    b. Preparation in a related area (for example, additional prepa-
       ration in elementary education)
    c. Completion or equivalent of an educational specialist degree
       leading to certification as a curriculum and instruction leader
       with courses and experiences in the following areas:
       (1). Curriculum, including the:
            (a). Theories of curriculum; models of curriculum
                 development
            (b). Knowledge and ability to apply skills of social
                 research, including problem identification and
                 the collection and analysis of data, in program
                 planning
            (c). Abilities to develop direction for a school system
                 relating to local, state, and national needs
            (d). Possession of skills and abilities to construct
                 educational programs
            (e). Abilities to identify appropriate criteria to evalu-
                 ate programs
       (2). Instruction, including the
            (a). Abilities to apply the theories of instruction and
                 supervision to the improvement of instruction
            (b). Knowledge of evaluative procedures to assume
                 successful implementation of appropriate instruc-
                 tional procedures
            (c). Recognition of differences in style and learning
                 rates of students with varying backgrounds and
                 cultural, ethnic, social, economic, and religious
                 backgrounds
       (3). Leadership, including
            (a). Processes and purposes of organization (organi-
                 zational theory)
            (b). Management skills to provide the human and
                 material resources for facilitating curricular and
                 instructional changes
            (c). Abilities to prioritize, in relation to district/
                 state/national goals, and possess decision-making

skills within a framework of sound human expertise and fiscal resources
(d). Leadership skills in mobilizing the talents and
abilities of coworkers (human relations skills
included here).

Certification Process

Based on the recommendations of the responses from certification officers and professors, the formal certification of curriculum
leaders should be administered through an appropriate state department of education office. Certification should follow the completion
of the recommended and filed program of studies for a curriculum
leader from universities accredited and approved to offer the program and the degree level. Programs should be designed through
the active participation of practicing curriculum leaders in the
state, through their role as advisory committee members, participants, and co-workers in field activities and members of the evaluation team.

There should be a systematic sequence of courses, workshops,
and institutes for curriculum leaders, to enable the continued
upgrading of their preparation.

Finally, it is recommended that this monograph and in particular the contents of this section be disseminated to the following
groups for their review, debate and eventual action:

1. ASCD Professors of Curriculum

2. NCATE Professors of Curriculum

3. State certification officers

4. Governance boards and membership of each ASCD affiliated unit

5. ASCD governance bodies and membership at large.

Where Do We Go from Here?

Subsequent steps should involve three major thrusts: validation, dissemination, and implementation. Substantive implementation will require preparation of a definitive description of quality
performance in curriculum worker preparation areas. Dissemination should occur within ASCD membership as well as other net-
works which influence education.

The distribution of this document among ASCD members accounts for one aspect of dissemination. Beyond this, however, formal action by ASCD will be needed to provide the educational enterprise with these descriptions of curriculum worker certification, role, and function.

Key education committees in the U.S. Congress should be informed of curriculum worker role and function and certification recommendations. Legislation to include these recommendations should be requested. Congressional action should be requested to require states to incorporate these recommendations into regulation, legislation, and policies governing education in the states. Simultaneously, efforts should be launched to inform state education associations and education committees in state legislatures. The working group should begin immediate dialogue with the chief state school officers' association. Affiliated unit presidents should contact education committees in respective state legislatures. In all these cases, efforts should be directed to incorporate curriculum worker certification requirements and curriculum worker role and function into statutes and regulations governing education in the states.

Among universities preparing curriculum workers, ASCD should inform professors of curriculum of recommendations for certification and role and function. University programs should provide training experiences leading to competencies in recommended certification categories.

ASCD should become a resource agency to assist universities, state education associations (SEA's), and local education associations (LEA's) with implementation of curriculum worker role and function descriptions and certification requirements. This will require preparation of performance descriptors to indicate proficiency in each preparation area. In summary, the next steps would seem to require that ASCD generate an impact on the universities, SEA's, and LEA's with regard to curriculum worker role, function, and certification.

In conclusion, the role of the curriculum leader, as we view it, is to provide leadership and management expertise essential to planning, developing, implementing, and evaluating the curriculum. It is generally conceded that the curriculum leader must have the personal characteristics, professional preparation, and professional experience to assume that role.

6 An annotated bibliography

MAENELLE DEMPSEY AND LUCY DYER

THIS BIBLIOGRAPHY cites research and references dealing with curriculum, curriculum planning, and curriculum workers. Most entries are dated within the past five years. To reasonably limit the scope of the task, entries from school administration, supervision, teacher preparation, teacher competency, educational psychology, role theory, and organization theory were usually not included unless they contained specific reference to curriculum.

Entries were identified through the ERIC index, dissertation abstracts, and the general experience of committee members. The professors of curriculum were surveyed for their reactions to an early draft of the bibliography.

While this bibliography cannot be a complete listing of accumulated research and thought regarding curriculum, it will contribute to a definitive referent for curriculum workers, their role and function.

Books and Pamphlets

Association for Supervision and Curriculum Development. *Leadership Through Supervision*. 1946 Yearbook. Washington, D.C.: the Association, 1946. Presents the earliest ASCD effort at a role description for the educational supervisor. Demonstrates the rhetoric of the "human relations" supervision of the 1940's.

Association for Supervision and Curriculum Development. *Action for Curriculum Improvement*. 1951 Yearbook. Washington, D.C.: the Association, 1951. Presents the tasks necessary for curriculum development. The connection between the tasks and the workers who accomplish the tasks is only implied.

Association for Supervision and Curriculum Development. *Leadership for Improving Instruction*. 1960 Yearbook. Washington, D.C.: the Association, 1960. Reports on the possible applications of leadership

72

studies from sociology and management toward identifying role prescription for instructional leaders.

Association for Supervision and Curriculum Development. *Role of Supervisor and Curriculum Director in a Climate of Change.* Washington, D.C.: the Association, 1965. Describes curriculum worker in terms of functions at various levels of educational organizations. Provides background for but does not include specific information on individual certification or institutional accreditation. Analyzes leadership responsibilities in an era of curricular reform.

George A. Beauchamp. *Curriculum Theory.* Third edition. Wilmette, Illinois: The Kagg Press, 1975. Discusses basic formulations critical to the efforts of the curriculum worker.

Warren G. Bennis. *Changing Organizations: Essays on the Development and Evolution of Human Organization.* New York: McGraw-Hill Book Company, 1966. Presents behavioral scientist's approach to analysis of organizations and patterns of change. Criteria for and roles of change agents are examined. Incorporates various schematic models and case studies. Notes provide excellent references.

Louise M. Berman. *Supervision, Staff Development, and Leadership.* Columbus, Ohio: Charles E. Merrill Publishing Company, 1971. Identifies process skills for curriculum workers and other school personnel. Skills parallel *New Priorities in the Curriculum*: perceiving, organizing and systematizing, communicating of personal meaning, showing concern, knowing, decision making, creating, and dealing with the ethical. Skills are presented as modified behavioral objectives with concomitant activities and hypotheses for testing.

Bruce J. Biddle and Edwin J. Thomas, editors. *Role Theory: Concepts and Research.* New York: John Wiley & Sons, 1966. Analyzes the concept "role" by developing a categorical schema that describes and relates the variables that make up the concept. A major portion of the book offers readings of research studies to demonstrate the viability of the schema. The book is considered the most authoritative text on role theory in sociology.

Leslee J. Bishop. *Procedures and Patterns for Staff Development Programs.* Athens, Georgia: Center for Curriculum Improvement and Staff Development, 1975. Identifies competencies for those conducting staff development. Procedural handbook for staff development based on needs assessment. Good checklists and references.

Arthur Blumberg. *Supervisors and Teachers: A Private Cold War.* Berkeley, California: McCutchan Publishing Corporation, 1974. Researches the interaction between supervisors and teachers using a modified version of Flanders' teacher-student verbal interaction categories. Looks at supervision as an educational psychologist.

Richard W. Burns and Gary D. Brooks. *Curriculum Design in a Changing Society.* Englewood Cliffs, New Jersey: Educational Technology Publications, 1970. Views the instructional administrator's role in terms of coordination. Applies Katz and Kahn's functional system components to education. Derives implications from these interrelated functional roles for the school system in the process of curriculum reform.

A few premises are dated, for example, the continuing shortage of teachers. Chapter 23 by Abbott and Eidel is especially pertinent.

Raymond E. Callahan. *Education and the Cult of Efficiency.* Chicago: The University of Chicago Press, 1962. Studies the influence of scientific industrial management upon educational administration during the first two decades of the twentieth century. Particularly important for understanding the early thinking of Bobbitt.

Fred D. Carver and Thomas J. Sergiovanni. *Organizations and Human Behavior: Focus on Schools.* New York: McGraw-Hill Book Company, 1969. Collects and organizes the writings of organization theory as it applies to schools. Most of the readings are dated, but this is a good introduction to the neo human relations emphasis to school administration.

Joseph M. Cronin and Richard M. Hailer. *Organizing an Urban School System for Diversity.* Lexington, Massachusetts: D. C. Heath and Company, 1973. Integrates program and structure in describing the Boston School Department. Describes roles and responsibilities within the largely decentralized school system. Impact of community groups and federal projects noted.

Ronald C. Doll. *Curriculum Improvement: Decision-Making and Process.* Third edition. Boston, Massachusetts: Allyn and Bacon, Inc., 1974. Describes desirable traits of an educational leader and states five tasks for curriculum leaders in chapter seven. Responsibilities are outlined along with competencies. Case studies are provided.

Peter Drucker. *Management: Tasks, Responsibilities, Practices.* New York: Harper & Row Publishers, 1973. Reviews the current assumptions and practices of management. Some chapters particularly address the management of public agencies such as the school.

Kathryn V. Feyereisen, A. John Fiorino, and Arlene T. Nowak. *Supervision and Curriculum Renewal: A Systems Approach.* New York: Appleton-Century-Crofts, 1970. Uses systems models to define roles of curriculum council and show interface with other school system roles. Chapters four, five, and thirteen most pertinent.

N. L. Gage. *Teacher Effectiveness and Teacher Education: The Search for a Scientific Basis.* Palo Alto, California: Pacific Books, 1972. Stresses the need for and production of scientifically-based knowledge about teachers. Analyzes research on teaching using a two-dimensional paradigm for the exploration of concerns, issues, and questions on which researchers on teaching have focused.

John I. Goodlad and Maurice W. Richter. *The Development of a Conceptual System for Dealing with Problems of Curriculum and Instruction.* Los Angeles: University of California, Los Angeles Institute for Development of Educational Activities, 1967. Shows that curriculum development derives from a set of values. Emphasizes importance of using consultant specialists. Follows rational curriculum construction model.

Neal Gross and Robert E. Herriott. *Staff Leadership in Public Schools: A Sociological Inquiry.* New York: John Wiley & Sons, 1965. Explores the principalship and its role. Emphasis on improving teacher performance. Based on findings of the National Principalship Study undertaken at Harvard in 1959. Indicates study's relationship to broader issues of role and organizational analysis and sociology of work and leadership.

J. Minor Gwynn. *Theory and Practice of Supervision.* New York: Dodd Mead & Company, 1961. Presents the intimate connection between curriculum planning and supervision. Chapter one sketches the historical development of models of supervision.

Andrew W. Halpin. *Theory and Research in Administration.* New York: The Macmillan Company, 1966. Represents thematically the historical development of the "new movement" in educational administration. Sections of the book concern theory and its application to research in administration, reports of research in the field, verbal and nonverbal communication, and the relationship of the scientific method to the preparation of educational researchers.

Robert J. Harnack. *The Teacher: Decision Maker and Curriculum Planner.* Scranton, Pennsylvania: International Textbook Company, 1968. Reports on the use of the computer to aid the teacher in curriculum building. Presents a position on the primacy of the teacher in curriculum work and outlines the rights and responsibilities of teacher *vis à vis* curriculum.

Ben M. Harris and John D. King. *Special Education Supervisor Training Projects.* Austin: The University of Texas, revised 1975. Presents conceptual model for generating competencies and lists generic competencies for preparing instructional supervisors in special education. Provides a philosophical base for the competency approach.

Ben M. Harris. *Supervisory Behavior in Education.* Second edition. Englewood Cliffs, New Jersey: Prentice-Hall, Inc., 1975. Provides a conceptual framework for relating curriculum development to teaching and supervision in chapters 1 and 2.

Virgil E. Herrick. In: Dan W. Anderson, James B. Macdonald, and Frank B. May, editors. *Strategies of Curriculum Development.* Columbus, Ohio: Charles E. Merrill Books, Inc., 1965. Collects the thoughts of Herrick as they pertain to the development of curriculum. The work particularly deals with the elements of curriculum design.

Philip L. Hosford. *An Instructional Theory: A Beginning.* Englewood Cliffs, New Jersey: Prentice-Hall, Inc., 1973. Reviews of instructional theory work including ASCD publications and those of Bruner culminating in the presentation of a general theory of instruction and explicit hypotheses regarding curriculum and instruction which should be tested by schools.

Dwayne Huebner. "The Leadership Role in Curricular Change." In: Marcella R. Lawler, editor. *Strategies for Planned Curricular Innovations.* New York: Teachers College Press, 1970. pp. 133-51. Describes curricular leaders' responsibilities in the following areas: knowledge of educational conditions, ability to exercise political influence, sensitivity to aesthetic environment, and cognizance of one's own humanness.

Bruce R. Joyce. "The Curriculum Worker of the Future." In: Robert M. McClure, editor. *The Curriculum: Retrospect and Prospect.*

The Seventieth Yearbook of the National Society for the Study of Education, Part I. Chicago: the Society, 1971. Views curriculum work as centering around the creation of human environments. Explicitly rejects the necessary connection of curriculum and schools as organizations.

. Bruce Joyce and Marsha Weil. *Models of Teaching.* Englewood Cliffs, New Jersey: Prentice-Hall, Inc., 1972. Presents some 14 models for teaching behavior. Particularly useful for teacher education since it implies that different teaching styles can be used by the same teacher for different purposes. The chapter on curriculum planning gives insight as to the use of the models in schools.

O. W. Kapp and David L. Zufelt. *Personalized Curriculum Through Excellence in Leadership.* Danville, Illinois: The Interstate Printers & Publishers, Inc., 1974. Regards the supervisor as a change agent with impact on curriculum development. Methods of clinical supervision are described; and the authors discuss evaluation of the teacher, instructional program, and supervisory process. Supplemental readings are included.

Edward Krug. *Curriculum Planning.* Revised edition. New York: Harper & Brothers, 1950. Answers the question, "What does it mean to work on curriculum?"

Marcella R. Lawler. *Curriculum Consultants at Work.* New York: Bureau of Publications, Teachers College, Columbia University, 1958. Reports on the work of the curriculum consultants of the Horace Mann-Lincoln Institute at Teachers College, Columbia University.

Arthur J. Lewis and Alice Miel. *Supervision for Improved Instruction: New Challenges, New Responses.* Belmont, California: Wadsworth Publishing Company, Inc., 1972. Clarifies relationships among functions and various functionaries, for example, the general supervisor, resource person, director of elementary or secondary education, and assistant superintendent for curriculum and instruction. Proceeds from theoretical delineation of curriculum, instruction, and teaching.

William H. Lucio and John D. McNeil. *Supervision: A Synthesis of Thought and Action.* New York: McGraw-Hill Book Company, 1969. Describes three basic beliefs regarding supervision, presented in closely defined, rather specific terms. The book additionally serves as an information source regarding changing views of supervision and the varied roles associated with supervisory positions.

James G. March, editor. *Handbook of Organizations.* Chicago: Rand McNally and Co., 1965. Collects the classic articles on organizational theory.

Corine Martinez, compiler. *A Selected Bibliography for Professional Supervisory Competencies.* Ben M. Harris, editor. Austin, Texas: Special Education Supervisor Training Project, Department of Educational Administration, The University of Texas, 1975.

Ralph L. Mosher and David E. Purpel. *Supervision: The Reluctant Profession.* New York: Houghton Mifflin Company, 1972. Explores supervision field, including its historical origins and current research. Identifies skills inherent in supervision and various methods such as counseling and group work. Notes responsibility of supervision in the area of curricular innovation.

Donald A. Myers. *Decision Making in Curriculum and Instruction.* Melbourne, Florida: Institute for the Development of Educational Activities, Inc., 1970. Presents an intriguing argument for the administrator as a "procedural taskmaster."

National Society for the Study of Education. *The Foundations and Technique of Curriculum Construction.* Part I and Part II. The Twenty-Sixth Yearbook of the Society. Bloomington, Illinois: Public School Publishing Company, 1926. Identifies the principles of curriculum-making that signalled the beginning of curriculum as a formal area of study.

Louis J. Rubin. *Improving In-service Education: Proposals and Procedures for Change.* Boston: Allyn and Bacon, Inc., 1971. Collected readings around the task implied in the title. Suggests that in-service education can be approached in ways similar to the education of pupils.

Seymour B. Sarason. *The Culture of the School and the Problem of Change.* Boston: Allyn and Bacon, 1971. Uses case studies to describe a model change process involving university and school cultures. Social psychology view of change.

J. Galen Saylor and William M. Alexander. *Planning Curriculum for Modern Schools.* New York: Holt, Rinehart and Winston, 1974. Summarizes the current practice and thought on curriculum development. A standard text.

Joseph J. Schwab. *The Practical: A Language for Curriculum.* Auxiliary Series, Schools for the 70's. Washington, D.C.: National Education Association, 1970. Argues the necessity of considering curriculum work as non-theoretical.

Thomas J. Sergiovanni and Fred D. Carver. *The New School Executive.* Toronto: Dodd, Mead & Company, 1974. Addresses the human aspects of educational administration. Examines organizational patterns in view of behavioral science research and pragmatic experience. Decision making is envisioned as a process that accommodates value, human, and organizational subsystems.

Edmund C. Short and George D. Marconnit. *Contemporary Thought on Public School Curriculum.* Dubuque, Iowa: William C. Brown Publishing Co., 1968. Collects most readings on curriculum as a field. Caswell's article is the classic statement on the role and function of the curriculum worker.

Hilda Taba. *Curriculum Development: Theory and Practice.* New York: Harcourt, Brace & World, Inc., 1962. Presents a comprehensive textbook on curriculum development from the Tyler rationale.

Daniel Tanner and Laurel N. Tanner. *Curriculum Development: Theory Into Practice.* New York: Macmillan Publishing Company, Inc., 1975. Examines the role of the teacher and supervisor in curriculum evaluation and improvement. Analyzes the curriculum field in the light of historic developments. Stresses the need for addressing macrocurricular problems through an aggregate model rather than focusing predominantly on microcurricular problems through a segmental curriculum model.

Ralph W. Tyler. *Basic Principles of Curriculum and Instruction.* Chicago: The University of Chicago Press, 1950. Organizes curriculum work around four questions the schools must face.

Glenys G. Unruh. *Responsive Curriculum Development: Theory and Action.* Berkeley: McCutchan Publishing Corporation, 1975. Presents a theory of curriculum development based upon a commitment to democratic ideals, humanistic values, and responsiveness to the needs of individuals and society. Shows how to unify sound theory and practice.

John R. Verduin, Jr. *Cooperative Curriculum Improvement.* Englewood Cliffs, New Jersey: Prentice-Hall, Inc., 1967. Discusses how *all* persons in education may cooperate in curriculum improvement. Responsibility for curriculum improvement becomes the focus for all levels of educators.

L. Craig Wilson. *The Open Access Curriculum.* Boston: Allyn and Bacon, Inc., 1971. Reviews the essential problems to be faced in opening the access of students to knowledge in schools. The first half of the book is particularly appropriate.

Periodicals

Lawrence A. Cremin. "Curriculum Making in the United States." *Teachers College Record* 73 (2): 207-20; December 1971. Presents the argument that the reform movement of the 60's operated in ways similar to the early days of curriculum reform.

Walter Doyle. " 'The Supervisor's Role in Negotiation': A Critique." *Educational Leadership* 27 (5): 475-79; February 1970. Contrasts professional and labor-management models of negotiation. Although in favor of supervisors and curriculum workers participating in negotiation, the author points out flaws in the professional negotiation process developed by the ASCD Commission on Problems of Supervisors and Curriculum Workers. Flaws stem from the commission's failure to explore the implications of defining these groups as professionals.

James K. Duncan. "Curriculum Director in Curriculum Change." *Educational Forum* 38: 51-77; November 1973. Fuses curriculum theory and role delineation. Identifies three areas of leadership expression: authority, power, and influence—each based on professional competence. Describes the interaction of each leadership area with the curriculum event.

James E. Eisele and Lutian R. Wootton. "Educating the Curriculum Specialist." *Educational Leadership* 29 (1): 50-55; October 1971. Suggests model for educating persons to implement a "problem-solving curriculum planning process." Defines four functions of the curriculum specialist and lists skills necessary to perform functions effectively. Training activities to develop each skill follow. Ties this into a field-based component.

Russell L. Hamm and William L. Walker. "Preparation of Curriculum Workers." *Educational Leadership* 28 (2): 69-71; October 1970. Recommends revisions of university preparation programs. Inspired by survey of Indiana curriculum workers. Emphasizes field-based experiences.

L. W. Hughes and C. M. Achilles. "The Supervisor as Change Agent." *Educational Leadership* 28 (8): 840-43; May 1971. Outlines strategies for supervisor of instruction to utilize in facilitating change.

Follows process model of change: awareness, interest, evaluation, trial, and adoption.

Francis P. Hunkins. "New Identities for New Tasks." *Educational Leadership* 29 (6): 503-506; March 1972. Views curriculum director as systems and communications expert. C. D. assigned responsibility for coordination of other system members who develop and sequence curriculum and for coordination of research into process of education.

Robert E. Jennings. "The Politics of Curriculum Change." *Peabody Journal of Education* 49: 295-99; July 1972. Discusses curriculum worker as change agent and his areas of influence and power in the school and community. Diagram of school-political system accompanying text. Somewhat Machiavellian.

Mauritz Johnson, Jr. "Definitions and Models in Curriculum Theory." *Educational Theory* 17: 127-40; April 1967. Analyzes the concepts "curriculum" and "instruction" and develops the planning demands of each area.

Barbara T. Mason. " 'Supervisor' or 'Curriculum Specialist'?" *Educational Leadership* 27 (4): 401-403; January 1970. Prefers term *curriculum specialist* to that of *supervisor*. Areas cited are consultation, negotiation, and accountability.

Walter A. Mickler, Jr. "New Roles Can Facilitate Change." *Educational Leadership* 29 (6): 515-17; March 1972. Suggests replacing supervisor with teacher educator and teacher evaluator for every school faculty. Mentions competencies and roles for each. Discusses their effect upon roles of other school system staff.

Franklin P. Morley. "Becoming an Instructional Leader." *Educational Leadership* 29 (3): 239-41; December 1971. Indicates personal traits and professional attributes requisite for effectiveness. Believes that professional competencies are acquired to a significant degree outside one's formal education and teaching experience. Includes coordination of supportive services and managing functional chronological cycles within the system as professional responsibilities.

James E. Rutrough. "Emerging Role of the Director of Instruction." *Educational Leadership* 27 (5): 521-25; February 1970. Reviews data from questionnaires sent to directors of instruction in Virginia. Information obtained concerned professional preparation, job roles, system organization, and instructional program.

Joseph Schwab. "The Practical: Arts of Eclectic." *School Review* 79 (4): 493-542; August 1971. Presents a course outline for developing the skills of instructional analysis.

Joseph Schwab. "The Practical 3: Translation Into Curriculum." *School Review* 81 (4): 501-22; August 1973. Recreates the necessity of the curriculum planning group and identifies the functions of the curriculum specialist.

Conrad F. Toepfer. "The Supervisor's Responsibility for Innovation." *Educational Leadership* 30 (8): 740-43; May 1973. Suggests guidelines for areas of supervisory involvement in identifying curricular needs, identifying local adaptations for proposed innovations, and assisting in complementary staff development. Urges teacher involvement.

Decker F. Walker. "The Curriculum Field in Formation: A Review of the Twenty-Sixth Yearbook of the National Society for the Study of Education." *Curriculum Theory Network* 4 (4): 263-80; 1975a. Reviews the assumptions and weaknesses of the foundations of the curriculum field.

Decker F. Walker. "Straining To Lift Ourselves." *Curriculum Theory Network* 5 (1): 3-25; 1975b. Presents prescriptions for a renewal of the curriculum field from the reality of the national scope of most curriculum development.

Fred H. Wood. "A Climate for Innovation." *Educational Leadership* 30 (6): 516-18; March 1973. Presents seven guidelines for the curriculum specialist's role in establishing a positive psychological climate for innovation. Based on research of Gross, Halpin, and Stein into characteristics of a desirable school climate.

Bob G. Woods. "The Preparation of Curriculum Specialists: An Analysis of the Opinions of Supervisors and Professors." *The Journal of Teacher Education* 22: 448-54; Winter 1971. Presents data from opinionnaire on designing a doctoral program for curriculum and instruction specialists. Respondents were curriculum professors and specialists. Areas considered were behavioral sciences, professional education, and internships.

Lutian R. Wootton, John C. Reynolds, Jr., and Jerrell E. Lopp. "Curriculum Content and Experiences: A Comparative Survey." *Educational Leadership* 31 (5): 431-34; February 1974. Gives follow-up on 1969 survey using same format as 1970 *Educational Leadership* article. Reports emergence of competency-based curriculum courses.

Lutian R. Wootton and Robert W. Selwa. "Curriculum: A Changing Concept." *Educational Leadership* 27 (7): 692-96; April 1970. Summarizes information from a survey of curriculum course offerings at teacher education institutions. Identifies course content, methods and materials used in these classes, and student population. Compares results with 1965 survey to predict trends.

Research Studies, Dissertations, Papers

Bruce J. Anderson. "Perceptions and Expectations of Certain Duties of the Director of Curriculum and Instruction as Determinants of Role Consensus, Role Conflict, and Role Ambiguity." Ph.D. dissertation. Charlottesville: University of Virginia, 1971. Presents data on curriculum director's role from superintendents, principals, supervisors, and teachers. Compares their perceptions with a previous study based on self-report data from curriculum directors. Anderson's respondents differed in perceiving the curriculum director as relatively uninvolved with writing, research, evaluation, personnel and supplementary services, school plant, public relations, and communications.

George A. Beauchamp and P. C. Conran. "Longitudinal Study in Curriculum Engineering." A paper presented at the annual meeting of AERA, Washington, D.C. (Northwestern University): March 1975. Describes the effects of the operation of a curriculum engineering system in a school system.

Harold Oliver Beggs. "An Analysis of the Role of Curriculum Administrators in First Class School Districts in the State of Washington." Ph.D. dissertation. Washington State University, 1972. Leads toward identification of competencies upon which to base certification. Task analysis outlines responsibility for curriculum development, in-service, guidance in selection of curricular materials, consultation, evaluation, communication, and input into budget decisions.

Ronald Allen Bretsch. "Perceived Role of the Curriculum and Instruction Coordinator as Related to the Presence of a Negotiated Agreement Role Description." Ed.D. dissertation. Albany: State University of New York, 1974. Presents categories of role functions for maintaining quality control, consulting, providing in-service, administering, and facilitating school-community cooperation. Advocates a negotiated role description.

Jose A. Cardenas. "Role Expectations for Instructional Supervisors as Expressed by Selected Supervisors, Administrators, and Teachers." Ph.D. dissertation. University of Texas at Austin, 1966. Investigates consensus within and among identified groups on supervisory job responsibilities which were designed to include curriculum development, in-service education, and organizing for instruction. The three groups show agreement on supervisor's role expectations and orientation.

Ronald Laurence Capasso. "A Role Expectation Analysis of a Curricular Generalist: A Case Study." Ed.D. dissertation. New York: Teachers College, Columbia University, 1973. Compares role expectations to actual role performance using interviews, surveys of oral and written communications, and on-site observations. Found little congruence.

W. Arnold Cooper. "The Ideal Operational Role of the Secondary School Curriculum Director." Ph.D. dissertation. Gainesville: University of Florida, 1970. Considers self-perceived role of intraschool curriculum worker. Responses focus on relationships with other school personnel, task analysis, and qualifications for position.

D. Friesen and G. Knudsen. "Graduate Programs for Curriculum Specialists." Presented at the Annual Conference of the Canadian Society for the Study of Education, May 29, 1973. (Xeroxed.) Presents a ranking of behavioral science and professional education items for inclusion in program. Includes copy of instrument and cover letter.

Dominick Joseph Graziano. "The Curriculum Director as an Evaluator." Ph.D. dissertation. Carbondale: Southern Illinois University, 1971. Presents self-report data from questionnaire used to identify five aspects of evaluative role: (a) assisting professional personnel in the adoption of innovative programs and practices, (b) encouraging adoption of innovative programs and practices, (c) aiding in the interpretation of the evaluation of programs and practices, (d) accumulating data and developing information about various programs in other settings . . . , and (e) explaining the rationale for developmental programs.

Gary A. Griffin. "Curricular Decision Making in Selected School Districts." Ed.D. dissertation. Los Angeles: University of California, 1970. Tests Goodlad's delineation of curricular decision-making levels: societal, institutional, and instructional. Questionnaires were sent to school system board members, administrators, supervisors, and teachers. Data showed a disparity between the institutional level decisions and the level of those persons making institutional decisions.

Gary A. Griffin and Ann Lieberman. *Behavior of Innovative Personnel.* Bethesda, Maryland: ERIC Document Reproduction Service, August 1975. Discusses characteristics of innovative educational personnel and factors that may affect innovative actions in the school setting. Speculates on behavior most appropriate to personnel considered to be innovative.

Billy Charles Hancock. "The Evolution of the Role of the Director of Curriculum." Ph.D. dissertation. Gainesville: University of Florida, 1971. Surveys literature focusing on relationship of curriculum director to other administrators, role, and curriculum tasks handled by other personnel. Includes suggestions for preparation of curriculum directors.

Howard Lee Harris. "Curriculum Leadership Behavior and Job Satisfaction: Their Relation to Structural Instability Within the Role-Set." Unpublished Ed.D. dissertation. New York: Teachers College, Columbia University, 1974. Compares leadership behavior of assistant superintendent for curriculum with job satisfaction of middle level curricular personnel under him. Uses sociological orientation in examining role and status sets.

William R. Hartgraves. "The Relationship of Principal and Supervisor Leadership Variables to the Implementation of an Innovation as Influenced by Organizational Variables." Ph.D. dissertation. University of Texas at Austin, 1973. Investigates effect of supervisor's and principal's competencies on implementation of curricular innovations. Supervisor involvement showed a positive correlation.

Warner Martin Houth. "A Factor Analytic Study of the Role of the Regional Curriculum Consultant." Ph.D. dissertation. Iowa City: University of Iowa, 1971. Uses Q-sort to examine role expectations held by local school districts personnel and the curriculum consultants themselves. District size affected role perceptions. Areas of consensus were conveying information on curriculum developments; providing in-service; and assisting teachers in preparing curriculum guides, developing and implementing units

Ellis Owen Jackson, Jr. "The Functions of the Director of Elementary Education as Perceived by the Superintendent of Schools, the Director of Elementary Education, and the Elementary Principal." Ph.D. dissertation. Columbia: University of Missouri, 1973. Presents data from the information sheet and questionnaires indicating many administrative and supervisory functions in addition to curricular concerns. Superintendent and director views are more similar than those of principal.

Michael Robert Jackson. "A Graduate Program for the Preparation of Directors of Instruction: A Performance-Based Approach." Ph.D. dissertation. Gainesville: University of Florida, 1971. Develops program from identification of seven task areas. Attendant competencies were the basis for learning components: formal courses, independent study, seminars, lab experiments, experimental activities, and field experience. Recommendations for process and product evaluation were specified.

Richard D. Kimpston. "A Competency-Based Preparation Program for Specialists in Curriculum and Instruction." *Competency-Based Education: Theory, Practice, Evaluation*. Athens: Department of Curriculum and Instruction, College of Education, University of Georgia, 1975. Stresses a rationale for a competency-based program, assumptions and processes in identifying competencies, strategies for competency identification and verification, assessment of program goals and objectives and plans for designing and implementing. (A paper presented at a conference on competency-based education, University of Georgia.)

Richard D. Kimpston, Marlene Mitchell, and William Stockton. "A Project for Defining Competencies for Curriculum and Instruction Personnel." Department of Curriculum and Instruction, College of Education, University of Minnesota, 1975. Identifies competencies in areas of assessing, designing, programming, implementing, and evaluating. Includes a survey to determine if competencies as perceived by College of Education faculty, public school and State Department of Education personnel. Project goals are to develop a competency-based curriculum, design a concomitant instructional system, develop a management system for the program, and establish compatible certification procedures.

Ivan Kleinman. "Organizing for Musical Growth in Public School Systems: A Delineation of the Role and Function of the Music Curriculum Leader." Ph.D. dissertation. New York: Teachers College, Columbia University, 1972. Categorizes behaviors of curriculum leader as purposing, monitoring, mediating, coordinating, and growing.

Daniel C. Link. "A Study of the Role of Personnel Responsible for Curriculum Development in the Local School Divisions in Virginia." Ph.D. dissertation. Charlottesville: University of Virginia, 1971. Reports actual and ideal involvement in the following work areas: planning, coordination, and evaluation of instructional program; personnel administration; in-service; instructional related services and activities.

Frederick William Luehe. "Functioning and Desired Roles of the Director of Curriculum." Ed.D. dissertation. Los Angeles: University of Southern California, 1973. Presents data from a survey of curriculum directors in state. Data consistent with many other dissertations in this area. Advocates line and staff responsibilities for curriculum director.

John Hayes MacNeil. "An Analysis of the Role and Function of the Director of Curriculum and Instruction Within the School System as Perceived by the Director and His Contact Groups." Ph.D. dissertation. Knoxville: University of Tennessee, 1973. Reports differences in role perceptions of curriculum supervisor among teachers, trainers, and employers. Role areas considered were supervision-administration, evaluation, preparation of curricular materials, personnel functions, curriculum development, enhancement of school-community relations, facilitation of research and evaluation, and provision of in-service training.

Leona Mirza. "Staff Perceptions of the Role of the Curriculum Director as a Decision-Maker in Elementary Schools." Ed.D. dissertation. Kalamazoo: Western Michigan University, 1972. Investigates decision making and influence in relationship to other staff roles. Notes differences between results from the questionnaire and data reported in literature a decade earlier.

James Dennis Moore. "An Examination of the Functions, Activities, and Areas of Competence of the Chief Instructional Leader in Selected School Systems." Ed.D. dissertation. New York: Teachers College, Columbia University, 1973. Uses self-administered questionnaire to determine responsibilities and competencies. High agreement among respondents, but scope of study too narrow to generalize.

Richard Louis Petersohn. "The Development of a Framework and an Instrument for Analysis of Supervision of Curriculum Development." Ed.D. dissertation. Athens: University of Georgia, 1974. Provides an instrument of 75 statements describing supervisory behaviors, combining processes, skills, and subtasks, which facilitate the major tasks of curriculum development. A jury of 60 experts from across the country responded to the semantic differential instrument with a six-point preference scale.

Louis R. Pucci. "A Study of the Role of the Curriculum Supervisor." Ph.D. dissertation. New York University, 1973. Combines statements from the literature into a composite role profile of curriculum supervisor. The questionnaire derived from this profile was administered to various levels of educators. Perceptions of superintendents and teachers were generally consistent with those of incumbents.

Teacher Corps Association Program. *Curriculum Specialist's Role in Enabling Interns To Acquire and Demonstrate Mastery of Teaching Competencies.* Madison: University of Wisconsin, 1973. Specifies the curriculum specialist's role in the Competency-Based Teacher Education Program. Includes objectives, tests, and activities.

William Everett White. "The Role of the Assistant Superintendent in Curriculum Improvement." Ph.D. dissertation. Lawrence: University of Kansas, 1971. Reports that respondent groups to questionnaire concerning curriculum-related duties of assistant superintendents were assistant superintendents, superintendents, and board presidents. Twenty-nine of the fifty-eight items were rated at the same level of importance by all groups. Some areas of role conflict reported along with confusion as to desirability of line or staff officer status for assistant superintendent.

Bob G. Woods. "The Doctoral Program for Specialists in Curriculum and Instruction in Designing Doctoral Programs in Education." John P. Noonnan and James D. McComas, editors. Bethesda, Maryland: ERIC Document Reproductive Service ED 055 031, 1968. Recommends changes in curriculum, institutional facilities, faculty, and organizational structure of doctoral program. Presents questionnaire data used in Winter 1971 article in *Journal of Teacher Education.*

Allen Frank Zondlak. "Perceptions of the Role of the Curricular Leader in Model Neighborhood Elementary Schools of Detroit." Ph.D. dissertation. Detroit: Wayne State University, 1971. Presents data from principals, curricular leaders, teachers, and paraprofessionals. Recommends the following areas of emphasis for curricular leaders: school interpersonal relations; staff, student, and community involvement; intraschool curriculum development; in-service.

Appendix

1. What is your position title? _____

2. How many years have you been in your present position? _____

3. How many years has the position existed? _____

4. If your curriculum responsibility does not include all areas and grade levels, indicate the area for which you have responsibility:

5. Place a check by the areas which are part of your work.

   a. ___Budget   h. ___Summer programs
   b. ___Community relations   i. ___Teacher evaluation
   c. ___Developing standards   j. ___Teacher negotiations
   d. ___Federal programs   k. ___Teacher supervision
   e. ___Inservice programs   l. ___Testing
   f. ___Program evaluations   m. ___Other: (specify)_____
   g. ___Staff meetings

6. What is the title of the person to whom you report? _____

7. How many years have you been in the district where you are presently employed? _____

8. What was the title of your previous position? _____

9. How many years have you been in education as a professional educator? _____

10. Do you aspire to another position in education? Yes_____ No_____
    If yes, to what position? _____

11. Check the educational positions you have held and the number of years in each:

          Years   Years

    ___Teacher _____   ___Supervisory _____
    ___Administrative _____   ___Other: _____

12. What certification do you now hold? _____

13. Indicate the highest degree you hold. _____
    year received_____

14. In what field was your highest degree taken? e.g., administration, psychology, curriculum, mathematics, et al.

Encircle the numeral you think best applies to the statements below.

15. Rate your competency to address the demands
of curriculum work:

Low   High
1 2 3 4 5 6 7

16. Rate your confidence to address the demands
of curriculum work: 1 2 3 4 5 6 7

17. Rate the importance of the curriculum work-
er's role as perceived by the community: 1 2 3 4 5 6 7

18. Rate the importance of the curriculum worker's role as perceived by the Board of Educa-
tion: 1 2 3 4 5 6 7

19. Rate the importance of the curriculum work-
er's role as perceived by the teachers: 1 2 3 4 5 6 7

20. Rate the importance of the curriculum work-
er's role as perceived by the superintendent: 1 2 3 4 5 6 7

21. What was your most successful curriculum decision in the past 12
months?

22. What do you anticipate will be the most critical curriculum problem
during the next five years?

23. Considering all aspects of your position, what kinds of tasks or issues
tend to most *detract* from your productivity as a curriculum worker?

24. Other comments about curriculum.

Contributors

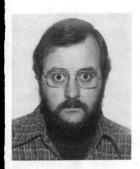

EUGENE BARTOO has been a mathematics teacher in various schools in New York State. He has been a research associate at the State University of New York at Buffalo where he earned his doctorate. And, he has been a director of curriculum and instruction. At present he is assistant professor in the education department at Case Western Reserve University in Ohio.

DONALD CHRISTENSEN has been a mathematics and science teacher, a high school principal, and a director of curriculum and instruction. He has held positions in higher education as well as consulting. He earned his doctorate at the University of Minnesota and is currently president of Christensen and Pulley, Inc., a Minnesota based consulting firm.

MAENELLE D. DEMPSEY has served as a practitioner in Georgia public schools, in higher education, and the Georgia State Department of Education. She has served on ASCD and ATE committees and commissions; has served on the *Journal of Teacher Education* Editorial Advisory Board; has been president of the Georgia Association of Teacher Education; and has served as editor for various publications from the Georgia State Department of Education. At present, she is the teacher education coordinator in the Georgia State Department of Education.

87

For 22 years, VERONICA KOLLAR has been a teacher in grades 1-8 in Pennsylvania. She has been a laboratory school teacher for two years, one of which was on closed circuit television. She is listed in nine directories of outstanding persons in education, for example, the *International Scholars Directory* and the *Two Thousand Women of Achievement*. At present, she is assistant professor supervising student teachers K-12 at Slippery Rock State College in Pennsylvania.

CHARLES A. SPEIKER has been a social science and history teacher, a director of curriculum and has held positions in higher education. He earned his doctorate at the University of Minnesota and is currently Associate Director of the Association for Supervision and Curriculum Development.

ALLAN W. STURGES has been an elementary and high school teacher, a high school department chairman and principal, and a department chairman and professor in various colleges and universities. Since receiving the Ph.D. from the State University of Iowa, he has worked as a consultant and studied in various foreign countries, and participated in in-service programs in curriculum development and evaluation. He is currently professor of education in the department of curriculum and instruction, University of Missouri-Columbia.

*2284-70
1977
5-18
C

*2984-10
1977
5-18
C

ASCD Publications, Autumn 1976

Yearbooks

Balance in the Curriculum (610-17274)	$5.00
Education for an Open Society (610-74012)	$8.00
Education for Peace: Focus on Mankind (610-17946)	$7.50
Evaluation as Feedback and Guide (610-17700)	$6.50
Freedom, Bureaucracy, & Schooling (610-17508)	$6.50
Leadership for Improving Instruction (610-17454)	$4.00
Learning and Mental Health in the School (610-17674)	$5.00
Life Skills in School and Society (610-17786)	$5.50
A New Look at Progressive Education (610-17812)	$8.00
Perspectives on Curriculum Development 1776-1976 (610-76078)	$9.50
Schools in Search of Meaning (610-75044)	$8.50
Perceiving, Behaving, Becoming: A New Focus for Education (610-17278)	$5.00
To Nurture Humaneness: Commitment for the '70's (610-17810)	$6.00

Books and Booklets

Action Learning: Student Community Service Projects (611-74018)	$2.50
Adventuring, Mastering, Associating: New Strategies for Teaching Children (611-76080)	$5.00
Beyond Jencks: The Myth of Equal Schooling (611-17928)	$2.00
The Changing Curriculum: Mathematics (611-17724)	$2.00
Criteria for Theories of Instruction (611-17756)	$2.00
Curricular Concerns in a Revolutionary Era (611-17852)	$6.00
Curriculum Change: Direction and Process (611-17698)	$2.00
Curriculum Leaders: Improving Their Influence (611-76084)	$4.00
Curriculum Materials 1974 (611-74014)	$2.00
Degrading the Grading Myths: A Primer of Alternatives to Grades and Marks (611-76082)	$6.00
Differentiated Staffing (611-17924)	$3.50
Discipline for Today's Children and Youth (611-17314)	$1.50
Early Childhood Education Today (611-17766)	$2.00
Educational Accountability: Beyond Behavioral Objectives (611-17856)	$2.50
Elementary School Mathematics: A Guide to Current Research (611-75056)	$5.00
Elementary School Science: A Guide to Current Research (611-17726)	$2.25
Eliminating Ethnic Bias in Instructional Materials: Comment and Bibliography (611-74020)	$3.25

Emerging Moral Dimensions in Society: Implications for Schooling (611-75052)	$3
Ethnic Modification of Curriculum (611-17832)	$1
The Humanities and the Curriculum (611-17708)	$2
Humanizing the Secondary School (611-17780)	$2
Impact of Decentralization on Curriculum: Selected Viewpoints (611-75050)	$3
Improving Educational Assessment & An Inventory of Measures of Affective Behavior (611-17804)	$4
International Dimension of Education (611-17816)	$2
Interpreting Language Arts Research for the Teacher (611-17846)	$4
Learning More About Learning (611-17310)	$2
Linguistics and the Classroom Teacher (611-17720)	$2
A Man for Tomorrow's World (611-17838)	$2
Middle School in the Making (611-74024)	$5
The Middle School We Need (611-75060)	$2
Needs Assessment: A Focus for Curriculum Development (611-75048)	$4
Observational Methods in the Classroom (611-17948)	$3
Open Education: Critique and Assessment (611-75054)	$4
Open Schools for Children (611-17916)	$3
Personalized Supervision (611-17680)	$1
Professional Supervision for Professional Teachers (611-75046)	$4
Removing Barriers to Humaneness in the High School (611-17848)	$2
Reschooling Society: A Conceptual Model (611-17950)	$2
The School of the Future—NOW (611-17920)	$3
Schools Become Accountable: A PACT Approach (611-74016)	$3
Social Studies for the Evolving Individual (611-17952)	$3
Strategy for Curriculum Change (611-17666)	$2
Supervision: Emerging Profession (611-17796)	$5
Supervision in a New Key (611-17926)	$2
Supervision: Perspectives and Propositions (611-17732)	$2
The Unstudied Curriculum: Its Impact on Children (611-17820)	$2
What Are the Sources of the Curriculum? (611-17522)	$1
Vitalizing the High School (611-74026)	$3
Developmental Characteristics of Children and Youth (wall chart) (611-75058)	$2

Discounts on quantity orders of same title to single address: 10-49 copies, 10%; 50 or more copie 15%. Make checks or money orders payable to ASCD. Orders totaling $10.00 or less must be prepa Orders from institutions and businesses must be on official purchase order form. Shipping a handling charges will be added to billed purchase orders. **Please be sure to list the stock number each publication, shown in parentheses.**

Subscription to **Educational Leadership**—$10.00 a year. ASCD Membership dues: Regular (subscr tion and yearbook)—$25.00 a year; Comprehensive (includes subscription and yearbook plus oth books and booklets distributed during period of membership)—$35.00 a year.

Order from: **Association for Supervision and Curriculum Development
Suite 1100, 1701 K Street, N.W., Washington, D.C. 20006**

THE
DEVELOPMENTAL
KINDERGARTEN

THE
DEVELOPMENTAL
KINDERGARTEN

Individualized Instruction
Through Diagnostic Grouping

By

FRED R. PETRONE, Ed.D.

Director
General Studies Program
College of Allied Health Sciences
Thomas Jefferson University
Philadelphia, Pennsylvania

CHARLES C THOMAS • **PUBLISHER**
Springfield • *Illinois* • *U.S.A.*

Published and Distributed Throughout the World by
CHARLES C THOMAS ● PUBLISHER
Bannerstone House
301-327 East Lawrence Avenue, Springfield, Illinois, U.S.A.

This book is protected by copyright. No part of it
may be reproduced in any manner without written
permission from the publisher.

© *1976, by* CHARLES C THOMAS ● PUBLISHER
ISBN 0-398-03506-7
Library of Congress Catalog Card Number: 75-35588

With THOMAS BOOKS *careful attention is given to all details of
manufacturing and design. It is the Publisher's desire to present books that are
satisfactory as to their physical qualities and artistic possibilities and
appropriate for their particular use.* THOMAS BOOKS *will be true to those
laws of quality that assure a good name and good will.*

Printed in the United States of America
R-1

REF
LB
1169
.P43

cop./

foc.

Library of Congress Cataloging in Publication Data
Petrone, Fred R
  The developmental kindergarten.

  Bibliography: p.
  Includes index.
  1. Kindergarten--Methods and manuals. 2. Individualized instruction. 3. Ability grouping in
education. I. Title. [DNLM: 1. Child development. 2. Teaching. LB1169 P497d]
LB1169.P43   372.1'39'4   75-35588
ISBN 0-398-03506-7

To "Babes"

PREFACE

THE developmental program proposes a fresh alternative for the kindergarten. Its limited aims are specifically focused into an attainable framework. By contrast, the typical program, in an almost frantic effort to expose children to a wealth of experiences, fails to concentrate its efforts effectively. Not all children need the same experiences; nevertheless, one usually finds the entire class engaged in the same activity. The dramatic adjustment from the fun and play of kindergarten to the everyday diet of reading, writing and arithmetic in the first grade, is often destructive of positive learning attitudes.

The raison d'etre of the developmental plan is to determine the effect of instruction on the ability to learn. Language, visual, listening, numerical and perceptual-motor skills are assessed upon admission. The formation of diagnostic instructional groups is generated from the initial evaluation. Immediate grouping not only addresses individual needs but also preserves precious instructional time. Small group instruction in the basic skills adds a new dimension to the role of the kindergarten teacher. Providing for the acquisition of basic skills (an essential ingredient of independent learning) is the primary responsibility of every kindergarten program.

The Rate of Learning Test, administered individually at the close of the year, determines the measurable learning gains which have accrued. Appropriate postkindergarten programming can be recommended based upon these results. The early "labeling" of children often associated with group readiness and group intelligence tests is thus avoided. It is through the marriage of curriculum and measurement that the developmental program marshalls the collective strength of the psychoeducational disciplines.

ACKNOWLEDGMENTS

A NUMBER of dedicated kindergarten teachers assisted the author in ways too numerous to mention. However, I would like to thank Miss Jessie V. Enevoldsen, Elementary Supervisor, Binghamtom City Schools, New York; Mrs. Jean Mesner, Reading Supervisor, Norristown School District, Pennsylvania; Mr. Carmen Storti, Upper Merion School District, King of Prussia, Pennsylvania; Mr. Clinton T. Smith, Superintendent, Susquehanna County Schools, Montrose, Pennsylvania; and Mr. Kenneth L. Rounds, Superintendent, Bradford County Schools, Towanda, Pennsylvania, for permission to evaluate kindergarten children in their respective districts.

I am especially grateful to Edgar P. Frear and Joseph A. Boyle, two friends and mentors, whose encouragement and interest will always be greatly appreciated. I would also like to mention the contribution of Dr. James D. Page, Temple University, and Dr. Horace A. Page, Kent State University, who critically reviewed the dissertation upon which part of this work is based. Orphia C. Chelland, Ph.D., Springfield School District, contributed much of the material on visual, listening and perceptual-motor skills and Joseph Stroman, Bensalem School District, provided many of the curricular suggestions, for which I am very grateful. Mr. Anthony Tomasco, of the psychology department at Cabrini College, offered advice regarding statistical procedures which was quite valuable. Mrs. L. E. Steiner must be thanked for typing the manuscript by the self-imposed June deadline. The fine photographer is William Raney, Cheltenham School District. Photographs were taken at the Candlebrook Elementary School with permission. Finally, I want to express appreciation to both my mother and wife, who kept after me to "get it done."

Fred R. Petrone

921 Academy Lane
Bryn Mawr, Pa. 19010

CONTENTS

THE
DEVELOPMENTAL
KINDERGARTEN

_____

CHAPTER 1

KINDERGARTEN SMORGASBORD

CREATIVE free play is the bedrock upon which Froebel ingeniously conceived the kindergarten. The American facsimile is a modernized version of its German counterpart of a century ago. Its image has not changed down through the years. From all outward appearances entertainment is its major thrust. A glance at the furnishings reinforces this impression: wooden blocks, dolls, a wagon, a miniature kitchen, trucks and assorted games. This popular conception also arises from the nature of observed activities: birthday parties, puppet shows, coloring and play. Emphasis upon learning, as commonly understood by laymen, is not readily apparent. Consequently, the stereotypes linger: an indoor playground, a convenient baby-sitting service, an educational frill. Nowhere is the portrayal characterized by necessity or importance.

Nor do the instructional objectives contribute to clarity or a unity of purpose:

to develop and maintain optimum health,

further his physical development,

extend his understanding of the social world,

enter into his scientific world,

grow in understanding of spatial and quantitative relationships,

expand his control of language,

enjoy his literary heritage,

express himself aesthetically through art media,

become acquainted with and learn to enjoy his musical heritage,

establish satisfying relationships with children and adults (Heffernan & Todd, 1960).

With such a diversity of goals the kindergarten lacks definitive direction and distinct focus. Subject to broad interpretation the inclusion of fads in the disguise of innovation is likely. Global, encompassing aims are indicative of theorists anxious to mold the whole child. Such a cherished, romantic ideal is a patently impractical, unrealistic dream. The half-day kindergarden provides little time to accomplish a fraction of the list. Opening exercises, rest, snack time, attention to personal needs, and dismissal consume one third of the three-hour session. This well intended, but misguided, effort to mold the whole child (in two hours a day) reduces the curriculum to a series of disconnected and unrelated experiences which lack continuity and depth. The 'needs' curriculum fails to develop a rationale for determining children's intellectual wants, and the teacher is left with no criteria for selecting among experiences for her precise group of children (Weber, 1969). A smorgasbord of loosely planned activities can no longer be justified.

Bruner's hypothesis (1960) that any subject can be taught effectively in some intellectually honest form to any child at any stage of development opened a Pandora's box for the kindergarten. Unfortunately, the dilemma of implementation plagues all theories and theorists. Instruction in any topic, regardless of sophistication, will be inappropriate for some; for in no group of five-year-olds is receptivity to learning similar. This fact was not noticed by some theorists. Attempting to extend this thesis beyond practical implementation, Robison and Spodek (1965) would add elementary concepts in sociology, political science, economics and anthropology to an already cluttered curriculum. The 'nonrestrictive' program (Headley, 1965) recommends a random selection of topics from the dictionary, using any letter of the alphabet. Randomization implies that a hierarchy of learning experiences fails to exist, that one activity is as good as another. Such a premise discards developmental research findings summarily. With teachers free to cafeteriorize the curriculum, the development of basic skills is left to whim or chance. Is it any wonder that the "blocks, paints, and clay curriculum" lacks intellectual content (Gans, Stendler, Almy, 1962).

Contradictory theories and practices abound. Learning theorists complicate matters by insisting that the most important factor in educational attainment is the specification of behavioral objectives and learning outcomes (Glaser, 1967). However, at a time when specificity is sought, "creative experiences... were elevated to an even more conspicuous place in the kindergarten curriculum" (Weber, 1969). Given the present state of measurement, determining the behavioral effects of creative expression is at best difficult, if not impossible.

A national poll (NEA, 1969) confirms the lack of an organized curricular offering. About half of all activities were unstructured exposures to experience; instruction did not occur through formalized classroom procedures (See Table I).

TABLE I

CURRICULUM EXPERIENCES INCLUDED

IN KINDERGARTEN PROGRAMS 1967-1968

	Structured	Unstructured
Social Studies	14%	65%
Science	15%	63%
Reading	41%	37%
Language Arts	31%	45%
Number Relationships	53%	31%
Health & Phy. Educ.	28%	55%
Art	37%	49%
Music	39%	39%

Abbreviated from National Education Association, "Kindergarten Education in the Public Schools, 1967-68" (Report 1969-R6) (Washington, D.C., National Education Association, Research Division, 1969), Table 10, pp. 20-21.

A free choice is offered in lieu of formal instruction in most curricular areas. For instance, less than one third of the programs surveyed offer directed language arts instruction; 15 percent offered no instruction in language arts or reading. The lack of basic skills instruction by over two thirds of the programs surveyed is a scathing indictment of their curricula.

What are the implications of a program which allows a free choice of many activities? Young children will always cling to enjoyable experiences and situations. Due to the fact that anxieties are easily aroused in five-year-olds, many are notably quick to avoid challenging endeavors. A child with poor motor coordination, for example, will likely refuse to play catch. Lack of ability creates avoidance behaviors; the very skills which need attention are adroitly avoided. Were the decision left entirely to the child, he would probably avoid the opportunity to learn. Some limitation on the abundant use of free time must be instituted unless we feel the child knows best.

BY-PASSING THE KINDERGARTEN

Our competitive mania with Russia, especially with their nursery schools, provided the impetus for massive federal funding of experimental preschools. Nursery school projects were duplicated on a national level. Researchers were delighted with the opportunity to test for significant differences. Although the increase in IQ resulting from the preschool exposure was first discovered in the forties by Beth Wellman (1945), unprecedented publicity accompanied the 'new' finding in the sixties.

Only the underprivileged youngsters admitted to the preschools benefitted, while thousands of their less fortunate controls were sacrificed for the sake of "science." Had the funds promoted the permanent establishment of kindergartens and nurseries for all deprived children, countless thousands would have been helped. Many programs were discontinued because of the extraordinary research expenses. Personnel costs to support such projects signalled their eventual doom.

Pressure for curriculum continuity emerged from the preschool. Service programs liked Head Start and Get Set emphasized enriching cognitive experiences as a means of improving basic skills. However, weaknesses in the basic skills are not a phenomenon peculiar to the underprivileged. Bentzen (1961) has estimated that as high as one third of all five-year-olds fail to develop one or more of the basic skills. If fully one-third would benefit from a change, the kindergarten curriculum should be reassessed with a high priority afforded basic skills instruction.

Irrespective of pressure, the antiquated kindergarten curriculum remains essentially intact, unaltered (NEA, 1970). Weber (1969) agrees that, "... the form of the curriculum itself remained relatively unchanged despite new ways of talking about it. One suspects that a kindergarten teacher from the twenties would feel comfortably at home in many kindergarten classrooms in the sixties. The content... equipment and supplies were exactly those developed in the twenties... The organization of the curriculum remained essentially the same."

As constituted, the kindergarten failed to meet the challenging diversity of cultural plurality found in our country. School directors were naturally slow to alter a program that provided for the majority. The desire to mold the whole child suited the middle class admirably; local educators avoided new directions which might alienate middle America. Practitioners informally agreed to ignore differences in personality and learning style of children not in the mainstream.

The lack of vitality and flexibility was no accident. Neglect forced the kindergarten to take a back seat. The thesis of neglect will be documented in the pages that follow.

A Local Program

The position held by many states is reflected by the Arizona law which permits local school boards to operate kindergartens if 'it will not interfere with the work of maintenance of efficiency in the grades.' Although twenty-nine states contribute to local operations, the amount is usually a token gesture. Twenty states provide absolutely no financial support. Half the states avoid their responsibility by failing to stipulate age of admission. By so doing, responsibility for funding and operation naturally falls upon the local district.

Marginal districts can ill afford kindergartens if other educational essentials are absent. If funds for mandated programs are short, local taxes alone will not bear the expense of kindergarten.

Marginal communities usually contain a large segment of the lower socioeconomic population and have a thin taxation potential. Consequently, the lower classes tend to live in areas where kindergartens are yet to open.

Nuisance and Inequality

Kindergarten attendance is subtly discouraged by pesky inconveniences. Registration fees and tuition are charged by one fourth of the districts in the NEA (1969) poll. Those of limited means have no money for tuition. In some instances transportation is not provided — another problem for parents. Unable to afford automobiles, they simply do not take advantage of the program.

The myth of equal opportunity is exploded early. Unable to supply the basic necessities, parents involuntarily fail to provide the needed educational experiences as well. Children of the poor frequently go about the house nude in the early years because clothing cannot be afforded. The poor have feelings too. Unwilling to face the embarrassment of registering an ill-clad youngster, these parents delay enrollment until the compulsory age of admission. The most needy miss the kindergarten opportunity.

Lack of Parental Involvement

Although parental participation is touted as essential to educational programming, present kindergarten practice leaves much room for improvement. Approximately 75 percent of the districts polled by the NEA (1969) offer no orientation for parents. The typical registration procedure requires parents to produce vaccination and birth certificates. Little or no effort goes into explaining kindergarten objectives. Tokenism in home-school relations is practiced by those wishing to prevent potentially meddling parents from influencing school policy. The absence of an open reception is indeed unfortunate; the opportunity needs only to be carefully planned to include parents.

Orientation is a vital matter. For the first time parents meet school personnel to whom they entrust their children. They should be introduced to the entire school staff: teacher, principal, nurse and counselor. Familiarity enables the communication process to flow freely. Having met the staff personally and broken through the professional ice, parents are freer to initiate contact when necessary.

The role of the kindergarten can be thoroughly presented in a well planned orientation organized by the principal. Registration could be combined with an informal coffee hour. Avoiding professional jargonese, school personnel would explain their function, enabling parents to understand what services and facilities are available to them. An informal atmosphere always provides a greater opportunity for questioning points of misunderstanding.

TABLE II

SPECIAL SERVICE PERSONNEL AVAILABLE

FOR KINDERGARTEN CHILDREN, 1967-1968,

9,766 SCHOOL SYSTEMS REPORTING

Special Service Personnel	*% Available*
Nurse	78%
Librarian	50%
Psychologist	47%
Physician	32%
Classroom Aide	30%
Counselor	27%
Dentist	17%
Kindergarten Director	10%

Summarized from National Education Association, "Kindergarten Education in the Public Schools, 1967-68," Research Report 1969-R6 (Washington, D.C., National Education Association, Research Division, 1969), Table 25, p. 39.

Detailed information regarding school operation prevents the possibility of confusion being transmitted to the children.

Isolation

Conditions peculiar to the kindergarten create the phenomenon of isolation. The kindergarten program is located in, but is not an integral part of the school. The classes are deliberately situated at one end of the building to avoid exposure to other children. The half-day schedule creates a self-contained atmosphere.

The isolation extends to the services provided kindergarteners. Table II reveals the limited services available to five-year-olds. School personnel usually initiate their services on first graders and hesitate to "waste" time on pupils who may eventually transfer. The preschooler is merely tolerated until the first grade, the point at which schools gear up to provide a full program.

The isolation has lead to supervisory negligence. Only one program in ten has a kindergarten director. Although the principal or elementary supervisor acts in a directive capacity, his first allegiance is to the entire program. Precious little time is left for the kindergarten. Yet almost one third of the kindergarten teachers do not hold the appropriate degree (NEA, 1969). It would seem logical that those inadequately trained would require greater, not less, supervision.

The curriculum is also largely ignored. In 1967 to 1968 only 6 percent of the kindergarten teachers were engaged in curricular study. The apathy surrounding curriculum revision and revitalization is corroborated by such data. Without supervisory impetus to examine viable alternatives and stimulate fresh activities, the kindergarten curriculum will remain stagnant.

Teacher Without A Staff

Much has been written about the teacher and her staff, but few visit the kindergarten regularly. Most of the standard school services are simply not available. Table II reveals that only the nurse, librarian and psychologist can be counted upon for periodic support. The specialists are only peripherally supportive and do not participate consistently in the program. Our schools have become top-heavy with layer upon layer of supervisory and guidance personnel whose primary function is advisory, and we all know how cheap advice is!

Although the classroom is the battleground on which the war to open minds is fought, only one teacher in four has an instructional aide. To wage the war on ignorance successfully, additional troops are needed at the front and in the trenches. Human potential evolves slowly through consistenly applied direct pupil-teacher contact, interaction and guidance. Administrators must rearrange their priorities. If at all, the war on ignorance will only be won by additional foot soldiers in every classroom.

That kindergarten teachers are struggling, often unsuccessfully, to prepare children for the learning process can be documented. The NEA (1969) poll of districts revealed that: one-third reported gaps in pupil learning, one-fifth evidence of social and emotional maladjustment, and one-half problems regarding educational continuity. Such extraordinary rates of functional difficulty provide incontrovertible evidence of program inadequacy contributing to individual malfunction. If present programming fails to accommodate numerous youngsters who enter, curricular reform and reorganization is in order. Swift ameliorative action would considerably reduce the number and degree of adjustmental difficulties faced by the kindergarten teacher. Unfortunately, we shall see that little imagination goes into alternative solutions. Old-fashioned purgatives are offered where modern surgical techniques are needed.

Traditional Solutions

Pressed to relieve the strained situation, administrators resort to the head-in-the-sand traditions of exclusion and retention. As kindergarten attendance is not mandatory, children are excluded for mental or physical immaturity, poor social-emotional development, limited background of experience, and poor language skills. Essentially, the child must adjust to the program as constituted; it is not designed to accommodate all five-year-olds.

Exclusion preserves the status quo. The additional year at

home will not likely enhance social-emotional security, nor improve language. There is no reason to believe that the family which failed to provide these basic needs in the first five years will suddenly do so in the sixth. Incredibly, the child whose needs are greatest is put up on the shelf for another year "to mature."

Exclusion may have detrimental side effects. Disturbed or neurotic parents have been known to punish offspring as a consequence. Rejection may be inflamed and escalated by exclusion. Unable to cope with the school setting, the helpless, bewildered child is additionally burdened with parental antagonism.

Exclusion is by no means the only snare; retention also awaits the beginner. Three quarters of the districts polled by the NEA retain kindergarteners. Repeating an entire year of the same treadmill which went badly the first go-round has little to commend it. Negative scholastic influences upon motivation occur early. Drop-outs are formed by inflexible educational institutions; they are not born.

Instructional alternatives are not available for the needy. Nor does the problem simply disappear. The weaknesses of present programs are further verified by numerous first grade retentions. In spite of social promotion, up to 15 percent repeat first grade every year (Dimond, 1959). When exclusion and retention are the "remedies," one can only conclude that kindergarten and first grade, as presently constituted, are not meeting the needs of many children.

COMPULSORY KINDERGARTEN

Fulfilling human potential is a meaningless cliché when little more than half of all five-year-olds attend kindergarten. If we fail to include youngsters at the initial stages of the learning process, what hope can be held for the years that follow. Thrown headlong into the educational mainstream without preparation, the needy soon discover the school an alien environment. Kindergarten is still a privilege and not the right of all preschoolers.

Culkin (1943) concluded long ago that we have hesitated to broaden the offering because taxpayers view it a luxury with vague objectives and nebulous results. Nor has the American

Association of Elementary-Nursery-Kindergarten Educators (ENKE) encouraged mandating legislation. ENKE publications deal almost exclusively with research, without elaboration upon implementation. If we lack conviction, what can be expected from the public? In the absence of a professional mandate we openly expose our uncertainty, apathy and low esteem of program need. ENKE must formulate modes of implementation, not act merely as a disseminator of information. Educational practice usually lags theoretical formulations at least two decades. Inequality of opportunity marches on as human potential withers on the vine.

The crucial role of kindergarten is gradually being understood by those aware of the significance of initial encounters and first experiences. Novice golfers no longer play without preliminary instruction. Bad habits are too easily incurred and too difficult to correct once established. The comparison also holds true for the learner. Kindergarten prepares youngsters for the confrontation with formal learning. Without an extensive period of familiarization, many more would find the encounter disorganizing and confusing.

We know that youngsters who attend kindergarten make greater progress in the first five grades, read faster and with greater comprehension, receive higher teacher ratings for industry and initiative, and establish better social relationships (McLaughlin, 1970). However, attendance alone cannot account for much of the difference. Parents who eagerly enroll their offspring usually evidence a strong educational interest, an attitude reflected by their children. Disinterested parents may fail to bother with enrollment if inconvenienced, thus transmitting scholastic apathy and impeding the motivation to learn.

KINDERGARTEN RENAISSANCE

A driving sense of purpose has not been established for the program. Before it can assume a vital role, a dramatic renewal of its character must emerge. When its principal purpose moves toward an individual analysis of learning patterns, the kindergarten renaissance will commence.

The standard program fails to consider the developmental levels of each child. Only if we first identify individual levels can instruction be designed to meet specific needs. Children with special needs can be found in *every* classroom. Shy, aggressive, immature, premature, slow, bright, isolated, disturbed and deprived children all have differing needs. Is there any child without some special need?

Differentiated instructional programming should begin immediately in order to fulfill human potential. Theorists who assume homogeneity among fours and fives will provide the standard smorgasbord curriculum for all. The typical program may be appropriate for the mature child from a stable family setting; however, not all youngsters are so fortunate.

EARLY IDENTIFICATION

Much has been written concerning early identification of children with extraordinary needs. Deficiencies in development cannot be remedied, if at all, until they are identified. Proposed methods include an extensive battery of tests impractical to administer without additional professional personnel (Ilg, Ames, 1965) (DeHirsch, et al., 1966).

THE DEVELOPMENTAL PLAN

An effective and economically feasible procedure would prepare the teacher to administer a five-minute developmental examination to every child upon admission and at the conclusion of kindergarten. The developmental kindergarten is a three-step plan whereby a scale which measures individual development is administered upon admission; instructional strategies are implemented throughout the year; and a measure of the rate of learning is undertaken at year's end. The developmental-diagnostic program measures the learning gains of each child in kindergarten.

The fundamental purpose of the diagnostic approach is an individual analysis of the child's ability to learn in a group setting. The instructional effect on learning and retention is assessed and evaluated. By its very nature the group instructional process will have a differential effect on children, speeding the rate of learning for some, impeding learning in others because of the nature of individual differences in children. For a small number of children the typical kindergarten may be disorganizing and learning is slow.

Based on the individual assessment of strengths and weaknesses, diagnostic instruction is instituted. Instructional procedures are specifically designed to complement the child's abilities. Children with similar deficiencies are grouped for instruction. Small group instruction is recommended, four to six in a group. Exercises designed to remedy weaknesses are applied consistently throughout the year. At the close of the school year, the Rate of Learning Test measures the gains which are the result of the diagnostic instruction.

On the basis of pretest and posttest evaluations, recommendations for the postkindergarten placement can be formulated. Those children demonstrating serious learning impedances after a year of diagnostic instruction should be referred for a complete medico-psychodiagnostic evaluation. A fundamental hypothesis of the developmental kindergarten is that the child who exhibits a slow learning pattern in kindergarten is likely to continue unless the factors causing the delay are detected and, if possible, remedied.

_____

CHAPTER 2

THE DEVELOPMENTAL PROGRAM

REGISTRATION

E NROLLMENT is typically an impersonal assembly line, bookkeeping entry where parent and child are invited, recorded, verified and pleasantly ushered out. Although the family milieu is known to have an extraordinary influence on behavior and learning, school personnel have been reluctant to obtain information on the child's development or the family history. Personal questions may be too easily interpreted as an invasion of privacy. Inquiries are studiously avoided unless and until a scholastic or adjustmental problem arises.

What effect does the prevailing rationale surrounding enrollment have on the management of individual differences? Although convention speakers regularly remind teachers to allow for individual differences, theorists are the first to admit that many schools merely offer lip service (Caswell and Foshay, 1957) (Almy, 1962). Precisely which differences to accommodate are rarely, if ever, discussed. How the kindergarten teacher arrives at a determination is a mystery, especially when so little is known about each child. Teachers meet a new class of thirty children armed with little more than ingenuity. If, during rest period, a child insists upon playing, should he be permitted or not? Such operational decisions must be made immediately. However, without background information as a frame of reference, the decision can only be intuitive, a fallible guide. Many of the judgmental errors of child management can be attributed to the lack of information available to the teacher (Hurlock, 1968).

Through the cumbersome trial and error process, teachers stumble upon the personality characteristics of children, often causing unnecessary aggravation, albeit innocently. Data regarding the individuality and special needs of each child continue to be overlooked, and information critical to the learning process is

16

ignored.

THE DEVELOPMENTAL INQUIRY

A developmental interview (Strang, 1959) conducted at registration has several important advantages. Taking time to interview the parent demonstrates the interest school personnel have for the well-being of the child. The parent is afforded an opportunity to establish a friendly relationship with the interviewer and to feel comfortable in the school setting. The cold formality of registration is broken and barriers to communication are lifted. The information obtained is of inestimable value for teachers as a guide to pupil management and instruction.

In the absence of a school social worker, the developmental interview can be conducted by the school nurse as an integral part of the medical history. Parents are usually willing to provide information regarding the child's past and present medical condition. Prenatal and postnatal care, premature birth, motor and speech development, high fevers of long duration, serious illnesses, and hospitalizations should be carefully investigated because medical history data distinguishes children who later turn out to be educationally handicapped (Owen, 1969). In most interviews normal limits can be established in less than ten minutes. A detailed history may be needed in the presence of a known severely handicapping condition.

Eliciting personal information regarding the family may be difficult, especially in cases of marital discord or family disorganization (Harris, 1961). Separated or divorced parents may not wish to discuss family matters and should not be pressed to do so. A very tactful, discrete approach, respecting the right to privacy, may breech the silence barrier. Two or three sessions may be needed before a parent is sufficiently comfortable to reveal personal affairs which may have had an undue influence upon the child. Obtaining information concerning disrupted families is essential to a full understanding of the child's behavior and ability to learn.

The parent must be assured that personal information will be held in strict confidence. Confidentialities should not be bandied about the faculty room over coffee. Teachers must respect the rights of parents not to have personal matters discussed throughout the school.

An informed teacher is equipped and prepared to provide for individual differences. Understanding the constitutional make-up of the child can prevent many adjustmental crises. The classroom can be restructured to accommodate those with special needs only if these needs are known. For instance, a child may well adjust socially but experience considerable learning difficulty. The two phenomena are often mutually exclusive. In the present state of the diagnostic art, learning disabilities are difficult to ascertain and frequently go undetected until the conclusion of first or second grade (Eisenberg, 1966). The typical primary program provides a medium in which learning aberrations germinate. The early instructional years are critical for the learner, and properly reconstituted they could prevent the development of many learning disorders. Early identification and early intervention are necessary to prevent learning disability (Fargo, 1968).

DIAGNOSTIC EXAMINATIONS

A preventive approach is facilitated by an intensive investigation of each child. A superficial screening examination may fail to detect developmental defects. The employment of competent, conscientious professionals will improve the quality of service rendered. The diagnostic examinations should be scheduled early in the academic years. Immediate detection may prevent the onset of adjustmental and learning disorders.

Medical

Only one third of the districts polled by the NEA (1969) provide medical exuminations. Any child can carry a subclinical illness which may then spread throughout the class. Absence due to illness is unusually high in kindergarten due to close pupil contact. Many five-year-olds have not developed an immunity to germ strains of other children.

A weak or frail child may be unable to generate enough strength to undertake learning activities. Children with nutritional deficiencies or those who miss breakfast regularly cannot take full advantage of the school experience (North, 1968). A thorough examination is essential to detect the presence of any medical conditions which may interfere with scholastic performance.

Dental

Without a dental examination, the school health program is incomplete. Less than one fifth of the districts polled conduct any such examination, which indicates that little attention is paid to oral hygiene. A program of identifying decay, abscesses, gum disease, and malocclusion is a necessary first step. Dentition also provides clues to the child's physical condition.

Of paramount importance is the parental follow-up by the school nurse, since parents are not usually present during school examinations. Information on the location of free or inexpensive clinics should be available for those who cannot afford private dental service. Regular brushing, low sugar intake and other principles of oral hygiene should be stressed. Brushing teeth requires a degree of manual dexterity which all five-year-olds should learn correctly.

Sensory Examinations

Appropriate functioning of vision and hearing is basic to scholastic adjustment. Satisfactory operation of the sensory channels is critical to receptive learning. An individual examination is necessary to ascertain the presence of any impairment which went undetected or was ignored by busy parents.

Examining the five-year-old presents a special challenge. Some do not fully comprehend the testing procedures. Confused and frightened, they fail to respond appropriately. This fact alone is suggestive of the child's immaturity. Nevertheless, to insure accuracy of results, a repeat examination may be conducted by the school nurse.

Audiometric

An individual audiometric screening at twenty or twenty-five decibels will determine whether the full range of signals are received. Auditory blockage may occur as a result of excessive wax, frequent colds, or infection of tonsils and adenoids. An otolaryngologist should be consulted if a deficiency appears in either ear.

Visual

Vision should be carefully checked for farsightedness, astigmatism, binocular incoordination, and fusion difficulties (Rosen, 1965). Near vision needs to be evaluated carefully, as much desk activity utilizes vision within twelve to fifteen inches from the

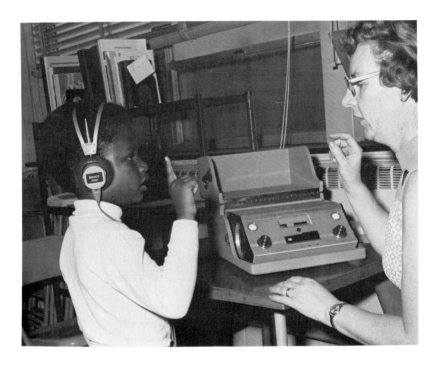

Figure 1. Audiometric screening.

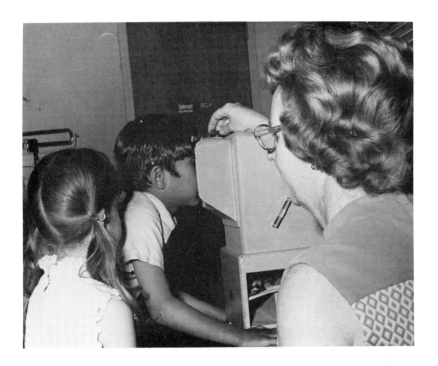

Figure 2. Vision screening.

eyes. Accurate use of near vision will enhance learning to color, draw, print and read.

The Massachusetts Vision Test, Keystone Visual Survey, and the Titmus Vision Screening are recommended as generally accurate methods of detecting visual defects. The commonly used eye chart at twenty feet fails to detect near vision weaknesses and can no longer be recommended.

The Importance of Follow-up

The detection of physical and sensory defects usually presents little difficulty if the examinations are conducted faithfully. However, parental follow-up provides the school nurse with her greatest challenge. The parent whose child needs corrective medical treatment may not have the financial resources to afford private care, which explains the presence of the ailment in the first place. The nurse should inform needy parents regarding available clinics and free public health services. If letters or telephone calls do not lead to corrective action, then a home visit is the only remaining method of impressing parents with the importance of immediate action.

Occasionally, parents refuse to act after repeated urging. Unreturned calls and unanswered letters are quite common in these instances. The school nurse may exhaust all means but to no avail. In one instance known to the author, parents refused to take their daughter with severe strabismus for an opthalmological examination. Confronted by the principal, they explained their inaction with excuses of work and lack of time. The girl, now in her third year, remains unable to read or write due to the visual disability. Emergency funds should be established for children whose parents refuse to take remedial steps. The school nurse can arrange appointments and escort children to the clinic during school hours. Of course, written permission is necessary before embarking upon such a course of action.

KINDERGARTEN — ALL DAY

Half-day sessions have always been considered poor educational practice, except in the kindergarten. The reason for the paradox is not clear since the arguments marshalled against double sessions are legion. Of the three instructional hours available, over one-third is consumed by custodial activities: rest, toileting, washing and cleaning up. Unable to resolve the discrepancy between the limited time and the numerous objectives, teachers are backed into a cafeteria offering. Experiences in social studies, science, language arts, number relationships, health, physical education, art and music simply cannot be scheduled with any degree of regularity. The very practical matter of storing project materials for two groups of children is cumbersome, especially if space is limited. Sequential projects and activities become difficult to execute. Instructional continuity is lost; a piecemeal operation is all that is possible, and a baby-sitting program emerges.

Consequently, many programs lack instructional organization. Over half of the kindergartens in the national survey reported no definite time allotment for instructional experiences; one-fourth reported activities without regular sequence. Extremely simple skills may develop without regular instruction. However, cognitive-conceptual skills cannot be reinforced or retained by activities which occur once or twice weekly. At the age of five, unless opportunities for reinforcement appear daily, retention will be minimal.

California and Hawaii have demonstrated enlightened educational leadership by establishing all-day kindergarten programs. Sequential, consistent instruction can be delivered without skimming or omission. Continuity, review and reinforcement are specifically designed into the instructional program. Individual and small group instruction are possible with twice the time available for each child.

THE DEVELOPMENTAL CURRICULUM

Three important criteria for curriculum design have emerged from instructional theory: (1) findings based on developmental psychology; (2) specificity of objectives (Bloom, 1956); and the measurability of terminal behavior (Mager, 1962). Goals which cannot be identified or measured cannot be evaluated, except subjectively. Objective evidence is usually preferable to subjective evaluation.

Piaget (1963) aptly summarized the necessity for curriculum reconstruction based on research: 'We wish to adapt teaching to the findings of developmental psychology as opposed to the logical bias of scholastic tradition.' Aesthetic experiences, woodwork and blockbuilding are part and parcel of the tradition of which Piaget writes. As recreation or free play such experiences can be justified; however, inclusion as a formal part of the instructional program is not supported by developmental research. Nor has evidence been uncovered to indicate that factual knowledge of social studies, geography or science concepts is important to the development of readiness to learn, except on a prima facie basis.

Specificity

The objectives of the curriculum should be specifically identified and the teacher provided with well-defined outcomes to be achieved by the learner (Bolvin, 1968). Methods and materials for instruction can then be selected to help children achieve these goals. The recent renaissance of the teaching methods of Maria Montessori is partially explained by its definitive program of sensory training. The objectives are clearly prescribed; activities which develop sensory skills are selected for instruction.

At the kindergarten level several skills have been identified which are critical to the learning process. The development of the basic skills (social, language, numerical-conceptual, listening, visual and perceptual-motor) is by no means advanced at five and should be developed further. The refinement of these skills is essential to speed the rate of learning.

Measurability

Any curriculum worth its salt should have components which can be objectively measured. These component elements must undergo a measurable change within the ten-month academic year; otherwise the effects of instruction on initial and terminal behaviors will be unknown. The academic year, September to June, becomes the time period or yardstick against which learning outcomes are measured. Only by developing objective methods of measuring terminal behavior can we hope to analyze inputs, generate information about the learner's characteristics, and provide feedback to improve the instructional process (Bolvin, 1968).

Rationale

The developmental curriculum has a precise focus, but an open structure. The skills to be developed are briefly sketched; the purpose is to free the teacher to exercise full judgment in the selection of activities. The major objective is to refine the basic social, sensory and motor skills. A minutely prescribed, spoon-fed program puts a straitjacket on the teacher, stifling creativity. Any lockstep procedure which spells out daily exercises is not flexible enough to meet the various needs of children at different levels of skill development.

Flexibility of teacher response is the *sine qua non* of intelligent instruction. The free exercise of judgment is essential to the instructional process as she adjusts her reaction to the performance of the children. Within the outline of the basic skills the teacher is entirely free to utilize her own ideas, select materials, and exercise professional judgment in response to pupil needs.

The developmental curriculum is presented in such a way as to provide general guidelines for each skill. For instance, visual discrimination can be developed in numerous ways. No single method of developing visual skills will meet the differing needs of children. Variegated instruction through the use of diverse materials is proposed as an alternative to repetitious drill. Drills need not be repeated two days consecutively but alternated with other activities in order to provide variegation. Variegation maintains a high level of pupil motivation, requiring the child to respond with greater flexibility. Variegated instructional techniques should improve the degree of reinforcement in learning.

A Balanced Offering

A variety of instructional strategies will enhance the learning process. Because of personal variability, individuals respond differentially to various modes of instruction. The independent child proceeds on his own, as the dependent youngster waits for adult direction. The highly animated child prefers motor activities which dissipate bodily energy. Instructional modes should be varied and alternated in order to accommodate as many individual learning styles as possible. Children also need time to adjust to a mode not in harmony with their personality.

Social and gross motor skills mature best in an open setting. Jumping, skipping, rolling and hopping occur spontaneously in free play. Unrestrained freedom of movement provides opportunities for social interaction of which sharing and taking turns are only two. Many social and motor skills are learned incidentally. Incidental learning is a primary mode of acquisition for the preschool child. Incidental events add to the child's storehouse of knowledge and account for the fact that play is so important.

"Open" since its inception, the kindergarten provides opportunities for children to explore their abilities and interests in the learning environment. The term *open* should not mean complete permissiveness. Unlicensed freedom under the guise of openness is difficult to understand, since we do not let children decide where to play, when to sleep and eat, without adult direction.

The developmental program limits the amount of time spent in creative, free play. Creative play periods are provided twice daily, with little restraint on the choice of activity or the use of materials. Spontaneous self-expression and opportunity for social interaction are primary objectives. Learning to play cooperatively, constructively and creatively is not automatic but must be developed. The energy release accompanying free play also satisfies emerging physical and bodily needs. Nevertheless, periods of activity are alternated with quiet, less active, structured activities. Young children are prone to overstimulation and hyperactivity. Prolonged sessions of any kind, open or structured, introduce boredom — the most deadly educational sin.

A number of youngsters cannot participate effectively in a completely open setting because of an inability to inhibit stimulus receptivity. Stimulus-sensitive children, overwhelmed by the ongoing hustle-bustle of an active program, become easily disorganized. Intermittent periods of quiet, sedentary activities with limited stimulation meet their needs. One can easily detect children who function poorly in an open setting by the uncontrollable running, screaming and hitting so characteristic of the overstimulated youngster. A time to relax and rest should be scheduled into every program.

Sensitive, anxious children from quiet, orderly homes (usually an only child) are initially confused by the noise and flurry of kindergarten activity. Frightened and shy, they prefer the warm comfort of home and mother's arms to the precarious uncertainty of making friends and playing with strangers. Time and experience combine to alleviate the anxieties of the only child who gradually makes the best of school. These highly anxious children do less well in an unstructured program.

Cognitive and conceptual ideas are more effectively communicated in a structured format. Abstractions must be presented simply, with the gradual addition of complex dimensions. An orderly, sequential introduction prevents confusion which would impede crystallization of the idea. Comprehension of the abstract takes shape gradually and must be carefully nurtured as one would a seedling.

As no one method of instruction is successful with all children, a sound instructional plan must include a variety of alternatives. Formal and incidental learning take place concurrently in a well-ordered program. A well-rounded offering provides a variety of instructional strategies: directed and independent activities, large and small group instruction, individual and cooperative participation.

Historical Tradition

For generations the pendulum has vascillated between emphasis upon the curriculum per se and the needs of the "whole" child. No serious attempt has been made to integrate or unify the curriculum and child-centered positions. Generalities regarding the need for science, social studies, woodworking and aesthetic experiences appear consistently in theoretical treatises. The following incident is instructive. A teacher indicated proudly that she had spent considerable time on the commonly taught social studies unit "community helpers." She was then asked by the author to elicit examples of community helpers. Not one member of the class could do so. A flabbergasted teacher could not understand, especially after having spent almost a month on the unit. Although children obviously recognize doctors, policemen and firemen as distinct entities, they fail to understand the abstract, group-inclusive nomer, community helper.

The foregoing suggests that abstract and randomly selected units of instruction continue to be offered year after year because we have failed to measure the effects of such instruction. Although theorists in the nursery school movement have gone off on a tangent (measuring IQ gains) their attempt to objectify gains which are the result of instruction is commendable.

Cardinal Principles

Curriculum experience should rest upon the principle of multiple sensory presentation. Only activities or topics which have both visual and auditory components should be selected. Simultaneous use of visual and auditory modes reinforces learning through conditioning, thereby increasing chances for retention. The principle of simultaneity is enhanced by the addition of other sensory components: tactile, kinesthetic and motor. For instance, learning about rabbits will be most effective by bringing an animal to class. The rabbit can be named, played with, fed and watered. Observing its colors and actions will elicit unbridled participatory discussion. Since not all children have seen rabbits firsthand, the learning experience is intensified through multiple-sensory exposure. Without the animal, however, pictures can serve as a substitute. However, pictures or photographs are not often life-size and do not stimulate the interest which intimate contact does. A visit to the zoo is an excellent experience to observe animals which cannot be brought into the classroom. Whenever possible, the object itself should be used in the instructional process.

Three-dimensional instructional materials are preferable. Manipulatives which can be touched, examined and played with reinforce learning. These materials include puppets, cut-out letters of the alphabet, cut-out numbers, puzzles, figures, shapes, cards and games. The use of workbooks can be justified if manipulatives are not available. The teacher has the responsibility to provide manipulative material whenever possible.

VARIETAL INSTRUCTION

Variegated instruction capitalizes upon two basic tenets of learning theory: frequency and novelty. It is well-known that frequent, brief periods of instruction result in greater retention. Prereading experiences are best divided into daily, fifteen-minute periods. Prolonged lessons include considerable time spillage with resultant loss of pupil interest and attention. Therefore, the standard instructional period should not often exceed fifteen minutes. The abbreviated lesson also accommodates the notably limited attention span of preschoolers. The ten- or fifteen- minute mini-activity enables children to undertake and complete a task in a relatively brief time span. Novelty is introduced by changing the instructional offering an average of four times per hour. Boredom is almost completely eliminated by varietal instruction.

The length of the instructional period is governed by the nature of response expectation. Activities which require minimal pupil response should not continue longer than ten or twelve minutes. Initially, storytelling and other listening experiences should be quite brief (five to seven minutes) and gradually lengthened as auditory attention increases. Children need frequent opportunity for physical activity to utilize bodily energy. Activities which engage the children motorically — playing, calisthenics and the like — may be continued longer. However, teachers are cautioned not to let such experiences drag on unnecessarily; time can be scheduled the following day.

The developmental program alternates sedentary and physical activities to provide a balanced program whenever possible. The standard twelve- to fifteen- minute instructional period is suggestive but should be violated by teachers. Activities which fail to interest, for whatever reason, should be discontinued immediately; activities which captivate interest and curiosity can be extended.

A word of caution regarding varietal instruction. Teachers should not stampede children from one activity to another in order to meet a rigid schedule or follow a curriculum guide. Speed is deemphasized; a comfortable pace is foremost. Children who work slowly are not pushed but given added time. Skills cannot be pressure cooked into children, as some believe, but develop slowly; the phenomenon of instant learning does not exist.

GROUPING

Historically, two patterns have dominated kindergarten instruction, free play and full class participation. When telling a story, singing, or directing arts and crafts, teachers use full group instruction because most pupils have had limited experience with classroom procedures. However, this well-meaning attempt to acclimatize does not effectively accommodate individual differences. The selection of a single activity for all may provide for the majority, but not the ever-present minority in every class. The mature child may find the activity satisfying, but the immature is confused by its complexity.

Classroom instruction is usually directed at the hypothetically "average" children in order to accommodate the largest number. Teachers must continually decide how to best divide time among individuals. Does she attend to those who ask for help and ignore others too shy to ask? Should she spend her time with those who seem to benefit from her help? Is she frustrated by those who make little progress thereby inclined to devote herself to others? Or does she democratically give equal time for all? Instructional procedures which provide alternatives need to be considered.

Small Group Instruction (SGI)

SGI enables teachers to spend time *unequally* among the children. Those who need additional guidance and direction are given that support on a continuing basis. The children are assigned to SGI based on scores obtained on the developmental pretest administered during the first weeks of school. The pretest provides important information regarding the present level of skill attainment. Areas of strength and weakness are pinpointed; instruction can be focused on specific needs. For example, children with verbal weaknesses are assigned to SGI in language. The teacher can now direct her attention to improving vocabulary, grammar and oral expression for this group. SGI is conducted in a formal manner, meeting daily, with specific activities designed for this group. These intimate sessions magnify the teacher's perceptions of pupil need. Daily contact solidifies a bond between teacher and pupil which dissipates anxieties. The dehumanization of large group instruction is avoided.

Learning is first a positive social-interactive process (with peers, parents and teachers) whereby behavior is altered as a result of the interactive effect. As both the quantity and the quality of teacher-pupil contact increases and improves, pupil performance and adjustment blossom. Insightful contacts stress positive interaction. Teachers must learn to resist the natural tendency to attend when behavior is annoying or asocial. Negative reinforcement is a detriment to learning. Providing constructive activities to which energies can be applied is preferable to punishment.

Effective SGI includes the services of an instructional aide. The aide oversees the activities of children not occupied by the teacher; she reads stories, supervises play and otherwise guides the remainder of the class. The presence of a second adult intensifies the instructional process through greater teacher-pupil interaction. Two adults working harmoniously set an excellent example to follow.

If the vast sums spent on expensive, prepackaged curriculum materials and learning machines were diverted to hiring aides, achievement levels might rise measurably. A child's personal needs cannot be discovered or met by exotic machines, but only by an understanding adult with time for human interaction. Chansky (1963) found that a free pupil-teacher relationship resulted in significant growth in reading. The insights gained from close pupil contact provide indispensable diagnostic clues which unlock the learning process. Children with the greatest needs have usually had limited, adult contacts of a positive nature. Therefore the need for positive adult guidance is important. Even if learning increments failed to materialize, the personal-social benefits would justify the expenditure. A sympathetic adult can satisfy human needs more than 100 machines and a dozen curricula. The interactive process is the catalyst which motivates; therefore, learning results as a consequence of humane-human interaction.

Without an aide, questions often go unanswered because the teacher is legitimately occupied or inaccessible. Youngsters quickly learn not to ask questions. Curiosity and spontaneity are stifled; apathy is assured. Without a second adult, there is too little time to treat children as individuals. Parental volunteers should be actively recruited; many would gladly serve. Administrators hesitate to recruit parents fearing leaks of a confidential nature into the community. Through a careful screening process and a probationary period, responsible adults can be selectively retained.

Class Size and Pupil Contact

Intensified pupil-teacher interaction may unlock the mystery of fulfilling learning potential. Katzman (1968) found that the ratio of students to staff members correlated significantly with school attendance and academic persistence measures in the Boston elementary schools. Noncrowding was associated with increments in reading achievement and the number of students passing high school entrance examinations.

The intensification of instruction speeds the rate of learning. The present twenty-seven to one pupil-teacher ratio can be reduced to a manageable fourteen to one by the presence of an aide. Increased pupil contacts by an understanding adult will improve the quality of the interaction process.

THE DAILY PROGRAM

Many variables influence daily planning and programming. The presentation of any schedule must always be tempered by judgment and flexibility. This schedule, as with any other, must be fitted to pupil needs and is offered only as a guide. Activities may be shifted, and time spans should be altered as the teacher observes the interest level and effectiveness of activities under way.

The full kindergarten day provides opportunities for including special occasions (field trips, birthday parties, etc.) without sacrificing basic skill instruction. Time allotments can be arranged to suit individual or SGI needs.

The developmental curriculum has limited, but attainable, curricular dimension and scope. The formulation of a sound model places a priority on the refinement of fundamental skills and concepts. The proposed kindergarten curriculum includes developing the following skills:

1. social
2. language
3. numerical-conceptual
4. visual
5. listening
6. perceptual-motor

Concentration on the basic skills will focus instruction on the fundamentals of the developing child.

A KINDERGARTEN DAY

9:00	Greetings	Opening exercises, plans for the day, calendar, weather, oral expression.
9:15	Fine motor skills	Coloring, drawing, cutting, pasting, printing name, and art activities.
9:45	Creative, free play	Opportunity for social play, cooperation, manners, and sharing.
10:15	Visual skills	Discrimination of shapes, sizes, colors, similarities, differences.
10:30	Lavatory, washing, snacks	Social participation, taking turns, readying snacks, cleaning up.
10:45	Concept formation	Portray, demonstrate and imitate concepts: up, down, in, out, front, back, etc.
11:00	Gross motor skills	Calisthentics, hopping in place, skipping, jumping, balance, left-right orientation.
11:15	Language skills	Oral expression, vocabulary, reading and discussions.
11:30	Indoor games	Learning rules of participation, and ability to follow directions.
11:45	Lunch	
12:15	Outdoor or indoor play	
1:00	Rest period	
1:30	Listening skills	Music, singing, rhyming sounds, letter sounds, rhythm exercises, and listening.
1:45	Language skills	Creative drama, play acting, role playing, and story time.

2:00	Daily review	Memory training, recalling activities of the day, reviewing experiences.
2:15	Open	Miscellaneous activities.
2:30	Dismissal	

CHAPTER **3** _____

SOCIALIZATION SKILLS

_____

EMOTIONAL CONSIDERATIONS

SOCIAL development rests upon emotional well-being. A satisfying emotional life founded on tender, loving care fosters social and cognitive growth. Second only to physical needs, the degree to which affectional needs are met play a predominant role in determining social behavior. Emotional stability rests upon a variety of nurturing maternal patterns. An infant's need to be loved is instinctive; the attachment behavior of infants is the dominant propelling force (Bowlby, 1969). Automatic sucking and clinging are initiated by the infant's seeking human contact and interaction. Smiling, cooing and crying attract the mother's attention. If alarmed, ill, fatigued, or in the prolonged absence of the mother, the infant intensifies attachment efforts. Anxiety develops if the mother fails to meet the infant's physical needs. Tensions, crying and overactivity occur as a result of ignoring the child's physical and affectional needs. "The infant's first sense of accomplishment comes from being able to attract the affectionate, comforting attention of his mother. This is his earliest success... antedating all later forms of success. The sense of being loved becomes in him a sense of being worthy of love" (Overstreet, 1951). Sullivan (1953) also stressed the importance of the empathetic relationship between parent and child, emphasizing that anxieties in the mother induced tensions in the infant.

Nurturance

A nurturing love is the basis upon which a strong parent-child relationship rests. Attention and care are reciprocated by total dependence and reliance upon the mother. Helplessness and fear of separation are components of dependence; crying and distress are common reactions to maternal absence. A sense of worth is

36

influenced by the amount of time and tenderness with which a parent will devote to satisfying physical and emotional needs. If cries and wishes are ignored, the child can only come to feel unworthy of attention and eventually develop a negative self-image.

With increasing maturity complete dependence gives way to independent strivings. Attitudes toward dependence and independence vary from culture to culture. In primitive societies where physical danger and psychological stress are greater, parents naturally overprotect their young for longer periods, encouraging a dependent attitude. Children with severe medical histories are also guarded closely by anxious parents who naturally wish to protect weak offspring. Unfortunately, the emotional damage caused by continued coddling may be as severely handicapping as the precipitating condition. Modern society encourages independence early, placing children in day-care centers and nurseries if mothers wish to work. A gradual weaning from dependence is essential to satisfactory emotional-social development.

Maternal Concern

Maximal care and attention may create greater social-emotional sensitivity in the child than minimal care. Over-zealous, smothering affections may lead to the development of an overly strict conscience, guilt feelings, low anxiety threshold, and inhibited behavior. Psychiatric offices are full of anxious, inhibited adults who were smothered into submission by overly indulgent parents.

But by ignoring the cries of the infant, love and affection are denied. Large (lower socioeconomic) families sometimes provide limited, inconsistent maternal attention. Quality care suffers when sisters or grandparents must supervise the young as the mother works to support the family. Such situations may well be interpreted as maternal rejection by the naive, young child. Minimal supervision may produce precocious independent strivings, impulsivity, overactivity, and the absence of a suitable conscience to moderate behavior. The anxiety associated with neglect limits attention and concentration, often interfering with the ability to learn. A child constantly on the alert to care for himself cannot relax sufficiently to increase powers of concentration. Such a defensive, on-guard stance limits behavioral flexibility and the ability to benefit from experience. It appears that negligence or the lack of supervision, not active rejection (beatings and physical abuse) leads to most asocial behavior. Prisons are full of males who were largely ignored as children and adolescents.

Satisfaction of bodily needs — feeding, elimination and sleep — is foremost. Positive experiences with the bodily processes are basic to physical and mental health. The method of feeding (bottle or breast) is incidental; the critical factor is the contented, comfortable feeling which accompanies being well-fed, played with, tended and loved. Ravenous overeating and anorexia are suggestive of anxiety.

Toilet training is initiated with a signal prior to elimination. A child trained too early, to convenience mother, is unable to control the sphincter muscle and cannot signal in time. Accidents will occasionally recur after training is established if the child is preoccupied in play, overexcited, ill, or simply does not wish to go to the bathroom at that moment. A defiant youngster will continue to have "accidents," responding to the impatience of an overly perfectionistic mother. Tensions between mother and child may begin with feeding and continue with difficulties in toilet training. A patient, understanding, accepting maternal attitude is essential for the development of a mentally healthy child.

Erik Erikson (1956) postulates basic trust or mistrust of parents, which infants generalize to the world at large, as the crucial relationship. The quality of the emotional interaction influences mutual trust. Parental affection, translated into meeting physical and emotional needs, results in the happy, cooing baby who loves, relates and confides in others. Infants whose needs go unattended become anxious, lose much body-restoring sleep and thereby upset the very sensitive homeostatic balance. A warm, predictable emotional climate is necessary for a healthy personality.

Nor is any particular method of child-rearing necessarily a significant factor in social-emotional development. Sears, Maccoby and Levin (1957) found that social classes differ in methods of child-rearing. Lower-class parents employ greater use of physical punishment, while the middle class predominantly use verbal persuasion. Irrespective of rearing style, a child can sense love, or its absence, in a parent.

Parental Conflict

No condition has greater detrimental effect on emotional development than family strife. Inevitably children are pawns in the struggle as parents engage in destructive moves on each other. Children innocently caught in the cross fire and immersed in the hate exchange, suffer damaging ego experiences which create inner turmoil. Conflicts over loyalty may engender parental wrath from both sides. Hostilities are vented on the children, who suffer from the denigration. The discord produces feelings of nausea, distress, anxiety and worthlessless. A child who cannot trust his parents has little reason to rely upon teachers.

Reversibility of Positive and Negative Reinforcement

Parents, overwrought and preoccupied with their own unhappiness, have precious little time for their children's needs. Such apathy has a devastating effect upon youngsters who seek and need continuing manifestations of affection. Those children who are unable to attract parental attention through normal behavior (crying, calling, pleading) resort to aberrant actions in desperation. Destroying household items, lying, aggressing, stealing and defiance begin as dramatic methods of attracting the attention and affection of parents. Attempts at suicide are considered extreme efforts of attracting parental love. The resulting punishment (normally negative reinforcement) is interpreted by the child as rewarding because parental attentiveness results from the asocial acts. Thus lying, stealing, aggression and destructive behavior become rewarded and are perpetuated, regardless of the severity of punishment. The reversibility of positive and negative reinforcement contributes to the production of delinquent and disturbed behavior. As only increasingly bizarre behavior elicits the attention (interpreted as care and love) so desperately craved, aberrant acts are reinforced through punishment. The asocial behavior is self-rewarding, attracts notoriety, and eventually becomes habitual. The prestige of nonconformity soon surrounds the individual known for unusual behavior. However, positive feelings of self-worth are destroyed in the process.

Self-awareness and Self-esteem

Bodily awareness begins the development of the self. The infant learns about his body through manipulative fondling and body use. At age two the child attends when called and recognizes his nose, mouth, hair, face, feet, hands and eyes. The self-initiated behaviors of sitting, crawling, standing, walking and running encourage independence and self-reliance. Independent activity leads to greater self-awareness. Learning to walk does not occur without falling, crying and standing to try again. The successes and failures are instructive, increasing personal awareness of skills and limitations. In the young, the self vascillates between overestimating and underestimating abilities; the ongoing process is one of continuing reevaluation and reassessment. Exploratory behavior often varies between impulsively seeking new experiences and fearful avoidance of others.

The correlates of self-esteem are based largely upon the impressions a child receives from others dear to him (Coopersmith, 1967). Positive and negative comments are interalized and accepted as fact. A child repeatedly called "stupid" believes it, unless later experiences contradict the impression.

Behavior in accord with parental wishes has a positive influence on self-esteem. The child unable to comply, for whatever reasons, suffers qualms concerning self-worth. Unfortunately parents sometimes set similar goals for their children (going to college), only to discover not all are willing or able. The inability or unwillingness to meet parental expectations has an essentially negative effect on the ego. A process of self-alienation begins; negative perceptions of the self are not easily shaken. If a child rejects parental goals, he risks falling into disfavor and estranging the supportive relationship. Much of the generation gap is due to differences in goals and interests of older and younger people.

Acceptance and internalization of parental standards are followed by attempts to comply with and meet these goals. However, the inability to fulfill expectations can also create feelings of inferiority and anxiety. Sons often avoid the occupation of the father due to the fear of comparison or a lack of interest.

Frustration and Anger

As personal needs and wants cannot always be met instantaneously, the ability to tolerate some delay in gratification is deemed essential to positive mental health. Social and emotional frustrations cannot be avoided; therefore, all children must develop methods of coping with frustrating experiences. Washing for dinner and going to bed both interfere with the joys of free play, often causing anger. A toy that will not remain upright as it is pulled causes frustration. The most common reaction to frustration is anger and sometimes hostility. Two anger episodes per day appear to be average (Goodenough, 1931); most incidents occurring before meals. Perhaps the well-fed child has fewer angry moments. As expected, colds, fatigue, digestive upsets, constipation and diarrhea contribute to an increase in outbursts of anger.

Anger can be internalized (biting self, somatic symptoms, head banging, tantrums) or externalized (hitting, biting, kicking, fighting). The adequate expression and control of anger is an important aspect of balanced emotional health. Outbursts will inevitably occur, but gradual control over the reaction to anger is deemed essential.

Frustrating incidents cannot be avoided and should be worked through. Social experiences often involve conflicting desires between and among children. As their experiences broaden, children develop strategies to avoid frustrating themselves and others.

Fear

In the normal process of growth, fear is a feeling that all children experience. Sudden, intense noises, sirens, bells or thunder can frighten children. Reassurance and cuddling will generally allay fears of a transitory nature. Parents must introduce fear (of hot stoves, of playing in the street) as a necessary precaution for survival. However, fears for personal safety often generalize. Falling prey to the imagination, which in the young mind has few limits, fear is wantonly extended to wild animals, ghosts, monsters, witches, sleeping alone or in the dark, and to countless other objects and unfamiliar situations.

Unusual or unpleasant experiences can become fearful. Being left alone for a considerable period often provokes worrisome fears. With increasing maturity many irrational fears disappear. Fears based on a real incident (a dog bite) may linger into adulthood.

Jealousy

Baldwin (1947) found legitimate grounds for jealousy toward the newborn. He discovered that maternal behavior often changed immediately before, during and after pregnancy. The intensity of maternal contact with siblings diminished, indulgence declined, and frequency of punishment increased. This alteration in treatment, associated with the upcoming birth, creates legitimate grounds for jealousy. Siblings naturally compare treatments, lest they be short-changed.

Jealousy has no place in the classroom. Equal treatment, sharing and taking turns prevents most occasions for the arousal of jealousy. Deprived children are naturally jealous when they see others with new clothes and many toys. Such feelings sometimes lead to stealing the personal property of others.

Jealousy among children is quite common and should be minimized. A child may try to control a friend, telling her that she cannot play or talk to anyone else. Personal possessiveness should be discouraged. Another common cause of jealousy is teacher favoritism. Children are extremely sensitive of the way teachers relate to them. Continuing favoritism toward a few "pets" while ignoring others destroys the possibility of fair relationships so necessary to assure self-confidence. Acceptance of personal, social or behavioral peculiarities tends to eliminate grounds for jealousy.

Anxiety

Crying is the first expression of anxiety in the infant. Withdrawal of love, scolding, fatigue, extreme excitation, unfamiliar visitors, and loud noises can also produce anxiety and crying spells. Learning to cope with anxiety is a normal aspect of daily life. When tensions are allayed by a supportive parent, anxiety in small doses is well tolerated. Tolerance gradually builds like an inoculation. Relief from anxiety, at the appropriate moment, provides the immunity needed to cope with the increasingly anxious occasions which must be faced in the future.

Stressful occasions should be kept to a minimum as frequent, intense bouts of anxiety immobilize the personality. Extreme anxiety freezes a normally flexible behavior pattern, undermines spontaneity and elicits perserverative, nonadjustive responses difficult to alter. Excessive stress can do physical damage to the highly sensitive nervous system of the growing infant. Disturbances in attention, concentration and sleep may result as the body fails to relax sufficiently to restore the homeostatic balance. Distractibility and hyperactivity are often concomitants of tension states in children.

Anxious moments and crying spells occur regularly in the kindergarten. The loss of a hat or a minor fracas can be upsetting. The teacher allays anxieties, reassures and emotionally supports the upset child. The classroom must be a pleasant, happy place to work and play.

SOCIAL PARTICIPATION

Creative free play and cooperative participation are two basic elements of the socialization process. The ability to accept the social constraints of group activity is the first developmental step. Daily social experiences of a positive nature increase the likelihood of satisfactory adjustment. As the daily routine is gradually understood, children know what to expect and become secure in the structure and limits imposed by the teacher. Social finesse emerges gradually, and patience is the byword, as each rule of social interaction is tested to the limit by children. Fluidity, flexibility and correctibility of behavior are indications of emotional well-being.

Vascillation

In the first days of the school year anxiety permeates the kindergarten. Although reactions vary, tears and homesickness are common, as many have not been away from the protecting comforts of home. Inquiries like, "Is it time to go home?" mask feelings of insecurity. Behavioral vascillation takes place as the children gradually adjust to social conditions. Those who were hiding their true personalities behind a veneer of shyness, when comfortable, tend to become over-confident, ignoring social rules. Vascillation tends to arise whenever children enter a new, unfamiliar environment. After the initial period of caution passes and anxieties are allayed, behavior in consonance with the real personality emerges. The initially nonverbal talk incessantly; the overly shy cannot be contained. Such overreacting eventually equilibrates as the period of unfamiliarity passes and the reaction to the new setting stabilizes.

Creative Play

Play is the child's medium of spontaneous self-expression wherein the ventilation of ideas, emotions and tensions are released. Trucks collide and naughty dolls are spanked as the imagination sparks the world of fantasy. Play affords relief from continual regulation and close parental supervision. The true joy of play is its unfettered freedom and ability to fulfill inner needs.

Self-directed play sharpens mind and body. Curiosity and free exploration combine self-expression with learning. Newly discovered words are sometimes repeated five or ten times consecutively, thus reinforcing their use. Sutton-Smith (1970) found that kindergarteners could give a greater number of creative responses to toys they had played with, indicating play stimulates learning.

The three developmental stages of play include solitary, parallel and social play. In solitary play fantasy is directed toward objects in the absence of a playmate. A child may talk to a doll, to an imaginary friend, to himself, or make strange noises. Parallel play takes place in the presence of a playmate but without interaction. Sandbox activities are often parallel as each child plays independently of the other. Talk occurs but the words are not directed towards playmates. Sigel and McBane (1966) reported that lower socioeconomic class youngsters who were impoverished in their play resorted to a high frequency of motor activity and block building (both parallel). Close observation will reveal those who are not ready for social interaction. The immature continue solitary play with toy in hand. Many hesitant but false approaches appear before the child gains sufficient courage to engage in social play. Feelers go out, but retreats are common at the last moment. Self-confidence and ego strength are necessary to undertake successfully the compromising give and take of peer interaction.

Role playing, one form of socialization, imitates adult life. Children alternately pretend they are nurses, doctors, mothers, Indians, etc. This interaction forcibly broadens an egocentric view to consider the interests of playmates. Through play many human relation skills develop. Learning to play together is a distinct preparation for adolescent social life. Companionship and friendship culminate as social relations mature. Peer influences intensify until they constitute a dominant force in adolescent behavior.

Participation in games requires some comprehension of the rules and therefore calls for a greater degree of mental sophistication than social play. Soviet kindergartens stress the use of games to improve social skills. Russian educators feel that games which require children to follow rules provide purpose and direction to social experiences. Games with simple rules can be conducted rather successfully if they are first explained and demonstrated thoroughly.

COOPERATIVE PARTICIPATION

Family relationships prepare the foundation from which social skills emerge. Interaction with parents, brothers, sisters, cousins and neighbors provide a social base for relationships outside the family. For instance, the only child who has had limited exposure to peers may therefore experience difficulty socializing. Confident and self-assured at home, the child may be shy, self-isolating or overly domineering in peer play because of the limited opportunity to develop the give and take of peer interaction. Youngsters who have not had to compromise, to accommodate others, find its necessity distasteful. Two or three years of peer exposure may be needed for appropriate social behavior to emerge. Satisfactory peer relations is the essential ingredient for positive participation in the group process.

Cooperative participation gradually emanates from within; it cannot be imposed from without. The teacher, much like the captain, sets the course and attempts to elicit the cooperation of each class member. The maturity to accept certain limits imposed by social participation is essential. Taking turns at the easel, sharing materials, and waiting in line are daily occurrences which preclude immediate gratification. A degree of self-denial contributes measurably to smooth social participation. Group procedures impose novel demands upon participants. Sitting, waiting for others, and listening to a story are only a few examples of experiences which must be patiently encouraged in those who have not had the opportunity to learn the very basic rules of social behavior.

Competition has no place in the kindergarten and is best left to adults. Unsupervised pursuits among children often turn competitive; first in line at the water fountain and at recess are but two of the competitive inventions. Parents often instill the need to be strongest, best or first. Odious comparisons among children undermine the self-confidence of many. Only self-competition can be justified. Improvement over past performance is certainly a legitimate goal. A comparison between initial and final performance is useful in determining what progress has been made.

Partners Learn to Cooperate

The selection of partners encourages closer interaction among children, especially in the early weeks when relationships have not had time to mature. A child may choose to work or play with anyone who accepts. In the absence of a choice the teacher may assign partners. Sexes are usually assigned separately because of common interests; however, members of the opposite sex are chosen occasionally. Teamwork and cooperation are the natural outcomes of the partnership. It has been found that kindergarteners working in pairs are more willing to persist in a given activity than those working alone (Torrance, 1959). The emotional support provided by another child enables the pair to pursue common goals for a longer period.

Many activities are conducive to the partnership principle. Most games, free play, the see-saw and picture books are fun together. As a partner, one must share materials, toys and games. Respect for the rights of others develops sooner because the partner's wants and desires need to be considered. Partners learn to be helpful and polite to each other.

Although surrounded by peers, children are nevertheless frightened at the prospect of loneliness, of not having a familiar friend to play and be with. By asking children to select one another as playmates, the partnership encourages closer relationships. Fears of loneliness are allayed. When the selection of a partner is a natural event, each child is relieved of the anxieties of loneliness.

Freedom of choice and flexibility are central to the partnership principle. Changing or leaving a partner is not discouraged; no one is obligated to play with a partner longer than he wishes to. When a child prefers to undertake another activity, he may proceed with or without his playmate. If a child tires of playing with someone, he is free to leave his partner without stigma. When lonely, he may approach another child and ask to be his partner. The purpose of the partnership is to encourage cooperative interaction, not force it. Freedom to work and play alone or in company is the perogative of every child. Partners are frequently rotated or switched; through rotation, intimate social contact with numerous classmates is possible. A child seeking a companion for a particular activity may ask the teacher, and volunteers are sought.

Invariably a few youngsters will be rejected in their efforts to obtain and retain partners in play. The teacher functions to alert the child to those aspects of his behavior and personality which alienate peers. So informed he may begin to understand what about himself interferes with establishing better relations with classmates. Such understandings emerge slowly in five-year-olds and must be periodically reinforced. For instance, a child who rather consistently takes toys from others should be shown how to share and take turns with materials. He should be instructed to say aloud or to himself, "I should not take toys." An intellectual awareness always precedes any behavioral change. The teacher should not make children aware of deficiencies without suggesting alternative avenues of behavior which overcome them.

The narrow, egocentric views held by children are gradually influenced by social relations with peers. Social interaction with partners initiates the process of considering alternative views. To some degree each child will be influenced by his companions. In order to play together the views of both intertwine and reactively influence one another.

Domination and Submission

A few youngsters will attempt to dominate by dictating the terms of the interaction. The self-assertive and strong-willed sometimes need to control and seem to enjoy ordering the shy ones about. Mislabeled "leaders" in group dynamics parlance, they fail to understand that classmates are entirely free to reject manipulative domination. The shy and withdrawn should be encouraged to assert themselves in order to limit such intrusions. The role of teacher is that of pacifier and judge, providing the social emollient which soothes the interaction.

The social practice of establishing and maintaining friends through gift-giving occurs with some regularity. Toys, personal items and sometimes money are given if a friend will play, excluding others. Covetousness by the immature masks the fear of loneliness — of losing the only available friend. Such children need to build greater self-confidence and self-respect before they learn that friends will be loyal without such incentives.

SOCIAL RESPONSIBILITY

The child gradually learns to care for himself but may continue

to have difficulty with buttons and shoelaces. The mature youngster initiates independent activities, is a willing participant, per-
sists until complete, and takes pride in his performance. He is also
willing to clean up, but may need occasional reminders to put
materials away.

In spite of occasional infractions, responsibility for social behavior improves gradually. Respect for the rights of others noticeably improves during the year. That everyone is entitled to a
turn and that one may be first but also last, are both realities of
group participation. Waiting one's turn for milk and cookies, for
the teacher's attention, to play, or to be heard are social skills
which emerge gradually. A degree of patience is necessary; the
needs of all cannot be accommodated simultaneously.

Sharing (materials and ideas) is a by-product of the social process. A child who will not give up riding a wagon should be
encouraged to do so by suggesting an equally attractive alternative activity. Children occasionally adopt materials as security
blankets, sometimes finding it difficult to relinquish their hold.

Helping is another social responsibility to encourage. Whenever an opportunity to help arises, children should be encouraged
to step in and aid in any way. The idea of helping one another is
emotionally supportive and comforting to all. Classroom helpers
demonstrate ways to be friendly and constructive.

Positive Contact

Teachers should seek opportunities to compliment each child,
whether for a new dress, well-combed hair, or a big smile. Opportunities for praise are limitless with a positive attitude. A completed piece of work may deserve praise, not for the end product
but for the effort expended. Children who have difficulty directing their energies constructively are guided into new areas of
activity as a means of finding success. A child will usually continue to try with a helping teacher at the elbow. Praise and emotional
support build self-esteem and improve pupil effort. The encouragement provided by the teacher builds constructive attitudes
and is accompanied by a spirit of self-renewal. Educators have

sought to improve motivation through exotic curriculum materials. The teacher creates a comfortable classroom climate for all. Taking time to converse with each child, to tie shoelaces, to help with coats, to stand by if his mother is late, is the kind of supportive warmth needed in the kindergarten.

When a child becomes temporarily unmanageable, isolation is the recommended procedure. Fatigue, anxiety or family difficulties can cause hostile, aggressive behavior to surface. Isolation is not a punishment but a rest period which enables the child to react less emotionally. When calmed, he is readmitted with a specific activity in mind to provide a constructive channel into which to direct his energy.

NONADJUSTIVE REACTIONS

A child incapable of cooperation directs energy toward activities unrelated to learning; abuse of classroom regulations is usually concomitant behavior. Conflicts with the teacher inevitably follow. The pupil then associates the teacher with unpleasantness; the teacher with learning; and learning with unpleasantness, in that order. A negative set toward learning is a by-product of the pupil-teacher conflict. Hostility and resistance to learning mount as the classroom gradually becomes a frustrating, alien environment. Seeds for the potential dropout are sown early.

The emotionally impoverished child endures gratification delays poorly. The child overwhelmed with unfulfilled self-needs has learned to survive by aggressive and/or withdrawing behavior, which have no appropriate outlet in the classroom.

Serious discrepancies in behavioral management between home and school may endanger cooperative participation. Inability to accept the transition from the intimacy provided by the family, to the classroom (group) setting, suggests a personal inflexibility which may also have deleterious effects on learning.

The immature, overprotected child may cry every morning for weeks, unable to function independently of mother. The spoiled child seeks continual assistance and reassurance from the teacher. No longer the center of attention, the child is uneasy, displeased.

Accustomed to undivided attention the child may sit idly, unable to initiate any activity unless the teacher stands by him. Division of the teacher's attention proves frustrating, and a childish resentment impedes social adjustment. Delayed gratification may evoke a tantrum or crying spell. The child who confuses the role of teacher as mother is apt to have difficulty with self-direction and learning.

In striking contrast the aggressive child (Redl, Wineman, 1957) dramatically interferes with other children in an alternating aggressive or threatening manner. Aggression followed by peer rejection escalates quickly and becomes a very difficult pattern to break. In many instances the teacher can moderate self-defeating behavior by providing opportunities to build relations anew. However, personal-social needs may be so compelling that little energy remains for learning. Fathers sometimes advise sons to defend themselves, to hit back and not to come home crying. However, such advice is often extended and misinterpreted by children as a license to initiate aggressive assaults. In chronic, severe cases, psychological and psychiatric intervention is essential before learning progress can be expected.

The isolated child (Gronlund, 1959) may roam aimlessly, anxious to avoid interaction. Fearful of participation, the isolate is quite content to play a peripheral role and may not speak to peers or teacher for weeks or even months. Social interaction may be slowly encouraged by urging classmates to play with the loner. By introducing the possibility of new friendships, defensive barriers may be lowered. That the shy youngster is not required to initiate social contact improves the possibility of social interaction.

Raised in a household with minimal supervision, the independent child may find the ordinary rules of social conduct difficult to accept. He may insist upon doing what he pleases, when he pleases (irrespective of the rights of others), and is likely to refuse directions from the teacher. He finds sharing and taking turns contrary to his wishes. The self-assertive claim ownership of classroom toys, refusing to share. Minimal maternal supervision does not develop the inner sensitivity needed for smooth group participation. A child largely ignored by parents will not usually place trust in another strange adult. Until the rudimentary social skills develop, formal learning takes a back seat; the psychic attention given to satisfy personal-social needs limits the energy available to learn. Youngsters unable to cooperate effectively often develop learning deficiencies.

Although satisfactory peer relations and cooperative participation are prerequisites for learning, evidence of such skills cannot be interpreted as guaranteeing the ability to learn at a satisfactory rate in a group instructional setting. Social skills and learning are characteristically different phenomena. A child may well adjust socially but fail to demonstrate measurable increments in learning. This possibility should be detected quickly, before the child spends additional time in school.

INSTRUCTIONAL UNIT
OUR HOME AND FAMILY*

I. PURPOSES
  A. Understandings
    1. Everyone has a home.
    2. There are many kinds of homes: trailer, houseboat, camper, tent, hotel, motel.
    3. A family lives together in a home.
    4. We have large and small families.
    5. A family usually has a mother, a father and children. Grandmothers and grandfathers sometimes live with us.
    6. We each have two names, our own name and the family name.
    7. We live and work together in our home. Each of us helps make a happy home.
    8. Children can help at home.
    9. Mothers help by caring for the children, washing, dressing, loving them.
    10. Fathers work for the food we eat and the house we live in.
    11. Fathers do different things.

*Abbreviated and used by permission of Mrs. Clara Rogers Domina, Orleans, Vermont 05860.

12. Children have fun at home with brothers, sisters and friends.
13. Our school family is our class. This family is made up of friends and partners.

B. Appreciations and Attitudes
(Elicit examples from the children)
   1. We love our fathers and mothers because they do things for us every day. What?
   2. We love our family because we play, have fun and help each other. How?
   3. A family helper does what is good, and not always what is fun. Why?
   4. Each of us is different. No two of us are the same. Each of us do good things and sometimes bad, but we try to do good for the family.
   5. Each of us must help to make a friendly, happy home by doing good things for our family. How?
   6. A happy family works and plays together. How do we work together? How do we play together?
   7. When we talk to friends and family we tell the truth. Through dramatic play emphasize the difference between truth and pretend.
   8. Through group activities develop attitudes of:
      a. Helpfulness and cooperation.
      b. Consideration and respect for other children.
      c. Pride in one's family and home.
      d. Acceptance of how other people live and work.
      e. Acceptance of self, abilities and limitations.

Oral Vocabulary

family	dinner	living room	kitchen
home	supper	cellar	attic
mother	grandmother	furnace	picture
father	grandfather	yard	name
sister	cousin	store	boy
brother	uncle	bedroom	girl
helper	aunt	bathroom	friends

II. POSSIBLE APPROACHES

1. Display pictures around the room showing different rooms in a house and members of a family either at work or play. Pictures will arouse curiosity and questions. The unit can be introduced through discussion.
2. The telling of a home experience may lead to group discussion.
3. Playing with dolls and doll furniture during activity time may bring about a discussion of how mothers keep house and tend their families.
4. The reading of a story about a home may arouse interest in their own homes and families.
5. Conversation about family activities may develop interest in reading about animal families.
6. Arrange a library corner with puzzles, books and games to stimulate interest.

APPROACH LESSON

Purposes
1. To introduce the unit on The Home.
2. To create interest in home and family activities.
3. To develop the attitude of acceptance of other people and of how they live and work.
4. To encourage these skills and habits:
   a. Good Listening — by listening to a story and by conversation with others.
   b. Courtesy — by talking one at a time and by listening when others are speaking.
   c. Ability to express themselves through conversation.

MATERIALS

A small house and family figures constructed from cardboard.

Puzzles, books and games.

Large dollhouse furniture.

Pictures of family activities.

Bulletin Board — "Our Home"

A silhouette of a house will be constructed from colored manila tag and used as a background upon which to mount pictures of daily family activities. Later, other groups of pictures might be used.

PROCEDURE

Talk about the small house displayed on the table.

1. "Does this house look like any of your homes?"
2. "If this were a real home, what do you think the family living here would be like?" "Would it be a large or a small family?" "Why?"
3. Each child tells a story about his or her home and family, detailing the family size and family members. Child is asked to tell what each family member does during the day. Family activities are explored in detail.
4. Demonstrate how families differ by encouraging children to talk of activities in their homes. Find pictures on the bulletin board that show what they do at home. Children may draw pictures under the caption "Things We Do At Home."

FOLLOW-UP LESSON

The understanding will be developed that "home" is really a happy family living and working together. There will be further discussion of family life and stories of family activities. Children will develop a story chart about the meaning of home.

III. SUBJECT MATTER
   A. Home
      1. What it means.
      2. Types of homes:
         a. Homes for human families.
         b. Homes for animal families.
      3. Rooms in the home:
         a. Living Room
            Furniture and use of room — table, lamp, chair, rug, carpet, drapes, curtains, shades, sofa, couch.
         b. Dining Room
            Furniture and use of room. Good eating habits.
         c. Kitchen
            Furniture and utensils — sink, range, faucet, re-

frigerator, cabinets. Use of room.
    d. Bedroom
        Furniture and use of room. Health habits — sleep
        and fresh air.
    e. Bathroom
        Cleanliness and good health habits.
    f. Cellar and attic
        Use of these rooms.
  4. Yard:
    a. Care of the yard.
    b. A place to play.
  5. Location of home.
    a. City, street, and house number.
B. Family Members
  1. Immediate members:
      Father.
      Mother.
      Sisters.
      Brothers.
  2. Relatives:
      Grandparents,
      Aunts,
      Uncles,
      Cousins.
C. Work of the family
  1. Father
    a. Where he works.
    b. Type of work.
    c. Why Fathers work:
      (1) Clothing — selection of proper clothing.
      (2) Food — selection of healthful food.
      (3) Fuel.
      (4) Pleasure — toys-entertainment.
      (5) Church — its part in making a good home and
            community.
      (6) Health.
            Doctor — how we keep well.
            Dentist — importance of caring for teeth.

        School Nurse.
- (7) Furniture.
- (8) Electrical appliances.
- (9) Lights, gas, water.
- d. How father helps in the home.
  - (1) Tends furnace.
  - (2) Mows lawn.
  - (3) Shovels snow.
  - (4) Takes care of screens, storm doors and windows.
  - (5) Helps care for children.
  - (6) Paints and repairs.
  - (7) Carries heavy things.
  - (8) Makes garden.
  - (9) Cares for yard.
2. Mother
   - a. Work in the home:
     - (1) Cares for children and teaches them.
     - (2) Cleans the home.
     - (3) Sews and mends.
     - (4) Washes and irons.
   - b. Work outside the home:
     - (1) Where she works.
     - (2) Type of work.
     - (3) Reason for working.
   - c. Work in the community:
     - (1) Church activities.
     - (2) Helps at school.
     - (3) Clubs.
3. Children
   - a. Caring for themselves:
     - (1) Personal appearance.
     - (2) Observing health rules.
     - (3) Taking care of toys and belongings.
     - (4) Taking care of themselves at table.
     - (5) Observing safety rules.
   - b. Caring for younger children:
     - (1) Dressing and feeding them.

          (2) Amusing them.
      c. Caring for pets:
          (1) Food for different types of pets.
          (2) Providing a place for them to sleep.
          (3) Kindness toward pets.
      d. Helping the home:
          (1) Doing errands,
          (2) Setting the table.
          (3) Wiping the dishes.
          (4) Keeping things in proper places.
          (5) Dusting.
          (6) Helping to care for the yard.
   D. Good Times in the Home.
      a. Happy Living:
          (1) Sharing in work and play.
          (2) Helping others.
          (3) Sharing materials.
          (4) Respecting property of others.
      b. Recreation:
          (1) Reading and telling stories.
          (2) Having picnics and parties.
          (3) Playing indoor and outdoor games.
          (4) Playing in the attic on rainy days.
          (5) Sports
          (6) Music, movies and television.
          (7) Dressing up and imitating grown-ups.
          (8) Taking trips.
          (9) Visiting and having company.
IV. ACTIVITIES
  A. Our Home
     1. *Conversation* about home and what it is. Develop understanding that home is a happy family, living and working together.
     2. Write a story chart together. Choose pictures of a home and family figures to use on chart.
     3. Construct a model home for the sand table. Use cutout figures or pipe cleaners for the family figures.
     4. *Discussion;* The size of the house. Have children tell

whether their house has one floor or two. Distinguish between one-family and two-family houses and apartments. Display pictures.

5. Have children bring snapshots of their homes or pictures of homes that resemble theirs. Make a chart and label each as Mary's home, John's home, etc.

6. Encourage children to look for pictures of types of homes. Make a class book of different homes, labeling each.

7. Begin booklets — "My Home." Draw pictures of homes. Each child will draw his home and might print a short caption under picture.

8. If possible, have an excursion to see a house under construction.

9. Begin the construction of a play house. Use orange crates or similar material. If possible, construct in one corner of the room a house large enough for children to play in.

Animal Homes

1. *Teach:* songs about familiar animals.

2. Compare the homes of animals to those of people.

3. Tell the kinds of homes animals in the neighborhood have. Compare the homes of different animals. Encourage children to tell about their pets and types of homes they have. Describe animals which are pets and the homes these animals have. Distinguish between the types of homes that wild animals and domesticated pets have.

4. Find pictures of animal homes. Construct charts or display pictures. Bring in birds' nests, etc.

My Room

1. *Discussion* — The rooms in a home. Encourage the children to tell the various rooms they have in their homes. Display pictures of different rooms in a house. Discuss the pictures, naming the purpose of each room.

2. Discuss what each one can do to make the home attractive.

3. Make a chart showing the rooms found in a home. Leave a space beneath each picture to paste the furniture needed.
4. Make individual books showing the rooms in each child's home. These would be cut from construction paper in the form of a house. Children could put pictures of their families and the rooms in them.
5. Bring furnishings for playhouse.
6. Have a discussion of health rules — Children might make a "Good Habits Book."
7. Look at filmstrips and discuss: Keeping Clean, Rest and Sleep.

Outside
1. Discuss caring for the yard and tell of the work involved. Encourage children to tell how they might help.
2. Talk about the yard as a safe place to play. Children need to know this information.
   a. In what city do you live?
   b. On what street do you live?
   c. What is the address of your house?

B. The Family
1. Encourage children to tell about their families, number of brothers and sisters, and whether they are older or younger. Bring out the difference in size of families and the fact that some families have grandparents living with them. Talk about other relatives who usually do not live with us but who come to visit.
2. As each child tells of his family, print the story for him on a large sheet of paper. Later he will draw a picture to accompany the story. These will be collected in a class book.

Father:
1. Encourage children to tell about fathers work.
2. Discuss why fathers work and how father helps family.
3. Discuss how fathers help the community.
4. Make a chart to show what fathers do for us.

5. Draw pictures of fathers work for individual books they are making.
6. Talk about how father helps in the home. Write a story of "How Father Helps" (Class experience chart).
7. Dramatize father's work and what fathers do at home.

Mother:
1. Talk about mother's work in the home and what she does to help us. Talk about work outside the home and reasons for working. Encourage children to tell of mother's work.
2. Draw pictures of "Mother's Work" for individual books. Mature children will be able to print a caption under each picture.
3. Write a story chart about "How Mothers Help."
4. Dramatize mother's work in the home.

How To Help
1. *Discussion* — How children help at home. Encourage them to tell how they help in their homes. Bring out how they can care for their belongings, for pets, for younger children and themselves. Indicate how this helps to make mother's work easier.
2. Learn how to care for pets.
3. Plant seeds and grow plants to take home.
4. Draw pictures for individual booklets showing how they help at home.
5. Make two charts: "We Help at Home"
"We Help at School"
Have children list ways they can help.
6. Have regular housekeeping duties for children to do each day at school.
7. Play house — emphasizing housekeeping duties.
8. Mimetics — Helping father
Helping mother

A Happy Home
1. *Discussion*-How can we make our homes happy? How can we make other people like us? Emphasize attitudes involved in happy living.

2. Encourage children to tell how they have fun.
3. Draw pictures of ways to have fun at home. Include these in individual booklets.
4. Have a party as we do at home. Make cookies for the party.
5. Dramatize fun at home.
6. Make a mural of "Things We Like to Do."
7. Make a chart showing children's birthdays.

Culminating Activity

Choose committees and plan a party to which the mothers may be invited. Write simple invitations to the parents. Encourage the children to do the planning and try to have simple refreshments that they can prepare and serve. Display the children's work at this time.

They might like to review what they have learned by having a television program. They could draw pictures of what they have learned, with an explanatory sentence under each picture. The picture will be pasted together and placed on two rolls. A television set can be constructed from a large pasteboard carton. A good reader may be chosen to announce or read the stories as the pictures are unrolled.

V. EVALUATION
  A. Pupil's Evaluation
    1. Have a "Friendship Box." Into the box the children will put the names of others whom they have seen:
      a. help others
      b. share
      c. take turns
      d. play or work nicely with others. Specify each week a positive attitude to look for in others.
    2. Have a large evaluation chart. Ask each child how he has improved.
      a. Am I helping others?
      b. Am I sharing?
      c. Am I taking turns?

      d. Am I playing and working well with others?

      e. Am I doing my best?

B. Teacher's Evaluation

    1. Have the children gained appreciation of the family group?

    2. Have they developed worthy attitudes?

    3. Have the children improved in their skills and habits?

    4. Was the unit carried out so that both the teacher and pupils have a feeling of accomplishment?

Figure 3. Cooperative communication.

CHAPTER 4 ————————————————————————

LANGUAGE SKILLS

————————————————————————————

COMMUNICATION may be simply defined as the ability to understand and be understood by others. Although appearance and behavior influence interpersonal communication, language alone provides the nuance to social intercourse and thereby plays a crucial role in human relations. The understandings achieved through language serve to mediate behavior. "We both speak the same language" is a cliche which indicates a great degree of communication. Language is a primary mode of social intercourse which enhances communication.

Competence in spoken language is a prerequisite for developing verbal ability. Loban (1963) found that the academically successful kindergarteners were those who ranked high in oral speech. Expressive skills are the foundation upon which verbal learning rests; lingual inadequacies impede the learning process. Language acquisition should be thoroughly understood by teachers who wish to provide effective instruction. An awareness of language theory and of the sequential milestones will cement a base upon which to build a sound language curriculum.

LANGUAGE ACQUISITION

Theorists explaining language development fall into three general categories: environmentalists, naturalists and interactionists. No single theory can account for acquisition completely. Position statements within each theory only partially explain the complex sequence of vocal emissions we recognize as language. The opposed divergent theoretical stances have shed additional light on the particular mechanisms at work.

Environmentalists (learning theorists) emphasize imitation, association and reinforcement as the important components. By rewarding oral utterances the child is encouraged to imitate adult models. Dialectal and ghetto speech are evidence of imitation and adult modeling. However, opponents are quick to point out that modeling is frequently ignored, that spontaneous speech occurs without definitive order. Furthermore, frequency of word exposure plays a limited role in acquisition; many of the high frequency words are acquired much later. The articles *a*, *an*, and *the* are heard daily but do not appear in early speech. Nor have learning theorists explained why children of nonspeaking deaf parents learn to speak as quickly as other children do.

Naturalists hold the contrary view that language is related to the growth of brain cells which evolved throughout the history of mankind. The elements of acquisition are rooted in physiological reactions and in response to genetically determined changes taking place in the maturing child (Lenneberg, 1967). According to this position, internal biological mechanisms develop naturally, independent of experience and intelligence. The critical period of acquisition occurs after walking has started. The speech explosion begins at approximately eighteen months when a vocabulary of less than fifty words increases to over 1,000 at thirty-six months. Such a phenomenal spurt presupposes a built-in physiological mechanism tied to a biological timetable. Naturalists have been criticized for failing to explain this phenomenon in greater detail and for ignoring environmental influences. The failure to delineate the precise role of environmental stimulation is a criticism which appears to have merit.

Piaget's (1957) cognitive interaction theory integrates elements of naturalism and learning theory. He believes acquisition occurs through two basic precepts: assimilation and accommodation. Assimilation is the process whereby environmental influences are absorbed, internalized. Through accommodation the child reacts individually, adjusting himself to external forces. The dynamics of internal reactions to external experiences molds cognitive structures. The child takes an active role in thinking and behavior; language is intimately tied to both. Spontaneous speech emerges as the child attempts to express his own feelings and thoughts in relation to others.

Each theory contains elements which contribute to an understanding of acquisitional processes. A combination of biological, environmental and interactional effects coalesce in a complex known as language. The precise contribution of each is un-known, and these generalizations fail to explain individual devia-tion and differential rates of growth. In the final analysis language is an individual growth process.

AUDITORY SELF-STIMULATION

Babbling is initially evoked by vocal stimulation impacting on a receptive nervous system. Triggered by an external vocal source, babbling is self-sustained through the auditory feedback mechan-ism. Montessori (1967) suggests that the auditory centers are spe-cially designed to capture words and language; so it may be that this receiving system is triggered by sounds of a particular kind — those of speech. The result is that words heard by the child set in motion the mechanism which excites the oral movements needed to imitate those sounds. The child reacts as if to respond. The significant increase in babbling which occurs between the sixth and eleventh month is thought to be in response to the voice of the nursing mother (Lewis, 1951).

Echolalia, the continuous repetition of sounds, utterances and nonsense syllables for the pleasure of vocal exercise, precedes recognizable speech. Early utterances are emitted solely for pur-poses of self-stimulation, not communication. Crying or smiling remain the primary means of communicating with mother. Ne-vertheless, all vocal emissions exercise the lips, tongue and jaw in preparation for the first spoken words which appear at the end of the first year.

Children demonstrate the ability to understand language be-fore the first word is spoken. In the latter half of the first year they knowingly attend to their name, understand the meaning of "no," and will look for the family pet when called. At one year most can point to bodily parts when named and follow simple directions like, "Come here." Associations are established be-tween the sound-label and word meaning. Language comprehen-sion and sound-object association are prerequisites for speech production.

Before the first words appear, most infants have received ap-proximately 3,000 waking hours of auditory stimulation. Many hours of language exposure are needed to discriminate sounds (phonemes) and integrate these sounds into meaningful word units (morphemes).

During the early years children are exposed to the language of the family but especially that of the mother, the primary language model. Mothers with high expressive speech rates usually have children who develop speech rapidly (Cazden, 1965). However, speech may be actively discouraged. In close quarters children are sometimes punished for speaking noisily because Father must sleep during the day, working nights. Inhibition interferes with the normal process of language acquisition and is thought to contribute to stuttering.

The First Words

In the second six months most children attempt their first intelligible words. Common objects or pets are usually named without elaboration: bow-wow, light, etc. Object naming continues into the second year. Not until about eighteen months are words put together into a sentence unit. "Me run" and other combinations appear.

Telegraphic statements indicate that word sequencing, which underlies the grammatical process, has begun (subject followed by verb). Two aspects of the word must be learned: the meaning and its sequential relation to other words, i.e. its position in the sentence. It appears that a number of factors determine the speed with which a word is acquired. It must be understandable, easy to pronounce, and readily incorporated into sentence patterns. Acquiring new words does not present the difficulty which sequential incorporation does. If almost a year passes between the time the first words appear and the ability to sequence begins, we can only assume sequencing is much more difficult indeed. Word sequencing will be further discussed in the section on spontaneous speech. For a summary of the chronological development of audio-lingual activity see Figure 4.

Although the purpose of speech is communication, the initial production of word combinations occurs with approximate syntax; however, comprehension is limited. The first words uttered are spoken thoughts and indicate an inability to engage in silent thought.

Months	
1	Activity and movement cease upon hearing a bell or other auditory stimulus.
2 - 4	Attends to human voice, turns head in direction of sound. Coos, gurgles, babbling begins.
6 - 10	Babbling increases. Child responds to name and points to objects named. Comprehension of speech begins.
11 - 18	Babbling diminishes, giving way to object naming. First intelligible words appear in isolation.
19 - 24	Object naming continues. Two-word, combined utterances appear in appropriate sequence. Ex: Me go. Telegraphic speech begins.
25 - 36	Telegraphic speech increases. Content words predominate. Ex: Boy run. Functor words omitted.
37 - 48	Basic rules of grammar imitated in simple sentences. Noun is followed by the verb. Private speech begins as child talks to toys and to self.

Figure 4. Appearance of audio-lingual activity.

Early speech (expressed externalized thoughts) is called egocentric because it is not directed toward others. Vygotsky (1962) was the first to notice that speech for social communication develops only after considerable egocentric talk. Comprehension emerges after three or four years of social interaction; increasingly words are used to mediate behavior. By the age of seven egocentric talk has largely disappeared as thoughts are gradually internalized.

Imitation and Spontaneity

Imitation is the ability to auditorily perceive the stimulus order of words for immediate reproduction. Accurate imitation does not depend upon sentence length but rather upon the complexity of the grammatical structure or verb pattern in the sentence (Menyuk, 1963). The meaningful content words, usually nouns, verbs and the high information words, are generally retained. Telegraphic speech predominates. Time to go home becomes "Me go home." Words which cannot be interpreted are ignored as sentences are modified to conform to the child's linguistic pattern.

The ability to imitate has little relationship to comprehension. Children can often repeat what they hear but fail to understand its meaning. In a study of over 1,000 imitations, it was found that hesitation, pauses, word emphasis, rhythm and intonation enhance imitation (Slobin and Welch, 1967). Preschoolers find imitation easier than speech production and comprehension. Imitation is largely an exercise of immediate rote memory which explains why three-year-olds can vocally reproduce sentences without comprehension. Imitative skills can be exercised through jingles, nursery rhymes and songs.

Speech is spontaneous and words are acquired in no particular order. Certain classes of words may be acquired earlier (nouns and verbs before adjectives and adverbs) but great variation exists. Words which can be easily incorporated into the child's linguistic system appear early. Word sequencing and comprehension play a greater role in speech production than imitation. Ease of comprehension and sequencing determine the age at which a word will appear. Therefore, each child's developing vocabulary differs as spontaneous speech and linguistic processing vary.

ORAL GRAMMAR

The acquisition of grammar develops slowly continuing well into preadolescence. Only after the age of four does the awareness of grammatical features begin (Scholes, 1969). Incorporating words into a sentence requires an integration of word knowledge and word sequences, plus the inclusion of connecting words: *and, but, or.* The irregularity of syntactic classes in English complicates grammatical structures, contributing to the delay.

Although they can be generally understood, most preschoolers speak with considerable imperfection because words enter the speaking vocabulary without a full set of syntactic features attached (Cazden, 1968). Signs of immature speech include one or more of the following:

1. plurals added to nouns and pronouns: hims, yous.
2. the addition of ing to verbs: I seeing you.
3. intransitive verbs used transitively: I falled down.
4. inaccuracy with regular and irregular plural forms: mans, mines, childs.
5. incorrect use of verb form: comed, runned.
6. overuse of pronouns.

If oral vocabulary is meager, incorrect forms linger as the same words are inappropriately applied to numerous situations. Contextual generalization (Braine, 1963) partially explains the acquisition of word order and grammar. Sequencing is facilitated as words frequently reappear in similar patterns and combinations which eventually become familiar.

In young children one estimate of oral language fluency is sentence length. At the age of three the average sentence contains four words, increasing to seven words at age six (Templin, 1957). Sentence length increases at the rate of one word per year. Such a slow rate of growth indicates the difficulty with which word combinations are incorporated into oral expression. Apparently, grammatical structures are only very gradually acquired. The ability to string words together into a correct sequence cannot be rushed. Consequently, it is no surprise to find sentence length and sentence structure unimproved by brief periods of instruction. Ammon & Ammon (1971) found that after six to eight weeks of instruction, vocabulary revealed signs of improvement. A conclusion that can be drawn from this research is that vocabulary enrichment should be a short-range goal and the improvement of syntax and grammar a long-range goal of any language program.

Because grammatical structures are not readily acquired does not mean that consistent instruction throughout the school year will not have a beneficial effect. Learning to communicate through improved oral expression is a lifelong process.

ORAL LANGUAGE PROGRAM

Experiences in oral expression need little justification, as scholastic performance is clearly related to expressive fluency. Therefore, a creative program of oral self-expression should have a first priority. Youngsters with lingual inadequacies parrot inappropriate phrases, often fail to comprehend directions, and sometimes resort to nonverbal participation. Shyness and personal oversensitivity often accompany those with limited speech patterns. Opportunities for self-expression by the inarticulate must be nurtured in a warm atmosphere to avoid embarrassment, the prime inhibitor of language growth.

Small group instruction is an ideal vehicle for encouraging creative expression. A conversational dialogue between the teacher and a few select pupils will serve to introduce, expand and reinforce correct oral patterns. Cowe (1967) found maturity of speech most influenced by adult discussion of concrete topics with children. The self-expressive program should provide numerous opportunities to manipulate, process and arrange words into sequentially meaningful patterns.

Expressive fluency can be encouraged in numerous ways. Conversation is stimulated by greeting each child individually upon arrival. Personal experiences provide an unlimited source of ideas for discussion. Each child can speak personally of family experiences, television programs, weekend activities, and incidents with peers that exercise recall and stimulate creative self-expression. Topics likely to elicit oral participation are listed at the conclusion of the chapter. Note that conversation relates to familiar, everyday experiences.

Animation provides an opportunity to reinforce verbal experiences. Imitating a variety of animals, or playing cowboys and Indians, offers a host of associated motor activities to accompany and complement the verbal concepts that are introduced. Role playing, pantomiming and play acting enhance and vitalize an otherwise ordinary discussion.

Classroom discussions should be utilized, not for the collection of facts (of questionable long-term value) but for the expansion of self-expression through verbal and associated motor activities. The scope and variety of language is broadened by vocabulary exposure, word usage and word sequencing. Learning to use new words to communicate ideas should be a central goal of oral expression.

Labeling

Although estimates vary, the average five-year-old has approximately 2,500 words in his speaking vocabulary. Immediate retrieval from a fund of freely flowing words is necessary for comfortable conversation. However, with a limited vocabulary bank to draw upon, speech can be hesitant and repetitive. A halting, groping for words often leads to frustration. Children with limited expressive skills resort to crying, screaming or hitting as alternate means of communication. The inability to label impedes language development and eventually leads to severe academic weaknesses (Langer, 1967). Labeling is a fundamental language skill which must be carefully nurtured to enlarge the vocabulary bank.

The kindergarten should be literally cluttered with hundreds of objects or pictures of objects to be labeled. Identification and discussion of toys, pets and of common or unusual objects will increase auditory-visual association skills. A unison response by the children increases the stimulus intensity which aids retention of label-naming. A thorough, descriptive elaboration follows labeling to insure comprehension and to attach additional associations to the label. For instance, if a model airplane is demonstrated, its color, shape, size and function are fully explored. Comparative ideas are encouraged, expanding an awareness of a variety of items with similar properties. A reply to the question, "What else flies?" enlarges the concept of flight. Incorrect answers provided by the teacher are corrected by the alert youngsters.

Beyond Labeling

Knowledge of the name alone may not provide sufficient associational information to use the word orally; therefore, a thorough discussion for purposes of elaborating comprehension and expanding word usage immediately follows labeling. Building word associations presents the more difficult challenge. The label will not likely be retained unless some distinguishing characteristics or features are associationally attached. For example, bears: climb trees, live in the forests, eat berries, hibernate and have fur coats. Armed with knowledge of its distinctive behavior and salient features, the word (bear), with conceptual meanings attached, can then be used effectively in a sentence.

To increase oral vocabulary a comprehensive understanding of the labeled item is essential; its use, function or purpose must be developed before it can enter the speaking vocabulary. Correct use of the word in a sentence is usually a good indication of comprehension.

Interpreting Pictures

Although pictorial presentation is never as vivid as a live subject (rabbit or turtle), pictures represent the first level of abstraction. As many of life's experiences are representational via films, radio, television, books, etc., recognizing items or objects through pictures reinforces visual memory.

Each child is encouraged to begin a picture scrapbook; cutting and pasteing become fun activity. Naming and discussing the pictures may be followed by printing the name below it. Creative, fantasy and imaginative stories about the pictures are encouraged. An extensive collection of pictures from magazines and newspapers provide an excellent source of diverse pictorial materials.

Fantasy and fun stories can be built around unusual or humorous pictures. The free flow of ideas through imagination stimulates creative oral expression. The stories need not be factually correct; in fantasy anything goes. Curiosity and mental imagery enhance motivation when freed to function openly. Under the bulletin board caption, "What is it?"pictures of unusual animals or strange objects are posted. The curiosity of children will do the rest. Pictures may be cut in half with only one portion displayed for identification. At the end of the day, the matched half is mounted.

ORAL EXPRESSION

Errors in oral expression are expected in the young. Improper word sequencing, omission of word endings, and errors in verb tense are quite common and only gradually acquired (Menyuk, 1969). Speech is encoded through a dialectal frame of reference and emerges from the child's developing audio-lingual system. The profusion of adult dialects insures the likelihood that correct grammatical constructions will not be acquired naturally. Therefore, formal instruction in oral grammar should not be overlooked.

The basic elements of correct oral expression constitute the backbone of a sound preschool language program. The teacher listens for the grammatical errors of each child as he speaks to discover his instructional needs. Those with limited expressive fluency need daily language sessions, preferably in a small group, throughout the year. Less frequent opportunity for oral instruction will have little noticeable effect.

Action Verbs

Brown (1957) found that over half of the verbs spoken by younger children are action verbs. The action can be visually portrayed to enhance the mental image and improve retention. A list of verbs the children can demonstrate through activity include calling, crying, sweeping, running, rolling, pulling, pushing, sliding, swinging, pointing, throwing, hugging, loving, eating, licking, looking, walking, cutting, sawing, hammering, talking, kicking, waving, meeting, writing, sleeping, swimming, jumping, etc. The process can be reversed, portraying the action before asking for the verb. Also, children can be asked to complete sentences: A dog..., A man..., Horses..., Fish...,Boys are..., He is..., etc. Practice associating nouns with action verbs by asking, "What...sleeps?"...roars?"...eats?"...climbs?"....runs?"

Using Adjectives

Activities are so designed as to observe the child's reaction based on the use of adjectives. Books, pencils and crayons of different sizes and colors are readily available. Directions emphasize discrimination based on comprehension of the adjective. "Put the small book on the round table." "Give me the red book." "Take the big, red pencil." "Touch the small crayon." "Carry the thick book to my desk." To encourage accurate use of adjectives use a variety of beads, buttons, blocks and toys, always varying the description.

Pluralization

Preschoolers generalize that plurals are longer than singulars by adding "s" to the end of all singular words (Anisfeld and Tucker, 1967). Comprehension of number can be evaluated by the following procedures. With a number of pencils, books and crayons on the desk the teacher asks "Give me a pencil." "Give me the pencils." "Give me a book." "Give me the books." "Give me a crayon." "Give me the crayons." Vary the objects and order of presentation to relieve boredom. The child replies orally as he complies. "Here is a pencil." "Here are the pencils." Exercises are repeated until the difference is grasped. Nouns which do not add "s" when pluralized should be emphasized: foot, feet; child, children; tooth, teeth; mouse, mice; man, men; woman, women.

Overgeneralization of the plural form creates faulty agreement between subject and verb. The "s" is added to the verb in the singular, to the noun in the plural. This rather fine distinction should be expressly taught and not left to chance. Portray the difference dramatically in order to visualize the idea and thereby improve comprehension. Example: "John runs." "The two boys run." "Sally walks home." "The girls walk home." "Mary paints." "Mary and Bill paint." "John plays tag." "The boys play tag."

Auxiliary and Irregular Verbs

Correct use of the verbs to be (am, is, are, was, were) and to have (have, has, had) is essential to proper oral expression. Usage in combination with action verbs develops slowly. Pluralization and tense accuracy should be stressed. Examples: "Mary is eating candy." "Mary was eating candy." "We were eating candy." "I am eating candy." "I have a hat." "We have hats." "He has a dog." "He had a dog." Developing questions with auxiliary verbs also deserve our attention. "Is she your friend?" "Was he with you?" "Were you home?" "Have you a hat?" "Were you eating candy?"

Irregular verbs also need special attention as they recur regularly in everyday speech. Verbs that change word form completely present the greatest difficulty. A few rather common irregular verbs include do, did, done; fall, fell, fallen; go, went, gone; buy, bought; drive, drove, driven; and see, saw, seen. Combining auxiliary and irregular verbs correctly in a sentence is quite difficult for preschoolers; instruction should be delayed until simple usage is mastered.

Comprehending Statements

Teachers sometimes believe that failure to follow directions is due to inattention; often the idea is not completely understood. In a complex sentence, word choice or word arrangement may be the confounding culprit. The following procedure will pinpoint those who misunderstand directions. Begin very simply, giving each child a chance. "John, touch my desk." "Jane, sit on the long table." "Mary, shake hands with Shirley." The children soon discover that the noun which precedes the verb acts upon the noun following the verb.

The Simon Says game is also valuable as a means of determining verbal comprehension. Directions may be increasingly complex, asking for three or four activities consecutively. "Simon says: touch your chin, clap your hands, close your eyes and hold your head." Periodic opportunity for exercise should improve comprehension skills.

Asking Questions

Statements can be made into questions by reversing word order. The teacher provides a statement and the pupil rearranges the words into a question. "John is coming." "Is John coming?" "Jane will go." "Will Jane go?" "Mary is here." "Is Mary here?" "He is working." "Is he working?" "She is playing." "Is she playing?" Statements of greater intricacy are attempted after mastery of simpler examples. "He has had fun." "Has he had fun?" "You are going home now." "Are you going home now?" The procedure can be reversed by providing the question and asking for the statement. Another variation provides the youngster with the initial part of the question. "Is the dog . . . ?" "Will Mary . . . ?" "When will . . . ?"

A variety of questions should be practiced orally using the interrogatives: what, when, where, who, why, how and which. The verb to do is also useful formulating questions. "Do you like it?" "Does he want more?" "Do you like me?" Tag questions detect comprehension. "John did it, didn't he?" "Mary is coming, isn't she?" "You like me, don't you?" Fluency with questions can be improved through persistent instruction.

Positives and Negatives

Affirmative and negative statements are basic grammatical constructions. Children can learn to convert positive statements into negative and vice versa. If at all possible, the actions should be animated to assist understanding. "John is eating." "John is not eating." "The class is sitting." "The class is not sitting." "Mary is standing." "Mary is not standing." Negatives are also developed using the prefix *un*. "Pile the blocks." "Unpile the blocks." "Button your sweater." "Unbutton your sweater." "Cover yourself." "Uncover yourself."

Possessive, Passive and Reflexive

The possessive form can be developed by asking the child to:

"Get me Mary's crayons." "Give me John's hat." "Touch Joe's desk." "Find Betty's gloves." By observing the activity we determine comprehension. Such exercises should increase the ability to grasp usage of the possessive form.

Passive sentences reverse normal word order. The first noun is acted upon by the second noun. With a toy car and bus the child is asked to demonstrate: "The car is hit by the bus." "The bus is passed by the car." "The bus is hit by the car." "The car is passed by the bus." Considerable practice is needed to improve an understanding of passive forms.

Reflexives can be animated to maintain interest and improve comprehension. Adding *self* to pronouns is not a difficult exercise and grasped quickly by most youngsters. "Mary pinched herself." "John saw himself in the mirror." "John hurt himself." "Mary tapped herself." "Betty scratched herself."

Comparisons

As comparisons are relative estimates between two conditions, an understanding of comparative terms is not easy. In the comparison, include the word *than*, i.e. taller than, bigger than. The two items to be compared should be visibly present to enable the children to see what is meant. Clearly demonstrate the dimension upon which the comparison is made. For example: "This glass is wider than that glass." "This book is bigger than that book." A list of common comparisons include hot, cold, warm, big, short, tall, thin, sad, happy, pretty, quick, high, low, little, small. With experience children understand the effect of adding *er* to a comparison word. Superlative comparisons (biggest, warmest) should be avoided until mastery of a simple two-way comparison is well developed.

Conditional Statements

Five-year-olds tend to listen to the main clause, ignoring the conditional or subordinate clause. With careful instruction youngsters can learn to listen for the condition. The following conditioners should be practiced periodically: when, if, as soon

as, before, as, and after. For example:
   "When I stand up, clap your hands."
   "After Sue opens the door, everyone stand up."
   "If John gets his milk, you can get yours."
   "As soon as I turn around, go to your seats."
   "Sit down before I ring the bell."
The tendency for the action to occur before the condition is understood can be overcome with practice. Examples should incorporate observable events which can be corrected and repeated in the event of error.

Encouraging Conversation and Discussion

Spontaneous conversation is encouraged throughout the day. As the children work, play and participate in group activities, talking is natural to the social process. Talk becomes the primary medium of communication, gradually replacing touching, pulling, pushing, shoving and other forms of physical contact.

Classroom discussions directed by the teacher are conducted daily. The teacher acts as guide and clarifier to improve communication among the children. Opening exercises and plans for the day provide an excellent opportunity to exchange ideas and discuss topics the children may suggest. The success of "show and tell" is based upon the presentation of a concrete stimulus for discussion.

Far too many curricula treat oral communication incidentally and not as the basic language skill upon which reading, writing and spelling build. At five, children are learning to speak and converse. We must provide daily opportunity to enrich, expand and refine oral expression. An emphasis upon articulation is also clearly related to effective oral communication.

ARTICULATION

Intelligible speech is essential to communication. One researcher found that 25 percent of all six-year-olds in Seattle, Washington, misarticulated one or more sounds (Pendergast, 1966). If this sample is representative, then the percentage of five-year-olds who misarticulate must be higher. Such estimates support Templin's (1967) position that misarticulation is no respector of socioeconomic status, cultural background or intellect.

Misarticulation can lead to serious academic difficulty. Elliott (1968) found that the use of regular curriculums and ordinary teaching techniques failed to prevent the general academic decline of pupils with speech difficulties. The inability to articulate makes it less likely words will be accurately recognized in print. In one sample of poor readers, at least 95 percent misarticulated more than one sound and 50 percent discriminated auditory signals poorly; both conditions suggest the presence of a speech disorder (Sonenberg and Glass, 1965). Poor auditory discrimination, often associated with misarticulation, contributes substantially to difficulty in reading. The inability to distinguish sounds lessens the likelihood that letters representing those sounds can be identified accurately, thereby causing repeated errors in reading.

Improved articulation will have a beneficial effect on the ability to read, and therefore, should receive first priority attention. Developing articulation skills is an indispensable part of the kindergarten language curriculum.

According to Egland (1970), the five principal causes of misarticulation, singly or in combination, are

1. neuro-muscular impairment (physical or organic structure of speech: the brain and its nerve tracts; the organs of hearing and vision, the tongue, lips, jaw, teeth, palate, breathing mechanism, vocal cords, etc.);

2. anatomical defects (cleft palate, loss of teeth, malocclusion, irregularities in size and shape of the palate and partial excision of the tongue);

3. perceptual deficiencies (loss of hearing, faulty visual or kinesthetic cues);

4. low intelligence;

5. insufficient or faulty learning (due to faulty speech models, inadequate opportunity to practice, and a lack of environmental stimulation).

Misarticulation occurs in the form of substitutions (wed for red); omissions (egg for leg); distortions of sounds (s, z, ch, sh, l); and addition of sounds (s, sh, ch, l, r, j). The majority of children who misarticulate appear to have normal equipment for speech and language.

A concomitant side effect of poor speech is a weakened self-image. Children are prone to shun those whose speech cannot be understood. Isolation and embarrassment impede social-emotional growth. Speech which was acceptable at home is suddenly a liability, a source of discomfort and tension. Such distress reduces the use of speech in the classroom. Communication is impeded with a resulting abrasive effect on the personality. Compensatory behavioral patterns tend to emerge. Withdrawal, aggression or silent play are sometimes substituted for conversation.

What Can the Teacher Do?

Clarity is demonstrated by example; articulation is precise and careful. Emphasizing deliberate thought improves chances for clarity of expression. Misarticulations are recorded during discussions and conversations. To avoid embarrassment, correction does not take place before the entire class. Children with obvious articulatory deficiencies are scheduled for small group instruction with the teacher or speech therapist. Instruction is initiated by selecting minor errors amenable to swift improvement with a minimum of correction and practice. The ease with which these errors are eliminated encourages mastery of stubborn misarticulations which are firmly embedded in the speech pattern.

Articulation improves with age, except in those with severe speech disorders. Children with unintelligible speech should be referred immediately for a complete evaluation. Remedial efforts should begin in the kindergarten because correction is usually less effective at a later age.

READING IN THE KINDERGARTEN

Maria Montessori (1912) first introduced reading into the pre-school. She postulated a period of sensitivity at the ages of four and five, insisting that some of her five-year-olds could read "as well as those who had completed the first elementary." Instruction was never obligatory, and those children who did not express an interest pursued other activities. Montessori's views were not generally accepted by American educators who insisted that a six-and-a-half-year mental age was necessary for success in beginning reading (Washburne and Morphett, 1931). Unfortunately, this view has dominated the introduction of reading in American schools for four decades.

Recent research supports the introduction of reading into the kindergarten. In Denver, kindergarteners who were provided daily reading instruction benefitted from the exposure (Bond & Dykstra, 1966). Contrary to the preschool research in which the educational advantage disappears, Durkin (1962, 1963) found that early readers were at least one grade level better than regular readers at the end of third grade. A number of researchers (Morrison, 1968; Sutton, 1969) agree that kindergarteners who read maintained and increased their advantage over classmates throughout the primary grades. Reading can be taught effectively to a good number of preschoolers, but, of course, not to all.

Reading instruction is slowly filtering down from the elementary curriculum into the modern kindergarten. Forty-one percent of the kindergartens polled by the NEA (1969) offered some form of reading instruction, if only letters of the alphabet. This trend needs to be broadened in scope to include independent reading activities and SGI in reading for youngsters who are ready.

The modern kindergarten breaks the lockstep tradition whereby beginning reading instruction is confined to first grade. The extraordinary pressure to teach all first graders reading creates an unhealthy, anxious atmosphere for both pupils and teacher. In a survey of seventy-two schools, Hoggard (1967) found that 50 percent started into preprimers the first or second week of school, regardless of individual readiness. The lip service given individual differences is confirmed by the inflexibility of asking children to begin reading in the early weeks of first grade.

Teaching all kindergarteners to read is as inappropriate as teaching all first graders. Both rigidities are doomed because children simply do not arrive in neat, well-ordered packages which fit into arbitrary institutional patterns of operation. Too many routine academic procedures adopted by schools serve its convenience, not the children's. Some five-year-olds are ready to read, but others may not be ready until the age of six or seven because of a variety of verbal, perceptual or developmental weaknesses. King (1969) has concluded that young children need protection from extreme pressure to begin and the opposite extreme of prolonged delay. The reading program should not be organized so as to delay those who have started or deny the opportunity to those ready.

Learning to read is undoubtedly the most challenging task of the primary years, perhaps almost as difficult as learning to speak. Speech is an aural-oral integrative process, but learning to read demands a cognitive synchronization of lingual, auditory and visual modalities. Reading instruction occupies the greatest amount of time in the elementary curriculum; skill in reading will not improve without consistent effort by both teacher and pupil. In the short-term, reading is fraught with much trial and error, guessing, memorization, and numerous setbacks. Therefore, we should not ask that a youngster undertake the assignment lightly, unless assured a reasonable chance for success.

The practical problem of assessing readiness has plagued educators since the twenties. Reading instruction has not taken root in the kindergarten because of the inability to determine precisely which children are ready to begin. Readiness implies that we gradually ease children into reading when optimally mature, when their chances for success are greatest. Readiness will be explored in greater detail in conjunction with the rate of learning.

Updating the Teacher

Retraining the nation's 50,000 kindergarten teachers is essential prior to any systematic introduction of reading into the kindergarten. Preschool teacher training programs have historically ignored reading procedures and techniques of teaching reading. Unless teachers are thoroughly prepared and familiar with the reading process, as they were when modern mathematics was introduced (through in-service workshops), many will lack confidence in their ability to teach reading.

In a poll of 500 kindergarten teachers, LaConte (1969) found that individual and small group instruction is rarely used. Essential prereading skills were taught by only one third of this group. When teachers were asked to explain, vague replies about school policy were voiced. The haphazard treatment afforded prereading skills suggests that many teachers have little understanding of the rationale for individualized, prereading instruction. The teacher who neglects to prepare children for reading naively contributes to the fumbling and guessing which is so characteristic of beginners.

A systematic prereading program should be an essential feature of the kindergarten because many preschoolers have little understanding of the dynamics of the abstract decoding process. The prevention of numerous reading failures may well rest upon upgrading teacher competency. The critically important role of prereading and readiness skills must be especially well understood by kindergarten teachers.

Orientation to Reading

A systematic introduction to prereading should be an integral part of every kindergarten. Formal prereading instruction is notably effective preparing kindergarteners to read (Schoephoerster, Barnhart, Loomer, 1966). A daily session of ten or fifteen minutes provides the necessary orientation to the basic elements of the reading process. Many preschoolers hold a circumscribed view of reading and have limited expectancies of how to go about it (Reid, 1966). Children from nonreading backgrounds find the entire process a puzzling, meaningless, irrelevant activity.

An appropriate orientation program establishes reading as a desirable activity both in and out of school. Positive attitudes are developed concerning the necessity for reading in daily life. Reading stop signs, letters, packages, magazines and newspapers are essential in daily life. The prereading orientation provides a smoother transition between kindergarten and the "mandated" first year reading programs. The introduction to prereading skills will not benefit all children to the same degree due to the unique nature of individual differences. However, children should be aware that learning to read is necessary for a full life.

Identifying the Early Reader

Selection of children for reading instruction should be carefully planned. The Developmental Pretest (See Chapter 11) should be utilized as the initial screening device to select children whose repertoire of basic skills is well developed. Children with a superior rating (Table XII) have readiness skills equal to or greater than the average first grade pupil. These pupils are generally ready to read.

Children with a weighted stanine pretest score of at least fifty-one are recommended for reading instruction upon admission to kindergarten. The cutoff score of fifty-one was chosen to exclude children who may have isolated developmental weaknesses. The early reader will move swiftly through the reading readiness orientation program, learning to recognize letters of the alphabet with little difficulty.

A note of caution is necessary. Mere possession of the developmental skills provides no assurance regarding motivation to read. Motivational considerations play a significant role and frequently determine the amount of energy a child is willing to expend. Any child who indicates an avid or burning desire should always be allowed to proceed, regardless of pretest score, but permitted to discontinue if difficulty ensues and interest wanes.

A Lack of Interest

No symptom has greater meaning for the teacher than apathy. Children who display no interest in reading do so because unfamiliarity breeds a fear of the seemingly complex task. Those who fail to comprehend the intricacy of the symbolization process naturally fear its complexity and employ defensive avoidance strategies. When one hundred preschoolers were asked if they could read, almost all replied that they could, when in fact they could not. Upon further questioning, most admitted wanting to learn but others continued to insist they already knew how, so why learn (Mason, 1967). Disinterest, then, is a defensive strategy and a signal that the child is not ready or willing to undertake reading activities. We should not underestimate their ability to assess the difficulty of a task. Youngsters studiously avoid activities which appear difficult or personally threatening. The fear of failure generates a global avoidance reaction. Activities which include any risk of failure and embarrassment are not well tolerated. The egos of preschoolers are fragile indeed.

Children who display little or no interest in reading need not participate until they express the desire. A few may not indicate any willingness until the first or possibly the second year. They may be invited to observe or join those reading whenever they wish. The opportunity to be an onlooker enhances familiarization with reading, without pressure to perform.

As reading activities are encouraged, social pressure will do its work, moving the hesitant ones to try. The teacher must then discern whether the verbalization to read is a mere ploy or a sincere expression of interest. Such a distinction is not always easy but should be carefully assessed. A child who does not follow a verbal expression of interest with deeds, or who at the last moment changes his mind, is not pressed. Any child who begins and experiences serious difficulty, suddenly losing interest, may discontinue without onus or recrimination. Each child will let it be known, in good time, when he has developed sufficient self-confidence to approach the task. Hopefully, when the opportune moment arrives, we will capitalize upon it by providing positive opportunities for learning.

Teach Reading — Not a Method

The proliferation of reading methods and the controversy surrounding the strengths and weaknesses of different systems merely accentuates the weakness of adopting any one system. The method, be it basal, linguistic, modified linguistic, programmed or phonetic is incidental. No one method can possibly satisfy the differing needs of every child in the classroom. A system successful with one will certainly fail with another; the law of probability assures that. The idea that schools should use one reading system throughout the grades (promulgated by the publishing houses) is without scientific foundation. Such an inflexible approach locks the teacher and children into a straitjacket, assuring us of reading failures. A varietal, creative approach with a full complement of reading materials is needed.

The Classroom Library

Every kindergarten should have space reserved for a mini-library. Chairs, books, shelves and tables should give the appearance of a library reading center. A variety of magazines, picture books, nursery rhymes, hard and soft backed books are available for browsing, leafing through, or reading. The library is open to all children to stimulate an interest in reading; its use is encouraged daily.

Self-selection of material is permitted with adult guidance, as children sometimes select overly difficult reading material. The teacher is available to identify difficult words, explain stories, and answer questions. Each child begins reading for himself at his own level of accomplishment and comprehension.

Individualized Reading

The rationale for selecting an individual approach is based upon the benefits derived from the intimacy of pupil-teacher contact, not on any particular method of presenting words. Fostering teacher-learner contact cements a partnership which facilitates communication and mutual understanding. Only a limited number of children will learn to read in kindergarten. Therefore, the teacher should take time to confer with each of these children, providing small group guidance and instruction.

Through individual instruction the teacher adjusts to the reading pace of the learner. New words are introduced gradually as the child is ready to learn them, thereby assuring continual success. Teachers are cautioned to proceed slowly, emphasizing accuracy, but accepting errors as inherent to the learning process.

Motivation and interest are easier to maintain in a brief reading session. The child is asked to tell a one-sentence story or an event of interest which occurred at home or school. The teacher prints the words as the child speaks. The story is then read to the child who then rereads it to the teacher. The children are also encouraged to read to each other, help each other, and correct one another's mistakes, as they seem to be much less sensitive to correction by peers. The child may also illustrate the story above the printing. Words the child fails to read correctly are printed (preferably by the child) on small cards and learned as time permits. These stories are collected into a scrapbook and taken home to be read to parents.

Sound and letter association develop quite slowly and should be introduced informally. The beginner should know that each letter has a sound, and some letters have more than one sound. Since a profusion of abstract vocabulary confuses preschoolers, use of the following terms should be avoided by the teacher: blend, vowel, consonant. We can avoid their use by asking: "What does the letter b say?" "What does this word (dog) say?" In this way only sound, word and letter need to be understood, thus avoiding other complex terminology. Sound-letter association depends upon first recognizing the letter name and attaching an auditory stimulus to the visual cue, a complex assignment for youngsters. Associational integration of auditory and visual stimuli is a developmentally complex act. The error potential is great, especially if *either* visual or sound discrimination is weak. For instance, b and d, m and n, are letters whose auditory signals are extremely similar; therefore, discrimination is quite difficult. Sounds are introduced gradually and capitalized upon if the child points and asks: "What does this letter say?"

Speed and comprehension are elements of the reading process which should be addressed after the basic visual discrimination skill is well under way. The often expressed criticism that individualized reading neglects the development of sequential skills is patently absurd. Skills are taught as words appear which require their mastery; they need not be presented in an artificially predetermined sequence.

A LANGUAGE UNIT

Toys and Pets

I. OVERVIEW

   Communication is enhanced through conversation. Frequent opportunity for creative self-expression and verbal exchange enhances language growth. Describing the appearance and use of toys or the activities of pets challenges the linguistic organization of each child. The ability to describe a toy, pet or game with accuracy requires utilization of appropriate nouns, adjectives and verbs. These topics are familiar to each child and provide a base upon which to build verbal skills.

II. UNDERSTANDINGS

   A. Every toy, pet or game has a name.
   B. Toys, pets and games must be shared.
   C. Each has parts which make up the whole.
   D. We play with one at a time.
   E. We take turns with toys.
   F. We do not break toys or hurt pets.
   G. We are careful of other's things.

III. APPROACH

   A. Toys and games (from home or school)
      1. Give name.
      2. Describe appearance in detail.
      3. If a game, give rules for playing.
      4. Pick friends to play with and demonstrate to the class.
      5. Sharing means taking turns.
      6. Play carefully to avoid breaking toys.
   B. Dolls
      1. Give doll's name and age.
      2. Color of dress and hair.
      3. Describe parts of dress — bow, frill, etc.
      4. Tell of doll's actions — talks, cries, etc.
      5. Where does she sleep? Live? Play?
      6. What does she eat?
      7. Why is she happy, funny, good or bad?
   C. Pets
      1. Name of pet.

2. Bring in color photograph.
3. Describe appearance — color, size, age, etc.
4. Describe physical features — paws, mouth, tail, feet, etc.
5. Can it do tricks?
6. Describe actions — eating, sleeping, etc.
7. Compare the pets of two children. Which is bigger, smaller, younger, older, taller, thin, heavy, etc.
8. How did you get the pet?
9. Who takes care of pet? Who feeds it? Who cleans litter box? What does he eat?
10. Tell of incidents with the pet.
11. Why is the pet fun to play with?

Vocabulary can include the names of animals, pets, toys, games and dolls; only a few are listed below.

rabbit	mouse	trucks	dolls
chick	frog	fire engine	dresses
dog	parrot	bicycle	duck
cat	fish	racer	hamster
parakeet	guppies	motorcycle	horse
canary	kitten	cars	
turtle	horse	minibike	
pony	hot rod	airplanes	

IV. DISCUSSION

A special bulletin board holds the photographs of family pets with the names printed below. Each child is given the opportunity to tell about his pet and answer any questions. Small pets which can be managed may be brought to school for brief periods with parental permission.

Comparing pets presents a great opportunity to expand verbal expression. Two children are asked to compare how their pets differ and what similarities exist. Use of comparative adjectives and adverbs is encouraged: bigger, smaller, taller, shorter, taller, thinner, heavier, faster, slower, louder, fatter, etc.

SUGGESTED LANGUAGE ACTIVITIES

A. We depend upon the telephone for many important services.
1. Use pictures to illustrate the important uses of the telephone. These include:

    a. talking to friends and relatives.

    b. getting information by asking questions.

    c. emergencies.

    d. important calls for mother or father relating to work or shopping.

B. Label and name as many objects in the room as you can. Objects in stores can also be named.

C. Tell a story about a recent TV program. Each child takes a turn to tell a story.

D. Converse about clothes the children are wearing. Explore color and design — stripes, dots, etc. Discuss clothing in detail: jacket, sleeve, buttons, pockets, collar, etc.

E. Breakfast or lunch — important meals of the day.
    1. Discuss what constitutes a good breakfast, lunch, dinner.
    2. Collect pictures of the basic food groups: milk, eggs, meat, cereal, bread, fruit, juice, etc. Label these pictures.

F. Object box — child reaches in and pulls out an object, labels and tells its purpose or use. Box may contain: nail, screw, eraser, scissors, key, ruler, fork, toy hammer, brush, feather, etc.

G. Picture box — assorted pictures cut from magazines are placed in a box. The child selects one and describes the action or scene in detail.

H. Dramatizing Storytelling

Whenever possible, teachers should select stories to read which can be dramatized by the children. Not all portions of the story are amenable to creative expression. A greater understanding of the story is effected by visualization of the action. Opportunity to portray characters in the story are rotated so that all participate. In unison or individually the common action verbs in the story may be imitated: mopping the floor, dusting furniture, tagging, driving a car, sleeping, and sweeping.

The children should be encouraged to imitate various characters: policeman, doctor, cowboy, Indian, etc. "What am I?" is a game of pantomime. The children guess who is being imitated. Talking and acting about feelings is also emotionally satisfying: happy, say, crying, smiling, frowning, fighting, helping, laughing, exciting, etc.

I. Drawing the Story

Two or three children are selected to go to the board and draw a story as it is told. "Once upon a time there was a house on a hill..." Stories are drawn as they are read by the teacher. Visualizing the story improves retention and memory.

J. Providing Words for Sentences

The teacher volunteers two words which are used in a sentence. Given the words *dog* and *cat*, a sentence is constructed without help. As the children are able to construct sentences combining two words, more are added.

K. Say and Do — Do and Say

Oral comprehension can be detected by observing the action of the children. Children are encouraged to think of an action, say it, then do it. The entire process can be reversed by first performing an action then stating it verbally. The child may say "I will sit down," then does so. After the children become proficient, the idea of tense is introduced. Past and future tense are introduced into the statements. "I will get a drink," or "I did open my desk." Much practice is needed for kindergarteners to use present, past and future tense accurately.

L. Topics of Conversation
  1. Getting to know your family
     a. Brothers and sisters' names.
     b. Their age and size.
     c. Their likes and dislikes.
     d. Their games and toys.
     e. What they do for fun.
  2. Visitors at home
     a. Relatives.
     b. Friends.
     c. Neighbors.
  3. Friends
     a. In the neighborhood.
     b. In school.

M. Ideas for Prereading

An effective method of introducing new words is through the daily routine of opening exercise. The words can be read aloud in unison. The following is printed on an easel in large letters:

Today is Monday.
It is sunny and warm.
We have 13 girls and 14 boys.
This week's letter is C, c.
My name is John.

The daily routine and repetition of opening exercise permits the exposure of many new words in an informal atmosphere.

Labeling objects within the classroom is also a favorite way of introducing new words. Periodically the labels are removed and flashed to the children to determine whether the words are recognized. Classroom activities also provide excellent opportunities for creative stories. Feeding the fish in the aquarium and telling about the classroom pet (rabbit) become excellent topics for stories to read.

N. Rhyming Words

Nonsense rhymes and nonsense sounds can be fun as the children attempt to match the sounds: cat--rat, boy--toy, fat--zat, joy--loy, etc.

O. Puppetry

Using puppets also adds the visual dimension to any story. Animation and excitement are generated by recreating: The Three Bears, Three Little Pigs, Cinderella, Pinocchio, Jack and Jill, Little Miss Muffet and other nursery rhymes.

CHAPTER 5

VISUAL SKILLS

PERCEPTION has been defined as a process for receiving, integrating and decoding visual stimuli (Chalfant and Scheffelin, 1969). Initial percepts appear as undifferentiated, gestalt impressions. At the age of four, partial details are noted and at five integration of parts and wholes begins. However, many preschool youngsters remain unable to systematically scan an array of figures and discriminate its features accurately (Elkind and Weiss, 1967).

The precise application of vision is critical to the learning process and should not be left to develop incidentally. Recognizing the figure of a circle is a visual-cognitive act sharpened by deliberate exercise. Allen (1969) effectively improved both spatial and figure-ground perception of mildly retarded children through visual training. The average five-year-old would also benefit from a visual program of instruction opportunely offered during this period of swift visual maturation. There is perhaps no greater way to maximize human potential than to complement the ongoing process of perceptual growth.

VISUAL PROCESSES

Processing combines ocular-motor and cognitive functions. Steps in visual identification include orientation of the head and eyes, object scanning, tentative cognitive classification, and feedback from external sources to confirm the percept. The ocular-motor functions of convergence, binocular fusion, tracking, and systematic scanning undergird cognitive awareness.

Convergence on a distant point minimizes the inward pull on the eye muscles for directional focusing. However, near vision (within arm's length) places a considerable burden on young, immature eye muscles. For a number of academic activities maintenance of near vision focus is critical. Those with a limited con-

Figure 5. Alphabet discrimination.

vergence span fail to sustain focus because of eye muscle fatigue. In many families few opportunities to exercise near vision may arise prior to school. Unless the child has been exposed to considerable near vision activities (drawing, coloring, etc.) teachers cannot assume the presence of adequate near vision attention span.

Binocular fusion can be defined as the coordinated, functional use of both eyes. However, if the acuity of either eye is greater, a tendency to rely upon the better eye exists. Ignoring the image in the weaker eye may lead to functional blindness. Symptoms include covering or shutting one eye, tilting the head to sight, soreness and rubbing. Sometimes only an opthalmologic examination will reveal the absence of binocular fusion.

Tracking is the ability to sight and follow an airplane, bird or object in flight. Young children track by turning their heads and should gradually learn to rely upon eye movement. Direct those children who have difficulty tracking to hold their heads still and follow a pencil flashlight with their eyes. Vary the direction and distance of the light from the eye. Watching a beanbag toss is also a good tracking exercise. Vary this activity by substituting a balloon, then a ball.

Because initial eye fixations tend to be random, important details are often missed. The untrained eye needs additional time to fix on more than one point in order to perceive all aspects of the stimulus. According to Gibson (1956) the multiple fixations needed for complex stimuli take longer than one-half second. In order to distinguish between similar appearing stimuli (run-ran), multiple comparative sightings are necessary. Systematic-analytic scanning is the skill which improves visual accuracy by alternating vertical-horizontal sweeps and sightings of the stimulus. Scanning skills can be developed through appropriate instruction for those who need it. When scanning becomes habitual, identification and discrimination improve. The visual repertoire of every child should include the habitual application of analytic scanning.

Discrimination

The act of distinguishing one stimulus from among others is a fundamental learning process (Chalfant and Flathouse, 1971). The ability to contrast and retain a distinction facilitates the possibility of a differential response. Numerous experiences with pictures, puzzles, magazines, toys and games exercise visual skills that tend to improve discrimination. If only slight differences exist between stimuli (m-n, p-d), repeated presentation is essential. Fine discriminations require considerable concentration and visual memory. Therefore, the introduction of stimuli should be carefully and deliberately controlled. In simple discrimination no more than two letters should be presented for comparison. Complex discriminations of multiple stimuli are deferred until success with simple discrimination has been demonstrated.

Figure-ground differentiation is the ability to separate figures visually from a background of competing stimuli. Extraneous elements often create interference effects which distract from focusing upon the principal figure. Objects embedded in a busy background are difficult for the immature eye to detect. The absence of systematic scanning also contributes to poor figure-ground differentiation. When salient characteristics of the principal figure are pointed out, discrimination is facilitated.

Form Perception

Recognition of form commences with a gross gestalt image, free of detail. The basic element of form is the line. Lines drawn with increasing thickness create new shapes. The following lines should be identified: thin, thick, broken and curved. Each line should be practiced extensively, with time to visualize and label. When drawn free-hand, these lines evolve into complex designs.

The common figures (circles, square, triangle, diamond, rectangle) can usually be identified after a few exposures. Animal shapes are distinctive and easy to identify: giraffe, elephant, dog, cat, etc. Many common objects have distinctive shapes (houses, boats, buildings, telephones) and need only be labeled. The figure or object must be labeled to give it significance. The cognitive label differentiates and classifies the object-form as distinct from other percepts.

Size differentiation is a basic aspect of form. The terms big, bigger, large, larger, small, smaller, should be developed. Because size is relative, children fail to understand how both a button and an elephant can be big. These terms should be utilized in numerous contexts to demonstrate the full range of comparative use.

Bodily orientation, directional awareness, and three-dimension depth perception are basic components of spatial relations. Because positional and directional terms are relational and not fixed concepts, their understanding evolves only in a variety of diverse settings. For example, *in* and *out* can be applied to houses, rooms, boxes, bags, etc., and therefore cannot be fully grasped by a single example. By careful demonstration (in appropriate spatial orientation) the following positional-directional terms can become meaningful: front, back; in, out; upper, lower; before, after; top, bottom; left, right; forward, backward. Instruction should be addressed to the variety of situations in which these terms can be applied.

The vertical, horizontal and diagonal positions are almost imperceptible directional shifts to the preschooler. Young children will often fail to distinguish between a rectangle placed vertically or horizontally because positioning is the only cue. Rotations (p-d) and reversals (J-L) are also positional shifts which should not be ignored. Through repeated manipulation of letter forms and other visual-kinesthetic exercises, proper directional orientation will emerge.

Visual retention is the ultimate measure of learning. The ability to recall the visual configurations and to associate the auditory labels is a complex visual-cognitive task. Visual memory is the amalgamation of an arsenal of separate skills operating cohesively. Convergence, fusion, tracking, scanning, discrimination and spatial relations are basic elements of the visual process which contribute to visual memory. By exercising and practicing each skill individually, we hope to improve visual retention.

EYE-HAND COORDINATION

Facile eye-hand use involves the integration of two sensory systems maturing at independent rates. Consequently, visual-motor skills develop very slowly over a number of years. The continuing difficulty five-year-olds encounter with tying shoe-laces, buttoning and zippering confirms the view that much practice is needed to make these precise movements.

Activities which exercise fine finger movements are excellent preparation for printing and writing. In many programs, children are taught to print their first name, irrespective of prior fine motor activity. In large measure the amount of previous experience with pencils and crayons will determine how well the printing is performed and not the teacher's instructional skill. Creative art is an excellent medium through which eye-hand coordination can be improved.

Creative Art

Kellogg (1972) recommends daily sessions of spontaneous art (self-directed and self-taught) as a primary means of improving eye-hand coordination. When produced under nonstress conditions, creative art allows for daily variation in performance. Daily attention to the forms, shapes and lines extends visual perception and attention to include fine details. From the initial scribbling emerges a graphic record of developing manual dexterity, visual acuity and ability to retain the graphic forms repeatedly made. A sense of personal satisfaction also emerges from the production of free-hand drawings and creative patterns.

According to Kellogg, the first drawing stage begins at three. Implied shapes gradually become shapes in outline form. Two or more forms are merged into designs; ultimately pictorials are produced by a rearrangement of these simple shapes. Through daily creative art activities, the fine coordination needed to make accurate line connections evolves. Joining lines accurately is among the more difficult pencil-crayon skills.

Formless scribbling initiates the process of self-directed hand control. Scribbling is encouraged and the productions are called designs. We accept (positively) whatever product results from these initial efforts as opportunities for self-expression and maturity.

Imposed art activities tend to bore to the point of frustration. Avoid pattern drawings, stereotyped cutouts, copying and printing on a line. Eliciting a creative effort takes considerably more teacher time and patience than simply passing out commercially prepared worksheets or coloring books. Creation is an individual process, some speed along as others dawdle. Although dawdlers need stimulation, the rewards from a self-initiated piece of work are usually more satisfying.

Fantasy, imagination and self-expression are the cornerstones of creative art. The logical use of color is ignored; apples are blue and houses are purple. Drawings need not appear like any object. A giraffe's neck on a human body "to see the whole world" is a perfectly natural anatomical creation. Children enjoy explaining their work if a teacher expresses genuine interest. These imaginative drawings, having no relation to reality, should be proudly displayed, irrespective of quality.

Artistic expression can also be therapeutic. The timid, lonely child may win friends through graphic expression. The release of tension through artistic endeavors generates constructive ego feelings. The cathartic effect may result in greater satisfaction with oneself.

A variety of art media can be utilized to practice eye-hand coordination. Initial contacts with crayons, paint, chalk and clay are naturally exploratory. Hand and finger-painting cultivate manual dexterity and control. Painting with the first finger imitates the pencil movement.

Crafts lend variety to the art offering, reducing the possibility of boredom. Many simple items can be made from bags, plates, milk cartons, pipe cleaners and construction paper. Children may have preferences for certain media. Those who find painting messy use crayons until they become comfortable with paints.

Creative art stimulates and activates a variety of visual-perceptual processes. Art activities unconsciously train the eye to control the hand. As eye-hand coordination matures, scribbles become curves, circles, half circles, squares and diagonal lines. In various combinations these lines and shapes make up the letters of the alphabet. Such experiences are preliminary preparation for printing and writing. Through creative art the eye and hand are synchronized.

DISCRIMINATION AND READING

Beginning reading is primarily a visual discrimination, visual retention skill. Basal readers repetitiously present the same few words for identification. An immediate visual-vocal response is essential for word recognition. Because the ability to discriminate varies considerably, those with weak visual skills will be unable to differentiate whole word configurations. Discrimination of word and letter forms is a basic prerequisite to successful reading. Therefore, visual discrimination training should have a distinct place in the kindergarten curriculum.

Instruction in visual discrimination skills should precede the formal introduction of reading. However, research is clear regarding the effects of short-term programs. Participation in brief (six to eight weeks) visual training sessions will result in little or no gain (Elkind, Horn and Schneider, 1965). Unless teachers persist throughout the year with regular, if not daily, visual discrimination exercises, improvement will be negligible.

Sorting the Alphabet

After considerable opportunity manipulating the various geometric shapes, letters are introduced. Each child is given several copies of cut-out letters to separate into piles. Similarities and differences among the letters must be recognized for accurate sorting. Sorting affords an opportunity to visualize the part-whole configurations and develop spatial orientation. Only after success with differential sorting and separation should letter naming begin.

A Letter A Week

Introduce the letters at the pace of *only* one a week. Each day the letter is reviewed by manipulation, coloring, copying and tracing. Focus emphasis upon the details of the shape which distinguish it from other letters. Attention is also directed at spatial orientation. Children are free to select the letter they wish to learn, and often choose letters which appear in their first names. If the children have no preference introduce the letters whose symbols in upper and lower case are similar. Letters with different lower case configurations tend to confuse beginners.

Rotations and Reversals

The lower case letters are difficult to learn because many are similar in appearance and a few are identical except for position. The tendency to rotate and reverse letters is so common among beginners that it may be considered normal. Easily confused letter pairs include d-b, d-p, c-e, n-u, m-w (Rankin, 1968). Difficulty with spatial positioning may occur with the following letters: b-p, q-d, f-t, d-b, p-q. Vertical extension (n-h, q-d, a-q, a-d) also needs particular emphasis. These rather fine distinctions among lower case letters must be carefully delineated and periodically reviewed. Teachers sometimes forget that children also forget.

My Name is...... JOHN

With the help of the teacher, reading can begin by learning to recognize the names of classmates. Each week a child is selected to present his name to the class. For instance, the name JOHN is printed on the board by the teacher. Each letter is spoken in unison by the entire class as it is printed. The name and each letter are reviewed daily throughout the week. The child may wear a name-tag and walk about the room asking others to read his name. John goes about helping others learn his name. The process of understanding the relationship between letters and letter sounds begins without directly teaching sounds. At the end of the year many letters and names are recognized at sight. Learning names makes reading highly personal, building fellowship among the children. Teachers need not be concerned if a number of children in the class have the same first name; the repetition is not harmful, but reinforcing.

Our schools reflect society's need for high speed, instant learning. However, no matter how hard we try, learning simply cannot and will not be instantized. The recognition of letters and words is a difficult, time-consuming and often unrewarding task. Children need time to focus and reflect before venturing a response. We allow little time for ingestion, causing too many cases of verbal indigestion. They too quickly learn to parrot a memorized meaning without grasping the substance. Because of the limited response time due to pressures to complete the curriculum, children reply to be through, having little concern for accuracy. We sometimes fail to acknowledge, by the way we teach, that a delayed, correct response is preferable to a hurried, erroneous one.

EXERCISES IN VISUAL SKILLS

A. Form Perception
   1. Identify forms and shapes by labeling.
   2. Make a kite out of construction paper. Attach a string to the center and add a tail from yarn or strips of paper. Decorate.
   3. Make an American flag out of a rectangle.
   4. A variety of geometric shapes can be imaginatively converted into objects, people or animals by simple additions.
   5. Find a large circle among smaller circles, a large triangle among smaller triangles.
   6. Compare picture sizes asking which is bigger, smaller, larger, etc.
   7. With varied sized sticks, pencils and blocks ask for a small pencil, a big stick, a large block.
   8. Name objects in the room that have the shape of a circle: clock, round table; a square: book, paper, seat of a chair.
   9. Identify birds by shape and color: cardinal, hummingbird, blue jay, robin, woodpecker, eagle, owl and pigeon.
   10. Detect differences in facial features by noticing a happy, sad, crying, sleeping and frightened clown.
   11. On a flannelboard group farm animals: cows, chickens, horses, pigs, turkeys and donkeys.
   12. Give each child a picture to talk about.
   13. Recognize persons in different clothing: clown, policemen, fireman, pilot, postman, doctor, spaceman, farmer, etc.
   14. Match letters. Give each child five copies of two letters of the alphabet to separate into piles. Repeat with other letters.

15. Make a ball out of clay and identify the shape as round.
16. Sort triangles, squares, rectangles and diamonds into different piles.

B. Discrimination

1. With a colored piece of construction paper match objects in the room with the same color.
2. Draw circles on white paper. Color each and name the color.
3. Name the color of objects in the classroom.
4. Sort beads of different colors into piles.
5. Place pieces of yellow, red and blue construction paper in a bag. Each child selects a piece from the bag and matches it with colors on the table.
6. Identify shades of color, using terms dark and light, as in dark red, light red, dark blue, light blue, dark hair, light hair.
7. Describe shapes using terms: fatter, thinner, taller, shorter, etc.
8. Identify objects according to material (wood, paper, metal, plastic, glass) and texture (smooth, rough, furry, soft, hard).
9. Match similar looking words: find-mind, tries-tried, run-ran.
10. Match pictures, objects, playing cards, shapes, designs, symbols, letters and words.
11. Describe clothing worn by children. "Who is wearing a red dress with green flowers?" "Who is wearing a red shirt?"
12. Describe what can be seen from the classroom window.
13. Identify

Foods:	*Vegetables*:	*Fruit*:
bread	corn	apples
milk	peas	banana
cereal	lettuce	grapes
cake	carrots	watermelon
ice cream	beets	lemon
pie	tomato	cherry
butter	pumpkin	plums
bacon	onions	strawberries
eggs	peppers	orange

Birds:	*Fish*:	*Animals*:
owl	whale	giraffe
robin	crab	zebra
hummingbird	octopus	elephant
cardinal	shark	monkey
blue jay	swordfish	tiger

Birds:	Fish:	Animals:
pigeon	porpoise	lion
eagle	eel	fox
crow	stingray	bear
parrot		deer
parakeet		camel
canary		kangaroo

C. Spatial Orientation

The following terms should be illustrated by using a variety of materials (books, pencils, tables, chairs, etc.) to explore the idea of position: *above, below, in, out, up, down, under, over, top, bottom, front, back, left, right, forward, backward, beside, on.*

1. "Put the block on the desk."
2. "Put the ball on the table."
3. "Put the chalk in the box."
4. "Put the big block on the large triangle."
5. "Put the big box on the little circle."
6. "Put the red book at the bottom of the pile."
7. "Put the small book on top of the table."
8. "Hold your hands above your head."
9. "Put your right hand behind your back."
10. "Put your left hand over your head."
11. "Put your hands up, down."
12. "March forward and backward to music."
13. "Stand on the left side of your chair, the right side, behind and in front of your chair."
14. "Touch your left ear, your right ear."
15. "Stamp your left foot, put your left foot down."
16. "Take a step forward, a step backward."

D. Scanning

1. Name the objects in a picture with many items.
2. Name what you see on the left, on the right, at the top and at the bottom of the picture.
3. Scan a pattern to detect the irregularity: XXXOXX
4. Complete a pattern already started: 00100—.
5. With beads and flannelboard cutouts create new patterns.
6. Make patterns of string or yarn.
7. Complete a sequence of alternating letters: A C A C A —.
8. With heads held still, the children try to sight a pencil

flashlight that is moved across the room.
9. With heads held still, the children watch balloons in the air.
E. Figure Ground Perception
1. Make a collage on colored cardboard. Use buttons, string, feathers, pipe cleaners, yarn and other items.
2. Make a farm mural. Paint the sky and background on brown wrapping paper. Paste or staple pictures of farm buildings and animals.
3. Make a snow scene. Cut white paper into various shapes and paste on colored paper.
4. Build a snowman from three different sized circles and paste on a colored paper. Draw landscape and make scarf and hat from cloth.
5. Make a bunny from cotton. Paste cotton balls on construction paper. Add leaves and flowers made from colored paper.
6. Paint sky blue and grass green as a background for a clothesline. Clothing, birds, clouds, sun and kite are added.
7. Children point to objects in pictures named by the teacher.
8. Use buttons as the center of flowers. Cut and paste petals on colored construction paper.
9. Identify figures or objects in foreground and in background.
F. Visual Memory
1. With eyes closed the child describes his clothing.
2. Each child recalls a television cartoon or story.
3. Show and hide. Three items are observed. After the eyes are covered, an object is removed. The child names the item that was removed.
4. Items placed in a bag are named after the bag is closed.
5. Recall the details of a picture after its removal.
6. Expose a geometric form and ask the children to reproduce it.
7. Children listen to a sentence or story and draw what they heard.

8. A child examines various objects: crayon, pencil, eraser, nail and button. After he turns his back, several items are removed. He tries to name them.
9. Match patterns of dominoes.
10. Teacher arranges pictures in a row and asks the order to be repeated.

G. Art — Eye-Hand Coordination
1. Using a pencil or crayon make scribble drawings. Give it a name and create a story.
2. Illustrate a story, poem or song with crayons or paints.
3. Cut out pictures from old magazines and paste on construction paper.
4. Take turns easel painting.
5. Make masks using paper bags to represent circus animals. Fold bottom against the bag and insert hand to operate like a puppet. Paint eyes and paste ears.
6. Make a paper chain of many colors to hang around the classroom. The entire class can cut strips of paper with scissors.
7. Using scissors cut a fringe from paper, then cut corners off. Learn to cut curved lines and finally cut along lines with angles and curves.
8. With a continuous line make a design. The design is completed without removing the crayon from the paper. Demonstrate, then select different colors to complete the design.
9. Make different shapes and sizes of clouds by cutting out white construction paper. Paste on blue background and color the remainder.
10. Give each child a leaf to trace on white paper. Color the tracing. In the fall use different colored leaves.
11. Make figures and designs from toothpicks.

CHAPTER **6** _____

LISTENING SKILLS

▬▬▬▬▬▬▬▬▬▬▬▬▬▬▬▬▬▬▬▬▬▬▬▬▬▬

A STREAM of signals commences at birth which impinge on the receptive auditory network to stimulate language. An intact nervous system sequentially integrates attention, discrimination, retention and expression. These components play a complementary role fusing the auditory system.

According to Dykman (1971) auditory attention or listening has four principal dimensions: alertness, stimulus selection, focusing and vigilance. Directional awareness indicates an alert auditing mechanism. Turning the head toward the sound is indicative of the alert reaction in preparation for reception.

Stimulus selection and focusing are self-excitatory, volitional acts of arousal which go beyond the initial alert. Stimulus intensity effects receptivity. Loud whistles and sirens are difficult to ignore as whispering attracts little attention.

Comprehension plays an important role. An understood remark may elicit a response; however, a complex sentence will often be totally ignored. Selection and focusing are most apt to occur when stimuli have meaning or when a novel sound arouses curiosity.

Elements of alertness, selection and focusing contribute to vigilance which is the maintenance of concentration in spite of distractions. Attentive energy coalesces in vigilant concentration.

Auditory attentiveness can be expected to vary considerably among four- and five-year-olds as both maturation and constitutional factors are crucial. The youngest will need a greater variety of experiences to maintain participatory effectiveness. The highly distractible, immature child with a maturational lag often moves quickly from one activity to another without organization.

Little is known concerning the influences of maternal care and family relations on concentration, if any. A warm, nurturant

109

family with a comfortable routine seems to allay tension, an enemy of attention. However, an excitable, over-stimulating family life may produce numerous diversions and distractions which discourage attentiveness.

Except to reduce extraneous, potentially distracting stimuli, little is presently known that will improve attentiveness, except motivation. Attention seems to thrive on interest. Interesting activities have the effect of prolonging attention. By providing a variety of listening experiences, each child establishes his own level of attentional participation.

Auditory discrimination, the ability to detect differences among similar sounds, improves dramatically up to about the age of ten. Detecting the nuances which distinguish sounds is apparently a slow process which develops only after considerable maturation over a period of years. Only if these sounds are clearly discerned is an appropriate response possible. Failure to discriminate leads to a scattering of attention to any and all audible signals without discretion.

Discrimination is a fundamental language skill. Pronunciation is clearly influenced by sound differentiation. Children gradually learn to select meaningful sounds from the ocean of spoken words. Sounds with high frequencies (s and r), isolated syllables, word endings and phonemes often go unheard. Many number and letter sounds are indistinguishable to adults; telephone operators must amplify by saying, "p as in Peter." Repetition is essential because auditory signals cannot be studied like visual stimuli. Experienced teachers quickly learn to repeat directions automatically.

As great differences in sound discrimination exist (Wepman, 1960), the curriculum should provide extensive experiences which aim to refine careful listening. The preschool and primary program should nurture these skills by design. To miss this golden opportunity in favor of subject matter content (which will most assuredly be forgotten) is to ignore the developing child.

Processing auditory stimuli is a complex mental operation. Categoric labeling, serial ordering and translating the signals into organized, retrievable information is a multiple process. If the received stimulus cannot be related to stored information, a new category may be established. Categorizing novel stimuli facilitates associative bonding. Upon first seeing a dog and hearing the sound-label, dog, a visual-auditory gestalt forms without details. With additional experience the name gradually bonds other characteristics: tail, hair, barking, running, etc. Bonding facilitates the elaboration of concepts. Bonding is the process of attaching characteristic details to concepts.

Identifying (by labeling or naming) auditory signals enhances retrieval. Stimuli are processed by scanning stored data for related or similar associations. Memories which resemble or approximate the incoming stimuli are associated, sometimes incorrectly. In a discussion of Washington's famous cherry tree incident, a preschooler was heard to say that her daddy sings, "Don't sit

Figure 6. Attentive listening.

under the apple tree with anyone else but me." This remark represents the most relevant experience which could be associated with the topic. Learning and comprehension are based on relating previous experiences to new stimuli. Learning and comprehension crystallize when the present experience can be associated and bonded to memories in storage.

Memory is the recollection of previously experienced events. Retentive functions differ with individuals because of their multidimensional complexity. Recall is limited by the interfering effects of more recent events. However, in order for ideas, words and concepts to enter permanent memory, repeated exposure and usage is necessary.

The effectiveness of the auditory system reveals itself ultimately through verbal responses. Without a verbal reaction we cannot know what effect auditory stimuli have. Its proficiency is demonstrated through language production. The auditory-language network culminates in creative expression.

IDENTIFYING SOUNDS

Without a label, sound stimuli go unnoticed and ignored because they lack meaning. The absence of recognition renders the sound an undifferentiated stimulus. A necessary exercise for preschoolers is the labeling of a variety of sounds: water running, whistle, bells, siren, wind, engines running, etc. The associative label facilitates comprehension and retention. Sounds (thunder and wind) which have no visual components must be detected by aural discrimination alone.

Listening and Responding

The active listener learns. However, much of what is heard has no interest or meaning because of noninvolvement. No amount of storytelling will generate an attentive attitude unless pupil participation is elicited. Listening can only be verified by a verbal or behavioral reaction. Unless a response is an integral aspect of listening, inattention may result. "Tuning out" is a favorite habit of children and adults. Attentiveness is evoked through response expectation; preparation for action generates attentiveness. Careful listening is necessary for effective participation.

Listening for listening's sake generates boredom. Wilt (1950) and more recently Corey (1966) both found that students in the elementary school spend more than half the time listening, not doing. Too much teacher talk turns children off. Teachers must learn to listen before expecting it from children. Eye-to-eye contact informs the child that someone is attending. An attentive model sets an appropriate example.

Storytime is too often a period of sitting quietly before the teacher. Attention is activated by encouraging remarks and active questioning. Through interaction, stories come alive and excite the imagination. Gestures, imitation, facial expressions, dramatization and expression of emotion vitalize stories through sensory elaboration.

Rhymes

Nursery rhymes combine the art of storytelling with sound but have recently fallen out of favor. Modern curricula tend to emphasize story content (soon forgotten), deemphasizing word sounds and rhymes. The ability to detect and reproduce sounds that rhyme are basic discriminatory skills. Rhyming chains can be started by providing the first two words: feet, meet. Learning to detect words and sounds that rhyme is indicative of auditory discrimination.

The creation of nonsense sounds is an excellant method of constructing rhymes: fun, ton, mon, done, kun, run, bun, hun, pun, gun, etc. Nonsense sounds and words that rhyme are encouraged in order to develop a sensitivity to sounds. Creating nonsense sounds that rhyme increases spontaneity and pupil participation; the fear of being wrong is eliminated.

Nonsense riddles illustrate initial sounds. Wendy washes windows while William waits. Dirty dogs dig ditches deeply. Nonsense syllables can be used to demonstrate similar initial sounds: bis, big, bud, bad, ben, bir, bes, etc.

Throughout the preschool, "rhyme play" atunes the ear to sound unconsciously. Rhyming plays a central role in fostering auditory discrimination. Rhyming ability is excellent preparation for letter-sound differentiation.

Not all kindergarteners can detect differences in the sounds of the letters. Learning these multiple sounds is a most difficult task and should be introduced slowly and only to children with good to excellent auditory skills. Delaying sound-letter instruction may, in the long run, expedite the reading process. Through a conditioned tok-back technique, Chelland (1973) improved the discrimination of letter sounds with older children.

MUSIC AND LANGUAGE

Through the joyous sounds of music creative verbal expression can be enhanced. Syllables and words which fall on musically accented beats facilitate association and retention. "Sesame Street" and the "Electric Company" have both demonstrated the value of music as an associative learning device. Music provides experiences in the variations of sound, an exercise which may facilitate the identification of new vocabulary. Hearing can be refined through musical activities. Through music the nuance of sound emerges and the ear is atuned.

Musical exposure expands auditory awareness. The regular use of classroom instruments (drums, bells, sticks, flutophones, etc.) introduces a variety of sounds which extend the auditory experience. It is hypothesized that auditory discrimination can be improved by exploring sounds through music.

The basic components of music — volume, pitch and rhythm — should be explored. Volume can be presented using the terms loud, louder, soft, softer and quietly. Soft sounds (rustling leaves, the wind) and loud sounds (whistle, bells, sirens) demonstrate the difference well. Instruments played at different intensities will clarify the distinction. Commercially prepared records are recommended to illustrate the basic elements of music.

Movements coordinated with a rhythmic beat initiate the process of motor control. Beating drumsticks begins indiscriminately. The tendency to strike a beat without interruption or order can be gradually channeled into striking a beat on command or in time to music. Eventually a synchronized beat is produced. Simple patterns of one and two beats are followed by the more complex two-four and one-three time. The terms fast and slow are

Figure 7. Listening and singing.

explained relative to rhythm. Creative patterns are also encouraged.

Differentiating nuances of pitch requires a considerable degree of auditory concentration. The terms higher and lower are utilized to indicate the distinction. Choral singing, humming and careful listening facilitate an awareness of pitch. Learning to whistle can be instrumental in developing pitch. A time can be set aside to "whistle while we work." Controlled breathing and lip movements must be coordinated in order to whistle. Whistling calls upon the use of differences in pitch. Accurate pitch discrimination may be more closely related to vocabulary improvement than we realize. The sounds of many words are minimally difference (boy-toy); therefore, fine discriminations are essential.

Creative Movement and Music

Rhythmic melodies excite, animate, stir emotion and bodily activity in children. Mimetics, the act of portraying the action in a song or story, is an ideal means of synchronizing movement with music. Whether clapping, singing or dancing to music, the primary aim is to exercise motor control through musical experiences. Walking, marching, skipping, dancing and performing calisthenics, in time to music provide important opportunities to integrate the auditory-motor functions. Daily exercise will facilitate the development of coordinated movements to music. Bodily movements set in motion to music serve to exercise multisensory functions. However, the smooth integration of auditory, visual and motor functions cannot be guaranteed because sensory integration is an inner neurological process about which little is presently known.

LISTENING EXERCISES

I. OVERVIEW
   Provide a multiplicity of activities designed to expand reception and perception. In order to focus attention, limit the number of auditory stimuli presented at the same time. Activities should not continue longer than fifteen minutes unless the children wish to continue. Mastery of simple auditory tasks is the only criteria for proceeding to more complex ones.
II. AUDITORY ELEMENTS
   A. Listening
      1. Close your eyes.
         a. Bounce a ball. Ask how many times did it bounce? Vary the number of bounces up to four.
         b. Hold up a cup and spoon. When all eyes closed, stir spoon in cup and tap cup, asking, "What do you hear?"
         c. Illustrate the sounds of tapping, scraping and rub-

bing of pencils, paper, ruler and cards.
2. Demonstrate the sounds made when eating, sleeping, washing, working, etc.
3. Talkers and listeners are paired. Children take turns as talkers and listeners. The listener must wait until the talker has expressed himself fully before replying.

B. Locating sounds — directionality
Vocabulary: near, far, coming closer, going away.
   1. Listen for sounds outside classroom (automobiles, sirens, thunder, voices, etc.).
   2. Listen for sounds in classroom (shuffling feet, clock, bell, etc.).
   3. A child plays a drum moving about the room and the children point to the direction. Later eyes are covered during this activity.
   4. Detect sound source by placing a child in each corner with a different instrument. With eyes covered, direction is determined by pointing.
   5. With eyes closed identify: footsteps, barking, car horns, whistling, etc.
   6. A child moves about the room blowing a whistle. Point to the direction with eyes covered.
   7. Two children are placed in the center of a circle formed by the class. One is blindfolded as the other makes a noise or sound and tries to avoid being tagged. Vary by using a ball.
   8. Children are seated at their chairs with one hand over eyes. With the other hand they point in the direction of sounds they hear.

C. Sound Identification
   1. Present a variety of environmental sounds using recordings. An adequate signal continues for at least three seconds.
   2. First with eyes open, then with hands over the eyes, identify:

clapping hands	sweeping
tearing paper	raising windowshade
jingling coins	bouncing a ball

opening a window	rattling keys
knocking on a door	rustling paper
ringing a bell	moving desk or chair
whistle	snapping rubber band
pouring water	snapping fingers
tapping a bottle	hammer and saw
banging blocks	closing pocketbook
humming	crying and laughing
singing	pencil sharpener
radio	chalk on board
using scissors	crumple paper
drop an object	splash water
open-close drawers	shuffle feet
rub palms of hand	turn lights on
sighing	rub sandpaper

3. Discriminate tapping on wood, metal and glass.
4. Demonstrate a series of three identical containers, each of which holds different noise-producing objects: beans, sandbag, stones, bells, etc. Match the two containers with the identical sounding objects, blindfolded.
5. Higher or lower. The teacher strikes two notes on a piano. If the second note is higher, the children raise their hands; if lower, they point to the floor.
6. From behind a screen sounds are made with musical instruments to be identified.

D. Imitating
   Children enjoy parroting the teacher. Use a variety of words, numbers or sentences.
   1. Say what I say: sit, fit, bit, lit, kit, rit, etc.
   2. Repeat after me: 8-9-4; 3-5-7; 1-6-3.
   3. Say these colors: red, black, blue; green, white, red.
   4. Pantomime bodily movements and imitate actions and sounds.
      a. Animals: dog, cat, cow, chicken, monkey, ducks, sheep, bees, birds.
      b. People: doctor, policeman, postman, grocer, nurse, ballplayer, dentist, etc.

E. Sound Analysis
   1. Demonstrate both loud and soft sounds and what is meant by silence.

2. Discovering one's voice and that of classmates through taping is highly exciting. Play tapes to the class and identify the child speaking.

3. Same or Different. Pronounce two words which are the same or slightly different. Begin with initial and final consonants. Vowel differences are most difficult to detect.

4. Initial Consonants Different

bum-dumb	feel-steal	leaf-thief	beach-peach
cheap-jeep	hill-still	weep-seep	feed-bead
den-when	will-mill	weed-seed	lead-creed
coast-toast	fold-cold	lard-yard	sake-shake
fin-sin	mold-told	card-hard	wake-fake
fin-thin	sin-skin	some-come	zip-sip

5. Final Consonants Different

bum-bun	come-cup	rash-razz	sob-sop
bug-bud	had-hat	rag-rack	seat-seed
bus-buzz	leave-leaf	ride-ripe	steep-steam
bat-bad	pill-pit	rum-rug	steal-stole
home-hope	mush-much	rib-rip	tire-tide
tail-take	them-then	wing-wig	wish-which

6. Vowels Different

pit-pet	big-bag	led-lid	hit-hut
cup-cop	mat-met	bet-bid	big-beg
ball-bell	rod-red	pit-pet	sat-sit
cut-cat	had-hid	fit-fat	cap-cop
big-beg	hat-hit	pan-pen	bet-but
had-head	man-men	lip-lap	sip-sup

F. Following directions
The children learn to understand directions and the meaning of word order.

1. "Mary, close the door and sit at your seat."
"John, stand up and get a ball."
"Pretend you brush your teeth and comb your hair."

2. "Stand up, turn around, and sit down."
"Go to the front of the room then to the back of the room."
"Touch the first and last window in the room."

3. "Take the ball behind my desk and put it under your chair."
"Put your hand on the book, then put the book on your

hand."

Put the crayons on the paper, then put the paper on the crayons."

"Hop on one foot, bend down, touch your toes, then sit down."

4. "Right face, — left face."

"Forward, march, when I touch my head."

"Backward, march, when I ring the bell."

"In place, march, when I sit down."

"Right face, when I hold a pencil up."

"Left face, when I put the pencil down."

"Take one step forward, and two steps backward, then hop up and down."

5. "Make a sound like a bird, dog, pig and cat."

"Go to my desk, open a book and bring it to me."

"Go to the window, smell the flower and water it."

G. Language Sounds

Use oral rhyming to create nonsense sounds that rhyme. Follow the alphabet. Rhyme a variety of sounds.

1. boy, coy, doy, foy, goy, hoy, joy, koy, loy, moy, etc.
2. bine, cine, dine, fine, gine, hine, jine, line, etc.
3. Use any rhyming sounds.
4. Create oral sounds with same beginning sound.
   a. sat, sez, sed, sad, sem, sen, sej, sar, safe, sit, etc.
   b. dit, dat, ded, dim, din, deer, did.
   c. Continue with other beginning sounds.
5. Show pictures that begin with the same initial consonant.
   a. bat, ball, broom, barn, etc.
6. Sort pictures according to beginning sound.
   a. truck, tank, telephone, etc.

H. Auditory Sequencing

Children learn to order what they hear and repeat what was heard.

1. Repeat the numbers: 1-4; 3-2; 8-5.
   Repeat: 6-1-5; 4-3-2; etc.
   Repeat: 8-7-5-2; 7-0-1-6; 9-3-6-4, etc.
2. Repeat unconnected words: toy, bag, cow, boy, house,

truck.

Repeat; wind, sun, air, stars; ball, bat, baseball, glove.

3. Repeat sentences:
   a. I like milk.
   b. The house is red.
   c. My dog will eat soon.
   d. This ball is not very big.
   e. My uncle will not come to my house.
4. Animal sequences add the name of another animal as each child speaks:
   a. I saw a cat.
   b. I saw a cat and a dog.
   c. I saw a cat, dog and a lion.
   d. I saw a cat, dog, lion and horse.
   e. I saw a cat, dog, lion, horse and a mouse, etc.
5. The teacher reads a story and the children retell it in sequence.
6. Show a series of pictures and ask children to create a story.
7. Begin a story and ask how it may end.

I. Comprehension

Dramatize words, sentences and stories to portray their meaning.

1. Make incorrect statements; ask for an explanation of the absurdity.
   a. The boy walked on the ceiling.
   b. The boy ate under water.
   c. The girl with wings flew away.
2. Introduce the questions:
   a. who — me, you, her, him, teacher, father, etc.
   b. where — home, school, inside, outside, farm, city, etc.
   c. when — today, tomorrow, yesterday, now, later, etc.
   d. whose — mine, yours, his, hers, ours.

J. Rhythm and Melody

The child can imitate a rhythmic pattern with drums, sticks or clapping.

1. I-II, I-II, I-II, I-II.

2. II-I, II-I, II-I, II-I.
3. Create more complex rhythms using three, four and five beats.
4. With eyes closed identify: bells, tambourines, sticks, drums, flutophone, triangle, clapper, cymbols, blocks, etc.
5. With a drum the children step in time with the beat:
   a. clap each time a step is taken.
   b. fast beat — step in place.
   c. slow beat — one step forward.
   d. walk forward, backward, sidestep.
   e. walk on toes, heels.
6. With appropriate rhythms on records perform the following:
   a. running, skipping, galloping, hopping, marching, jumping.
7. Combine rhythm with calisthenics.
   a. Movement of arms, feet and hands in time to music.
8. Sing songs with simple melodies.
   a. "Old MacDonald"
   b. "God Bless America"
   c. "Ten Little Indians"
9. Matching tones in response to teacher's voice.
   a. Using la, la, child imitates teacher's pitch.
   b. Varying the pitch with each child ask "Where is John?" Child replies in same tone, "Here I am."
10. Matching voices.
    Using la, la, have each child try to match the teacher's.
11. Matching hums and tones.
    Using mmm and la, la, the child attempts to match hum and tone of the teacher. If child has difficulty, teacher accommodates to match child's hum and tone.
12. Auditory Association
    Learn to associate words that often go together in everyday speech.
    a. Tires go on a ____.
       Milk goes in a ____.
       The sun is ____.

The rain is ____.
A bicycle has ____.
The grass is ____.
The sky is ____.
We ride in a ____.
We sit on a ____.
We eat at a ____.
We eat soup with a ____.
We cut with a ____.
We button our ____.
We live in a ____.
Candy is ____.

CHAPTER 7 _____

PERCEPTUAL MOTOR SKILLS

THE simple act of reaching or grasping an object utilizes visual, kinesthetic and cutaneous receptors processed during the action. Initially these separate sensory systems within the perceptual process operate independently. The neural complexity of simultaneously processing more than one sensory mode accounts for the slow development of all motor activities. Smooth, coordinated movements depend upon the integration of multiple receptors. Visual, auditory and haptic senses are not sufficiently established in the young to be smoothly integrated into a coordinated motor activity without extensive exercise. Physical movements serve to mesh sensory functions by exercising the organization of multiple perceptual inputs. Opportunities for practice, in conjunction with maturation, contribute to perceptual motor skill.

The purpose of developing perceptual motor skills is to explore the broad range of human capacities, irrespective of other academic considerations. Children with serious academic weaknesses may overcome them as adults and succeed in many walks of life. The building of skills, whether on the athletic field or elsewhere, creates inner feelings of self-confidence and personal worth. Not everyone can be academically strong. The academic neurosis which places undue emphasis upon scholastic memory should be replaced by a philosophy which provides for a variety of diverse activities upon which to build individual skills. Personal self-worth and assurance can be constructed around success in a vari-ety of nonacademic areas. A sound program affords numerous opportunities to exercise a host of perceptual-motor activities.

MOVEMENT

Spontaneous movement fulfills the innate instincts of the in-

Figure 8. Exercising gross motor skills.

fant and first appears as diffuse, uncontrolled activity without direction. This natural spontaneity and random motion gradually give way to goal-directed behavior. Grasping the rattle or a glass of milk serves a more definite purpose. Repetitive exercise refines the activity. However, both spontaneous and goal-directed behavior continue throughout childhood and adolescence. The inner self is revealed through free, creative, expressive movement, and this childishness should not be suppressed.

Instruction in the control of motion has a very practical purpose. The elimination of dangerous activities (running in the street, touching hot stoves) is essential for survival. In all social experience some degree of inhibition is clearly necessary. Children should learn to inhibit movement through self-imposed control.

Gross Motor Functions

Raising the head, sitting up, crawling, standing and walking occur at much the same time in children from diverse cultures. By implication the motor timetable is biologically and genetically predetermined. Gross movements seem to depend upon neurophysiological maturation. Forcing a child to walk early does not significantly improve performance.

Motor activities gradually involve the use of vision prior to and during the action. Coordinated head and eye movements facilitate the alteration of inaccurate motor trials. Vision and movement eventually become interdependent. The muscular sense (kinesthetic) relies upon the visual mode for corrective action. In the very young, gross motor functions seem to have little transfer. Each movement pattern is learned individually.

A regular program of gross motor activities should include walking, running, jumping, hopping, climbing and calisthenics at different speeds. Calisthenics is perhaps one of the most effective ways of establishing effective motor control of the body. Daily, five-minute exercises in bending, twisting, stretching, reaching, pulling and pushing are excellent opportunities for group participation. Both indoor and outdoor physical activities should be scheduled. Those whose motor skills are noticeably weak should be afforded opportunity for additional practice.

An essential component of movement is that it be environmentally appropriate. Running into a street or about in a classroom is dangerous to self and others and therefore, is situationally inappropriate behavior. Remaining seated is essential when riding in a moving vehicle. Under given conditions movements are restricted and controlled to conform to the environmental setting for reasons of safety not understood by young children.

Our primary purpose is to improve balance, posture and coordination to the point where precise movement has a positive influence upon the personality. The inferiority feelings of many physically handicapped children are based on their inability to perform independently. Children can be extremely proud of their physical prowess. Developing precise movements in dance, art, music, drawing, painting, athletics or play is the basis upon which a sound perceptual-motor program rests.

Bodily Awareness

Self-awareness begins with the body. Through bodily functions and activities we learn about ourselves as we grow. Bodily feelings and self-perceptions are clearly related. Behavior is an extension of the self through bodily movement. The ability to hop, skip, jump and run builds self-confidence. Effective body control enhances the ego. The possession of physical skills influences peer relationships; its absence may lead to ridicule and lack of self-assurance.

Conflicting, ambivalent feelings about the body often result in extreme personal sensitivity. Negative references to size (squirt), shape, (fat, skinny) and appearance (ugly, big ears) are quite common in social interaction among children. A positive feeling regarding personal appearance and coordination facilitates peer socialization.

Balance

Fluid in the inner ear canals control balance, a basic body mechanism. Static balance is the ability to maintain a position on tiptoes, heals or on one foot. Calisthenics provide an excellent opportunity for practicing static balance. From a standing position numerous forward, backward and sideway movements can test balancing ability. Maintaining an upright position in motion, as on a swing or seesaw, is termed dynamic balance. Roller skating, jumping rope, riding a bicycle and ice skating exercise dynamic equilibrium. Most movements in athletics utilize body balance. Balancing objects (food trays, glasses of milk, etc.) are basic self-help skills which should be mastered early.

Bilaterality

The body has over 300 pairs of bilaterally symmetrical muscles which operate antagonistically to produce smooth, coordinated movements. Countless hours of exercise prepare these muscles to collaborate eventually as a team pair. Sport activities (baseball, dodgeball, etc.) develop the bilateral muscles. Catching the ball with both hands and swimming with a coordinated kick are complex bilateral activities. Without persistent practice specific skills which utilize bilateral movements will not develop. Coordination improves quite slowly over the maturing years. To refine the numerous agile movements of the arms, hands and fingers, a variety of experiences is necessary. Art activities (clay modeling, pasteing, cutting, crafts and coloring) exercise the fine bilateral muscles.

Laterality

In infancy perferential use of the left or right limb is absent. Not until approximately the age of four do any preferences begin to appear. Vascillation continues into the fifth and sixth year but by the seventh, laterality is rather well established. Children who develop lateral preference early are usually considered mature; however, evidence regarding this hypothesis appears inconclusive. It has been estimated that from 70 to 80 percent of the population has right lateral preference. The remainder favor the left side, and a few are ambidextrous.

Mixed lateral dominance occurs with some degree of regularity between the fine and gross motor movements. It is not uncommon for a child to prefer the left hand for throwing and left foot for kicking, but use the right hand for writing and eating. There is no evidence that mixed preferences create perceptual-motor difficulties.

Directionality

The ability to understand the multiple uses of the terms right and left is a cognitive-spatial skill. Correct selection of the right and left hand has no relationship to left and right turn. Both uses are separate and distinct and must be learned independently. As there are no fixed reference points, directions have few perceptual cues upon which to guide a response. A correct turn will depend upon the variable of the starting position. Such variability complicates the learning process for the preschooler. Because directions apply to diverse situations (down the street, down the cellar, up the street, up the stairs), the use of these terms cannot be fully grasped by a single demonstration. Therefore, directions like up, down, in and out should be explored through numerous visual exposures. Practice in a variety of contexts facilitates comprehension.

Reading utilizes the application of directional understanding. No other task requires the visual pattern of beginning at the left, proceeding to the right and returning to the left, down one line. The left-right-left visual pattern should be deliberately taught to all beginning readers.

By learning the various positional and directional terms, these rather subtle differences can be clarified. However, without vocabulary differentiation, comprehension is absent. When the correct direction can be elicited by a command, cognition is established. "Raise your right hand," has no meaning until it can be performed independently. Calisthenics provide an excellent opportunity to associate vocabulary with the visual cues of position and direction.

KINESTHETIC SENSITIVITY

Muscle movements of the arms, legs, feet and hands, including joints and ligaments, are monitored by an internal neural network. A change in position is accompanied by a corresponding signal to the kinesthetic receptors which feeds back to further control the motion. This tonal "feeling" is continually monitored by the receptors to detect and redirect position and movement.

Attaching visual and auditory cues to a muscular feeling serves to identify and classify the movement. Learning to walk occurs much before understanding the word "walk." This muscle feeling later becomes associated with the verbal signal. Bowel and urinary functions also have kinesthetic components. However, training requires that a verbal signal be given prior to elimination. Learning to signal initiates the process of controlling these bodily functions.

HAPTIC SENSES

The haptic system includes cutaneous and tactile sensations. Receptors on the entire surface of the skin receive tactile information. The face, hands and fingers appear to be the most sensitive areas. Temperature changes and pressure on the skin are quickly detected. The tactile sensitivity of children is revealed by the crying which often accompanies a very minor bruise.

The Kinsbourne and Warrington (1963-64) studies reported that half of the five-year-olds examined differentiated sensory input from fingers. Blindfolded, they could discriminate simple object shapes and detect which finger was touched by the examiner. Children receive tactile stimulation continually but without cognitive awareness and, therefore, should learn that tactile sensations have names. Cognitive differentiation will evolve by repeated demonstration of these terms: wet, dry, rough, smooth, hard, soft, soapy, greasy, sticky, gummy, rubbery, etc. Materials with different textures should also be explored: cloth, silk, dirt, fur, paper, sand, metal, glass, plastic, etc.

FINE MOTOR SKILLS

Coordinated use of both hands is among the most difficult for young children to perform accurately. Many a spilt glass and broken vase attest to the slow development of precise hand and finger movements. Skill with one utensil, a spoon or a fork, emerges rather quickly. However, mothers must continue to cut meat because managing a fork and knife simultaneously invariably leads to accidents up until the age of nine, ten and later.

The use of scissors is another complex bilateral skill, as eyes and hands must collaborate closely. Cutting begins without

Figure 9. Fine motor skills.

regard for direction or line. Construction paper is easier to cut because of its firmness. Use one-inch strips which can be cut by a single clip. With larger pieces, cutting requires moving the hand after each clip. Begin by cutting along straight lines; curved and zigzag lines are more difficult. Cutting out shapes (squares, diamonds, triangles, etc.) are reserved for those who have learned to cut around corners and diagonally.

Pegboards, form boards and puzzles provide a variety of interesting eye-hand experiences which are highly motivating. Block and construction play contribute to eye-hand coordination skills. Playing with marbles and jacks also exercises fine motor skills. In a supportive atmosphere, perceptual-motor skills are apt to emerge.

Printing and writing call for the most precise eye-hand coordination. Therefore, these skills develop quite slowly and only with consistent practice.

PERCEPTUAL-MOTOR ACTIVITIES

A sound program recognizes the uniqueness of each child's experiential background and differential ability. Within the framework of small group instruction, individualized activities are prescribed. Begin with activities which can be accomplished easily in order to build self-confidence, then proceed to those known to be more difficult.

The basic ingredient of a good program is the absence of stress to perform to certain expectations. Encouragement and praise for effort are important elements; criticism has no place on the agenda. Because we accept the notion of differential ability, not all are expected to do equally well. Peer criticism is discouraged. Vigorous movements are approached first. Exercises should conclude with a less strenuous activity whenever possible.

A. Body Parts

The purpose of learning bodily functions is to increase self-awareness and self-perceptions. Not only should the child be able to label the body part mentioned, but make a statement about it. Elbows bend, arms swing, etc.

1. Discuss each part in detail: hair — color, wavy, straight, etc.
2. Eyes — color, movement, open, shut, etc.
3. Teeth — to chew food, brush.
4. Nose — to smell, breathe.
5. Lips — move, to speak, eat, etc.
6. Continue with wrist, hands, fingers, feet, toes, chin, cheek, forehead, legs, mouth, shoulder, ankles, chin, fingernails, hip, stomach.

B. Body Movement

1. Stand up, sit down, close your eyes, open them.
2. Clap twice, once, etc.
3. Put your elbows out.
4. Place your feet apart, together.
5. Touch an arm, touch the other, continue with other parts of the body.
6. Place knees together. Touch right knee with left hand, reverse.

7. Increase the complexity: touch nose with one hand and knee with the other.
8. Cross arms and touch toes.
9. Touch your nose and your knee.
10. Gross Motor:
    a. Bodily motions — bend and stretch, reach, pull, push, twist.
    b. Roll on mats.
    c. Jump: in place, in time to a signal, make jump turns.
    d. Hopping: toward the board, over a line, over a rope, alternating feet.
    e. Gallop: around a circle, with right foot forward, then left.
    f. Leaping: over parallel lines, increasing the width.
    g. Skipping: in place, to a designated place, in time to a tempo and with rope.
    h. Pass an object around a circle from child to child.
    i. Play catch with a balloon, keep balloon in the air.
    j. Step over and between two board erasers.
    k. Draw two lines, have children jump over them. Spread apart and repeat.
    l. Imitate the body position of a partner.
    m. Ball activities:
       1. bounce a ball, bounce while walking.
       2. sit or kneel and bounce the ball.
       3. throw ball into a box.
       4. bounce or roll ball to partner, playing catch.
    n. Laying on back push self across floor using legs, arms, left arm and leg, right arm and leg.
C. Body
   The children lie down on large brown paper. Draw around each child with a magic marker, include details. Children use crayon to fill in the figures and features. Hang on the wall.
    1. Draw body parts in isolation. Ask that hands, legs, arms, feet, eyes, mouth, ears, and noses be drawn.
    2. Smile, frown, laugh, cry, show tongue, move lips, close one eye.
    3. Close eyes, open one, then another. Open, close mouth.

4. Learn to wink.
5. String beads, connect dotted lines.
6. Button and unbutton; learn to use zippers.
7. Lace shoes, tie knots with string and laces.
8. Twist your neck, then your wrist.
9. Nod your head, now turn it to the left, right.
10. Bend your knees, arms, elbows, etc.
11. Open-close: eyes, mouth, hand.
12. Wave your arms, stamp your feet, alternate left and right.
13. Skidoo: The children choose partners and stand facing each other. The following commands are given: face to face, back to back, right hand to right hand, left hand to left hand, elbow to elbow, knees to knees, right knee to right knee, left knee to left knee, and toe to toe. On command of Skidoo, children change partners.

D. Tactile Activities
1. Identify objects by using terms to describe them:

a. rubber — rubbery
b. sandpaper — rough
c. skin — smooth
d. road — bumpy and smooth
e. fur — fuzzy, soft
f. wood — hard
g. glue — sticky
h. cardboard — stiff
i. silk — shiny and smooth
j. paste — thick
k. soup — thin

2. Describe the texture of clothing while touching the cloth.
3. Identify objects in a box according to texture. Pull out to confirm.
4. Trace different forms and shapes with a crayon or pencil and color. Use spoons, cards and other objects.
5. Feel a variety of materials with different textures:
   a. paper, wood, metal, water, cloth (silk, cotton, wool) clay, powder, sand, leather, fur, sandpaper, pebbles, hair.
6. Common objects are concealed in a bag. Identify by touch. Use pencils, blocks, paper clips, forks, pegs and erasers.

E. Laterality
1. In a lying position:
   a. Move one arm, move a leg, move both arms in unison, move both legs.

b. Move both arms and both legs simultaneously.

c. Move left arm and leg (then right arm and leg).

d. Move left arm and right leg simultaneously. Reverse arms and legs.

e. With success in the above activities increase/decrease the speed of the movements.

2. Erect position:

a. With dominant hand squeeze a pencil, crayon, ball, sponge: throw a beanbag, put pegs in a pegboard.

b. With dominant foot do hopping relays, kick a beanbag.

c. Clench fist on dominant hand. Hold for three seconds.

d. Pick up blocks and other objects with dominant hand.

F. Bilateral Movements

1. Tap both hands simultaneously. Tap toes and heels.

2. Alternate tapping with left.

3. Clap hands, play patty cake.

4. Move hands clockwise, then counter-clockwise. Use chalk and blackboard for variation.

5. Move left hand clockwise and right counter-clockwise. Reverse hands.

G. Directionality

1. Touch your left ear. Touch your right.

2. Touch your right ear with your left hand. Reverse hands.

3. Touch your right elbow with your left hand.

4. Hold up your left hand. Right hand.

5. Point arrows to left and right.

6. Touch the right side of the door, the left side. Repeat with window, desk, chair, etc.

7. "Mary, turn left." "John, turn right."

8. In a picture with many objects, identify each.

9. Empty your left pocket, right pocket.

From left to right:

10. Place pegs in pegboard.

11. Place toothpicks on desk.

12. Place beads on desk.

13. Place straws and milk cartons on table.

14. Place crayons on paper.

15. Place felt objects on flannelboard.
16. Place letters of the alphabet.
17. Name objects in a picture.

H. Balancing
1. Stand on tiptoes as long as possible. Vary by closing eyes. Stay on toes increasing length of time.
2. Stand on one foot and swing the other leg forward, backward and side to side. Vary by closing eyes.
3. On a balance board, walk forward, backward and cross step.
4. Balance on one knee and foot using hands for support.
5. Balance on one knee and foot using one hand for support.
6. Walk on toes, forward and backward, and on heels.
7. Hop on one foot: forward, backward, sideways.
8. Take giant and baby steps without falling.
9. Practice cross steps and side steps.
10. Walk up and down a tilted balance beam board.
11. Jump in place, forward and backward.
12. Jump over a rope three inches high. Raise the level.
13. Skip without falling.
On a balance board:
14. Balance with arms outstretched, objects in hand, unequal weights in hand, arms over head and swaying.

I. Positional Concepts.
1. Touch the first block. Touch the last block.
2. Pick up the second block. Pick up the fourth block.
3. Give me the middle block. Put it under your chair.
4. Put the block in the desk. Put the block in front of the desk.
5. Put the wastebasket behind the desk.
6. Place the chair next to the desk. Put it near the window.
7. Demonstrate on top of, beside, in front, below, above, up, down, and between.

J. Fine Motor Skills
1. With a template trace a variety of geometric figures.
2. Use modeling clay to shape objects and letters.
3. Use scissors to cut construction paper.

Figure 10. Exercises in seriation.

_____

CHAPTER 8

NUMERICAL SKILLS

_____

I N the early years, incidental learning appears to be the dominant mode of mental acquisition. Knowledge is randomly acquired without apparent organization. The absence of any systematic, orderly acquisition suggests a prelogical thought process. Recognition, identification and simple association are the primary mental activities.

The descriptive property of number, because of its abstract and variable nature, develops quite slowly. Piaget (1928) long ago concluded that the inability to grasp the relativity of ideas is the principal obstacle to the development of mathematical reasoning in children. The fuid, relational nature of mathematical concepts defy comprehension after limited exposure. Differential results should be expected on a daily basis. Unfamiliar wording, novel directions, new examples, and forgetting contribute to inconsistent performance. Comprehension of mathematical concepts emerges only after repeated explication, demonstration and pupil exploration. According to Piaget (1965) the five-year-old needs extensive and repetitive experience with concrete manipulation of objects to understand number. Many preschoolers count by rote but have little grasp of numerical ideas. Understanding numeration is based upon experience with concrete operations.

GROUPING

Because children enjoy working together and learn from each other, a partnership system is recommended. Youngsters are naturally social beings often discontent with isolated desk assignments. Working with a partner encourages mutual exchange of ideas. The pair can freely explore prenumerical concepts, compare results, and challenge each other when ideas conflict. Partners can be reassigned as the need arises. Teams of three or four can be arranged when small groups are desired.

RESPONSE EXPLORATION

In far too many instances numerical answers are accepted without inquiry into the thinking process. The rote, imitative response flows all too freely from the mouths of babes. Through interrogation we explore the reasoning underlying a response. Questioning a response (whether correct or incorrect) encourages the child to examine his own thinking. If an answer cannot be explained or supported, the teacher knows immediately that comprehension is absent. This analytical approach reduces the tendency to respond in a rote manner. The fear of embarrassment before peers contributes to an atmosphere in which the need to be right usually supercedes the need to understand. Pupils rarely admit to the question, "Who does not understand?" The next section examines the role of manipulatives as an excellent means of understanding the mental activity underlying mathematical ideas. How a child uses manipulative material reveals his mathematical thought processes.

MANIPULATIVES

The daily use of manipulatives facilitates the organization of numerical thought by the simultaneous exercise of visual and tactile senses. A great variety of materials (milk cartons, buttons, erasers, plastic chips, straws, beads, pipe cleaners, blocks, paper clips, etc.) should be provided for sorting, classification and eventual counting. Sorting is the physical act, and labeling is the mental act of classification. Labeling is a basic intellectual skill upon which all subsequent learning rests. Identification and sorting initiate the logical processing of prenumerical ideas.

The perceptually bound preschooler is locked into the physical arrangement and physical space objects occupy. Any rearrangement alters perception which is interpreted as a change in number by the five-year-old. Worksheets and workbooks do not afford a concrete understanding of the logic underlying numerical abstractions. By sorting, rearranging and classifying the manipulative materials, the child is free to seek and arrive at his own solutions. Primary classifications include shape, color, size and activity.

Shape

Shape is a primary method of discriminatory classification. The common shapes include circle, half-circle, triangle, square, rectangle and diamond. Attention should be directed to those properties which distinguish each figure. Pictures which portray these various shapes should be readily available. The circle can be represented by tire, ball, wheel, balloon, buttons and the letter o. Repeated exposure to each shape is necessary to provide reinforcement for retention.

The shape of animals are frequently the primary discriminating feature. Learning to recognize the common farm and zoo animals, based on shape, is a pleasant exercise. Repeated exposure is essential to identify unfamiliar animals.

Color

Preschoolers can learn to recognize the common colors on sight, i.e. red, white, blue, green, brown, yellow, orange and black. Sorting plastic chips or pieces of construction paper and naming the colors is a first exercise. Not until accuracy is well established are shades introduced with the terms light and dark. Acute discrimination is necessary to detect nuances of shading. Not all are able to detect these fine differences. The color-blind child will, of course, have difficulty with certain colors in the spectrum. Teachers should be aware of this possibility which occurs primarily in boys.

Size

Size is a relative concept; *big* can be applied to a car or a button. Accurate usage depends upon prior knowledge of typical size. Introduce the terms big, bigger; small, smaller, using a variety of pencils, pens, erasers, books, blocks and crayons of differing size.

Numerous experiences with pictures which emphasize size differences will facilitate an understanding of its relational nature.

Logical inferences should be explored. If a truck is bigger than a book, then a book is smaller than a truck. Elicit comparison statements using: *bigger than* and *smaller than*. Many preschoolers begin with a trial and error approach, awaiting a cue from the teacher.

Activity

Actions associated with animals or objects offer another important mode of classification. Animals can be classed according to whether they run, fly, swim, climb, crawl or jump. Objects or things can be classed into numerous categories such as those that can be read, ridden in, opened, eaten, sat on, listened to, saved, played with, hit, touched, thrown, kicked. Activities are primary associational characteristics which facilitate comprehension of things and their purpose.

CONNECTIVES AND NEGATIVES

Understanding the differential use of *and, or, but* determines which property or properties to include when classifying. Using *and* involves processing at least two characteristics. "Touch a red square and a white circle." "Get a small box and a big box." Vary statements by including two properties without the connective. "Find a large, white triangle." Alternate directions with and without the use of *and*, to determine comprehension of its use.

The correct use of *or* indicates an understanding of the available option. "Tag John or Mary." "Get a red crayon or a blue crayon." Acting correctly on the option is evidence of comprehension. The use of *but* is exclusionary; *not* is implied in its use. "All please stand but Joan." "Collect all the books but mine." Comprehending the use of *but* develops slowly. Frequent oral exercise is essential to grasp fully its meaning.

Negatives reverse the basis for inclusive classification. The use of *not* breaks the pattern of seeking the property mentioned. "Pick up a triangle that is not white." By accenting *not* when

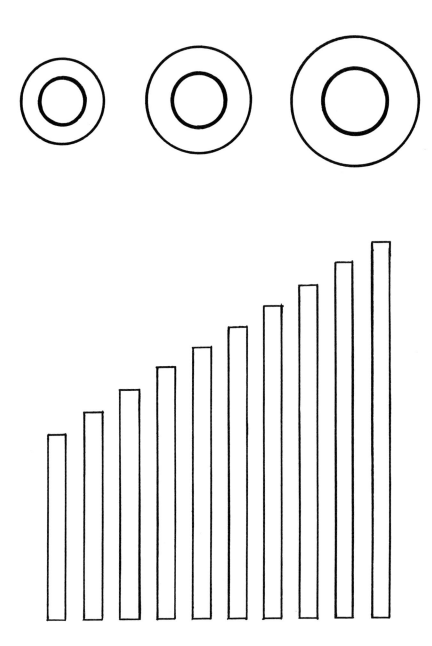

Figure 11. Seriation.

giving the instructions, the teacher cues the reversal task. Confusion is created by the fact that the property sought is not mentioned.

Processing statements indeed becomes complicated when both a connective and a negative are combined. "Give me the red and white cards that are not big." Only children with an excellent grasp of the language should be asked to react to such complex statements.

SERIATION

Ordering similar items according to size, from smallest to largest, is seriation. Five-year-olds generally order items on a trial and error basis. Begin with three items (sticks, pencils, circles, etc.) of noticeably different size. See top row of Figure 11. Gradually increase the number of items to ten, using a variety of manipulatives. Arranging more than five items is quite difficult because discrimination and ordering skills emerge slowly through a combination of maturation and practice. Reverse seriation involves placing the largest items on the left and arranging them in order of descending size. See Figure 12.

Ordering two sets of ten items is double seriation. Bats and balls are ordered one-to-one according to size, matching a bat for each ball (see Fig. 13). Frequent opportunity for practice should be provided. Ordering begins haphazardly, but eventually a trial and error approach will improve accuracy. If the set of bats is placed closer together than the balls, or if any are moved about, visual correspondence between sets is lost. Proximity is the criteria used by children who have not learned to count to establish correspondence. Counting is the most accurate way to establish correspondence between sets. Exposure to double seriation provides an opportunity to develop counting skills with manipulatives.

CORRESPONDENCE

Establishing equivalence of sets by one-to-one correspondence is a basic prenumerical skill. For those who have difficulty with

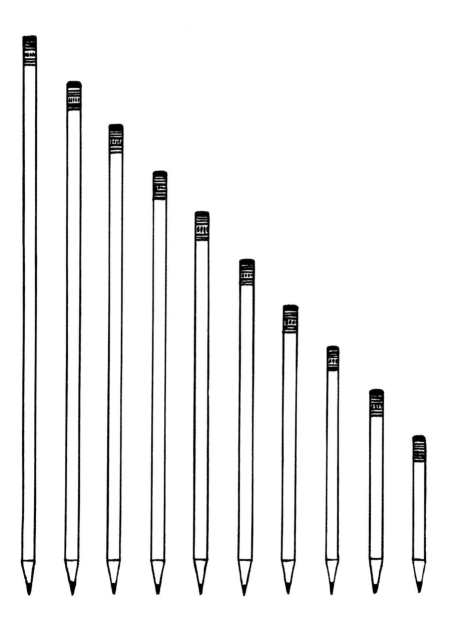

Figure 12. Reverse seriation.

sets of ten items, begin with sets of three or five items. Repeat the

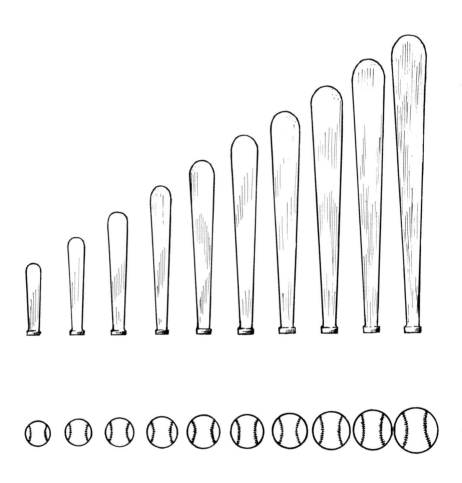

Figure 13. Double seriation.

procedure with three drinking straws and three half-pint milk cartons. When one-to-one correspondence is established, group the straws closer and ask, "Are there as many straws as cartons?" Alter the arrangement of cartons and repeat questioning concerning equivalence. When counting replaces reliance upon perceptual arrangements, numeration is established.

Matching similar sets (buttons with buttons) can cause confusion because the idea of sets can be lost during manipulation unless the color or shapes of the buttons are different. Sometimes one complete set is arranged and the idea of correspondence is lost. Dissimilar sets (glasses and books) or inequivalent sets (three saucers, four cups) do not lend themselves to quick correspondence. It is quite difficult to understand how glasses and books go together; therefore, matching is slow. Inequivalent sets are often treated as equivalent, with no attempt to exclude items. Only those who have been successful with one-to-one correspondence of ten items (double seriation) should be asked to match dissimilar or inequivalent sets.

PATTERNS

Copying or continuing a systematic array of figures exercises visual sequencing skills. Detecting regularities in the pattern is a first step in visually organizing and processing a display of items (see Fig. 14). A careful analysis of each item in the sequence is needed to establish a pattern. After a pattern is copied or completed, verbalization of the sequence is sought. "Two square beads, two round beads and two square beads again." Precise verbal formulations should be encouraged as a means of improving visual processing. The creation of original patterns and sequences enables each child to participate at his own level of maturity. Much practice is necessary to describe patterns accurately.

COUNTING

Introduce counting by rearranging the position of beads without altering the number in the set. After each shift in the arrangement ask, "How many are there now?" Demonstrate a variety of positions: horizontal, vertical, diagonal, scrambled, etc. (see Fig. 15). Preschoolers are optically distracted by the perceptual configuration. They will eventually learn, through practice, that the position of space occupied by the beads has no relationship to the

Figure 14. Simple patterns.

number. To avoid the possibility of rote responses, periodically change the objects to be counted, i.e. use buttons, blocks, plastic chips, dominoes, pencils, paper clips. Such a procedure reduces boredom and introduces the idea that many objects can be counted.

REVERSIBILITY

At the preoperational level, thought is irrevocably attached to

Figure 15. Counting beads.

perception. Therefore, any alteration in the position of items, such as buttons, sticks or beads, is erroneously interpreted as a change in quantity. Reversibility is the ability to understand that a change in the arrangement does not alter the number and that the process can be returned to its original state (see Fig. 16). The absence of reversibility suggests the need for additional manipulative, prenumerical activities. Comparing equal sets with variations in configuration should be practiced until it is understood that equality is retained in spite of shifts in position or arrangement.

MATHEMATICAL VOCABULARY

In the early years the multiple meanings of words are almost totally absent. Words with mathematical meanings are used but not in a mathematical context. For instance, the word *more* may be used to obtain more candy or more milk, but does not carry the connotive comparison *more than,* an idea of greater complexity. Correct oral application of each term evolves through repeated exercise in a host of mathematical settings. Visual, graphic, and manipulative demonstrations are deemed essential. Comprehension develops through exposure to a variety of numerical terms. The foundations of mathematical thought rest upon understanding the numerous expressions of quantity. Words like some-all, few-many, more-less, and most-least should have quantitative significance.

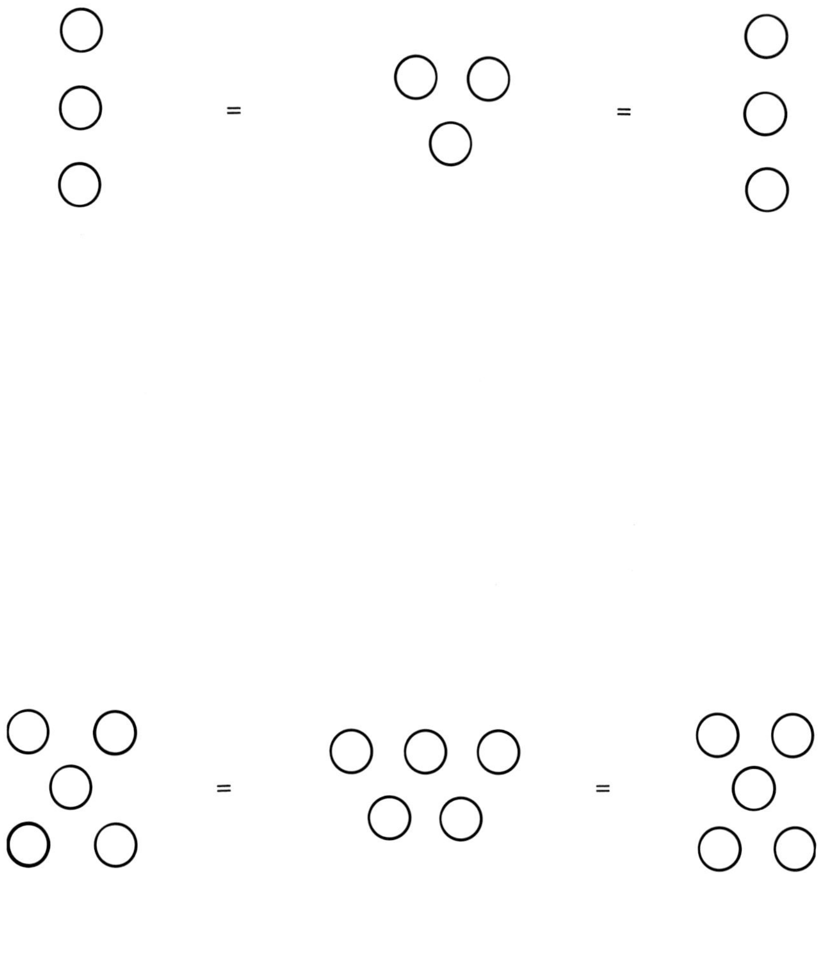

Figure 16. Reversibility.

Some-All

The distinction between these terms can be easily demonstrated with manipulatives. "Put all the pencils on my desk." "Get some crayons out of that box." Repeated practice is necessary to establish the idea that *some* and *all* are variable amounts. Demonstrate with a variety of manipulatives. Continue to vary the number of items to clarify distinctions in meaning.

Few-Many

Kindergarteners have a difficult time comprehending the variable amounts represented by *few* and *many*. Few should be demonstrated by any amount under five. Give each child manipulatives to hold and elicit statements using few. "I have a few pencils." "I have a few marbles." "I have a few beads." Assign partners, encouraging the use of *fewer than*. Complete sentences are preferable. "I have fewer pencils than Harry."

Any large number of items will adequately demonstrate the concept *many*. However, the idea that fifteen paper clips, twenty crayons and ten books can be *many* tends to confuse preschoolers. Its flexible, indeterminate use (a varied number of items in a slightly different context) alters the perceptual field which is then no longer interpreted as *many*. The use of *as many as* and *too many* should also be elicited. "I have as many pencils as you." "You have too many crayons."

More-Less

Use of *more* is easier to comprehend than *less*. Five-year-olds learn to use more candy or more ice cream rather quickly. Draw three circles and one square on the board and ask, "Are there more circles or more squares?" Assign partners, giving each a different number of manipulatives. Elicit statements using *more*. "I have more beads." Also introduce the comparison *more than*. "I have more blocks than Sally." "I have more than you."

Logic can be introduced with the use of *less* and *less than*. Give each partner a different number of plastic-shaped diamonds, squares, circles and triangles. Elicit comparison statements. "I have more squares than James; James has less squares than I." "I have less triangles than Mary; she has more triangles than I." Rotate partners and continue comparison statements. Those who cannot produce correct comparative statements should return to exercises in one-to-one correspondence.

Most-Least

Organize groups of three to work together. Give a different number of manipulatives to each member. Let each group determine who holds the *least* and who the *most*. Continue eliciting statements of *more than* and *less than*. Rotate group members and repeat, varying the number and types of manipulatives.

Volume

Young children interpret visual change to mean a quantitative change; such is often the case. Overgeneralizing the rule, however, creates the inability to observe accurately conservation of volume, as liquids and powder take the shape of vessels into which they are poured, thereby appearing to change.

Two identical glasses are filled to the same level with water. After the children agree that both glasses contain similar amounts, the water from one glass is poured into a taller, wider glass; a wider, but shorter glass; a taller, narrower glass; two smaller glasses. After each transfer, the children are asked which glass has more or are the amounts similar. To prove the amounts remain the same, pour the water back into the original glass. Sand and soil can also be used to demonstrate volume conservation. Snack time is most opportune to explore volume with milk cartons. The terms *full, empty, half empty* and *half full* should be used as they drink.

The young also interpret changes in shape to mean differences in volume. Begin with two balls of clay or putty of equal size. After agreeing the amount of clay in each ball is the same, one of the balls is transformed into a different shape. The children are then asked if the amount of clay is the same in the altered shape.

Figure 17. Conservation of liquids.

Numerous shape transformations should be demonstrated: long sausage; doughnut; flat pancake; broken into two pieces. After each transformation, return the clay to its original shape to demonstrate conservation. Direct their attention to the amount of clay, not the shape. Through repeated experience the realization will emerge that a change in form does not necessarily mean a change in quantity.

Distance

The variability of reference points complicates the understanding of distance. Two dolls are placed at different distances from a dollhouse. The children are asked to select the doll *near* the house. Vary the objects (toys, trucks, soldiers, etc.) and the distance to insure comprehension under diverse conditions. Use string or strips of paper to compare the distances.

Encourage use of the terms *near* and *far* when answering questions concerning distance. "Is John's desk near the window or the door?" The children are expected to answer in complete sentences. "John's desk is near the door." "Mary's desk is near the window."

Distance and direction can be developed by the use of classroom maps. The children are shown a map of the classroom indicating the location of teacher's desk, door, blackboard, desks, windows, tables, etc. Each day a toy is hidden and indicated on the map. A "detective" reads the map and tries to find the hidden toy. Distances can be measured using a string or a yardstick. New maps are drawn when furniture has been rearranged.

Length

The property of length can be demonstrated by letting youngsters run their fingers from left to right along the length of a table, desk or other object. Cut strips of construction paper to different lengths. Compare these strips; encourage statements using the terms *long, longer; short, shorter.* Attempt to elicit complete sentences. "The blue strip is longer than the yellow strip." "The red strip and the white strip are the same length." "The blue strip is shorter than the black strip."

A change in the physical position of an object is sometimes erroneously interpreted as a change in length. Therefore, objects should be measured in a variety of positions to reinforce the idea that length has not changed. Begin with two rulers, yardsticks or metersticks aligned in parallel. Use the phrase, the same length, as the children run their fingers along the length. Move these about and continue questioning after each movement. Compare the lengths of the yard, meter and ruler without resorting to the terms inches, feet or centimeter.

Logic statements can be introduced after the use of *longer than* and *shorter than* are understood independently. "If the table is longer than the desk, then the desk is shorter than the table." Introduce questions like, "Which is shorter, the pencil or the crayon?" "Which is longer, the train or the car?"

Height

Comparing children in the classroom is an excellent method of examining variations in height. Assign partners and encourage statements using *taller than* and *shorter than*. "Mary is taller than Arthur." Compare the heights of tables, chairs, animals, etc. Logic statements should only be introduced after correct use of *taller than* and *shorter than* is well established. "If Mary is taller than Arthur, then Arthur is shorter than Mary." Contrast with the use of *big*, indicating that an elephant is bigger than a giraffe but the giraffe is taller than the elephant.

Mathematical Vocabulary

The following terms are directly or indirectly related to numeration, quantification or classification. To become an integral part of the oral vocabulary these terms should be demonstrated in a multiplicity of diverse settings and repeatedly applied.

Numeration		*Size*	*Quantity*
add	same	big	
all	seven	bigger	enough
and	set		equal to
another	several	large	few
any	six	larger	many
			more than
both	take away	short	greater than
but	three	shorter	less than
	two		as many as
count	ten	small	how much
couple		smaller	how many
	zero		
dozen			
	Money	*Weight*	*Distance*
each			
eight	cent	heavy	far
empty	nickel	heavier	farther
	dime		
few	quarter	light	near
five	dollar		
four		lighter	nearer
full			
	Cardinal Order	*Height*	*Shapes*
half			
	first	high	circle
	second	higher	diamond
last	third		triangle
	fourth	low	rectangle
middle	fifth	lower	square
	sixth		
most	seventh	tall	
nine	eighth	taller	
none	ninth		
not	tenth		
number			
one			
once			
pair			

PRENUMERICAL AND NUMERICAL EXERCISES

A. Colors

Materials: Articles of clothing worn by the children.

Classifications: (1) color   (2) sex   (3) article name

1. Ask each child what colors he is wearing.
2. Using Simon Says ask all children wearing red to stand. Go through all the major colors asking children to indicate by sitting, raising the hand or other signal.
3. Introduce the classification of sex. What boys are wearing red today? What girls are wearing green? Proceed through all the colors, helping those who fail to recognize the dual classification.
4. Identify articles of clothing: dresses, trousers, sweaters, socks, shoes, shirt, coat, jacket, etc. All girls wearing red dresses, please stand up. All boys wearing blue trousers, please stand up. All those wearing black shoes, raise their hand, etc.
5. Multiple classifications should be introduced very gradually and only after much success with single classification. All girls wearing red dresses and boys wearing white shirts, stand up. All boys wearing black shoes and girls wearing white dresses, raise your hands.

B. Shapes and Sizes

Materials: twelve plastic blocks (three square, three circular, three rectangular, three triangular) each set a different size.

Classifications: shape — square, circle, rectangle, triangle.
                 size — big, bigger, small, smaller.

1. Label the shapes. Ask for examples of objects which have these shapes. Circle — clock; tire, ball; square — book, paper, ceiling, or wall tile; Rectangle — desk, boxes, pictures; Triangle — roof, mountain, pyramid.
2. Determine the properties of each shape. Circles are round. Squares have four sides of equal length. Triangles have three sides. Rectangles have two long and two short sides.
3. With string each child forms the shapes on the desk.
4. Trace the shapes on paper and cut them out with scissors. Create drawings from these shapes. A circle can be a sun-

flower; triangle — a mountain; rectangle — a cart; square — a book.

5. Detective. The teacher hides a shape behind her and the children ask about its properties. Does it have corners? Is it round? Are there three sides?

6. Introduce the classification of size. Which is bigger? What is smaller? Pick one which is bigger than the one I hold.

7. Classification by shape and size. Which is the bigger circle? Which is bigger, the circle or the triangle?

8. Is this circle bigger than this rectangle? Which is smaller, the square or the circle? Which is the biggest, the square, triangle or rectangle? Mixing shapes and sizes, repeat questions of comparison.

C. Patterns

Materials; beads (of same color) and string for each child.

1. Look for repeated patterns in the room and on clothing. Floors, walls, ceiling and designs often have repeated patterns.

2. Using round and square beads of the same color, string the beads, alternating shapes. Copy the pattern on paper.

3. Demonstrate a string of beads with no pattern.

4. String a pattern of two round beads followed by two square beads.

5. Create new patterns by adding cylindrical beads.

6. Create new patterns by using different colors.

7. Working as partners the children take turns creating patterns and continuing them.

D. Size Comparisons — tall, taller, large, larger.

1. "Who is taller?" Partners compare heights. Simple comparison statements are elicited. "Mary is taller." "John is shorter." Repeat until all have had an opportunity to participate.

2. "Which is larger?" Responses should include complete statements.

a. house or a canoe	k. yardstick or ruler
b. tree or a flower	l. penny or nickel
c. cat or dog	m. bead or block
d. car or truck	n. stone or rock

e. boat or canoe
f. goat or horse
g. cat or kitten
h. puppy or dog
i. watermelon or orange
j. banana or cherry

o. train or truck
p. father or son
q. daughter or mother
r. man or baby
s. lion or elephant

3. Arrange half the class according to size, tallest to shortest, as others watch. Arrange other half.
4. Arrange objects according to size. Use scissors, pipe cleaners, crayons, paper strips and cuisenaire rods.
5. Cut out paper "pancakes" each larger than the last. Stack with the largest at the bottom and smallest on top. Begin with five or six sizes, using the terms larger and smaller.
6. Stack books to illustrate different sizes.

E. Quantity — few-many, some-all, more than-less than, most-least.
Materials: beads, blocks, buttons, counting sticks, pebbles, straws, etc.
1. Begin questioning in groups of three children, each holding an unequal number of manipulatives. Repeat exercises almost daily.
   a. Who has a few beads? Who has many beads?
   b. Does Mary have more than John? Who has the most straws?
   c. Give me some blocks. Give me all the buttons.
   d. Who has the least straws? Most?
   e. Who has less sticks than Carol?

F. Counting — daily exercises
1. Count the number of boys and girls present each day.
2. Count body parts: arms, fingers, toes, nose, mouth, legs, chin, feet, head, neck.
3. Count items in the classroom: windows, tables, boxes, pencils, crayons, etc.

G. Volume
Materials: quart, ½ gallon, gallon, pint, ½ pint.
1. Identify the various sizes and label each.
2. Discuss sizes after labels are learned.

      a. Does the gallon hold more than the half gallon?

      b. Does the pint hold more than the ½ pint?

      c. Does the quart hold more than the pint?

      d. Is the half gallon more than a gallon?

H. Weight — heavy, heavier; light, lighter.

    Materials: Items with different weights: feathers, stones, etc.

    1. Which is heavier, a feather or a stone?

    2. Which is lighter, corn flakes or potatoes?

    3 Which is lighter, paper or wood? Book or paper? Chair or comb? Crayon or desk?

I. One-to-One Correspondence

    Materials: beads, counting sticks, paper circles and triangles diamonds, circles and squares.

    1. Match one-to-one beads with counting sticks, circles and squares, straws and milk cartons. Begin with three items in each set.

    2. "Are there more circles or more squares?"Question each accordingly.

    3. Draw three lollipops on the board. Ask the children to draw three children to eat those lollipops.

    4. Draw two baseball bats. Ask the children to draw two balls to match.

    5. Match sets of:

      a. students to books

      b. students to crayons

      c. books to magazines

      d. crayons to paper

J. Unequal Sets

    1. Demonstrate with five paint brushes and six empty paint jars. "Are there as many brushes as jars?" Place a brush in each jar to confirm. Provide the additional brush to establish equivalence.

    2. Repeat with four beads and five paper cups. Provide the additional item to match the sets equally.

    3. Distribute circles to all children in sets of five, four, three, two and one. Question using more than and less than. Who has more than two circles? Who has more than four circles? Who has less than three circles?

4. Compare sets of: boys and girls, windows and doors, pebbles and buttons, tables and chairs.

_____

CHAPTER 9

THE RATE OF LEARNING

‑‑‑‑‑‑‑‑‑‑‑‑‑‑‑‑‑‑‑‑‑‑‑‑‑‑‑‑‑‑‑‑‑‑‑

DISCARDING THE READINESS AND IQ MODELS

A SPECTRUM of physiological, developmental, environmental and psychosocial correlates influence the concept known as "readiness." Many theorists have isolated and identified a host of elements which include auditory discrimination (Thompson, 1964), visual discrimination (Barrett, 1965), anxiety (Cohen, 1961), self-concept (Wattenburg and Clare, 1964), physiological factors (Getman and Kane, 1964), perceptual-motor functions (Sutphin, 1964), language and perception (Weiner and Feldman, 1963) (De Hirsch, 1966), and developmental maturity (Ilg and Ames, 1965). Developmental factors which contribute heavily to the readiness model cannot be accurately assessed without an exhaustive individual evaluation which is costly, time-consuming, and often impractical. Environmental influences (motivation to learn, parental expectation, familial interests, socioeconomic status, parental stability, etc.) also have a significant impact on readiness but cannot be measured in the present state of the art. Since cognitive elements in the readiness model are also confounded by unknown emotional and personal-social dynamics, the accurate assessment of these contaminating variables is highly unlikely.

Children develop and therefore learn at different rates. Waiting for the hypothetic moment of readiness will be as inappropriate as systematically force-feeding the underprivileged. Both extremes miss the mark. What is too early for one is too late for a second, but opportune for a third. It seems that concepts are frequently introduced based on what we know about the "average" child. However, since no individual is average, we should begin instruction with what we know a child can do, not what we think he is ready for. Only after initial success do we gradually introduce increments of difficulty.

The lack of specificity surrounding the term "readiness" also clouds its use. Does it mean readiness to read? To write? To learn? Many use the term to connote general school readiness. There appears to be no agreed upon definition. Without precise usage its meaning is vague and blurred. Beller (1970) argues rather convincingly that the complex known as readiness will become meaningful only when we can ascertain its relationship to the rate of learning.

In the early years mental development is not a static phenomenon from which stable predictions of intelligence can be made. Honzik, et al. (1948) found IQ differences of more than fifteen points (some as high as fifty points) for over half of the individuals studied from preschool to adulthood. The variability of the mental rate of growth in each child renders reliable intellectual assessment at a given moment difficult at best. One year in a child's life between the ages of four and five comprises 20 percent of his life experience. Variations in daily experience account for the obvious discrepancy between preschool and adult IQ scores. Changes in height and weight can and often do occur sometimes in a matter of months. Since development is clearly a variable phenomenon in the young, intellectual growth must also follow the same uneven pattern. Maturation and change are constants which should be monitored on an annual basis.

Consequently, in the early years one evaluation will not provide a reliable, accurate assessment of the child's developing biological and intellectual processes. Prediction from a growth curve is usually more effective than from any one point (Caswell and Foshay, 1957). The developmental curve of an individual reveals the *rate* of growth and is a better index of what to expect than is any single measure of status at a given time. Each child has a genetically determined, individual growth rate which must be closely studied in order to understand him.

THE RATE OF LEARNING (ROL)

The ROL is a complex interaction of known and unknown variables. Wang (1968) has been unable to identify or isolate those factors which accurately predict the ROL. Since accurate prediction is not possible, an alternate recourse is to measure the ROL directly in the classroom. The ROL is that gain recorded on a posttest, over and above the scores on an identical pretest, which is the result of the standard instruction period of one academic year. The September to June instructional year is the yardstick against which learning gains are measured. Gains assessed over a shorter period have been found to be unreliable and nonpermanent (Coleman, 1966). The ROL differs from Carroll's (1963) degree of learning which is a simple function of the amount of time during which the pupil engages actively in learning. However, retention, the ultimate criterion for learning, is not accounted for. The ROL posttest measures retention directly after the standard instructional period of one year.

ROL — a Self-Comparison

Because each child's biological makeup and environmental experiences differ, we cannot justifiably compare one child's performance with another his age. The numerous subpopulations in our multicultural society (deprived, affluent, ethnic, chicano, black, etc.) render a fair comparison impossible. Brothers and sisters in the same family should not be compared because of genetic differences. It would appear that only identical twins from the same environment can be justifiably compared. Each child's ROL is confounded by both biological and environmental factors too complex to identify. The ROL will differ depending upon the skill to be developed. Verbal, lingual, manual, mechanical and mathematical skills will be learned at different rates by each child because of inherent differences in both ability and motivation.

Individual variability then is the typical pattern of learning. Periods of learning are invariably followed by plateaus of apparent consolidation. Plateaus appear intermittently and unpredictably in the learning cycle. However, plateau periods of nonprogress should not continue for an entire academic year, especially under the influence of direct instruction. Bloom (1964) theorizes that under normal circumstances measurable increments of learning should occur in intense learning environments.

Standardized achievement tests are based on the premise that gains can be expected within one academic year (ten months), plateaus notwithstanding. If minimal gains do not occur after an entire year, it is safe to assume that impedances to learning are operative.

The ROL is perhaps the most sensitive measure of the child's retentive-learning function. The ROL is to the kindergarten teacher what the thermometer is to the doctor. A slow ROL suggests the presence of impedance factors causing learning delays. Immediate steps should be taken to investigate the causes for a slow ROL.

The ultimate criterion for the ROL is the degree to which the child is able to retain what is taught. The ROL is a measure encompassing environmental, constitutional and instructional factors which influence the rate at which learning occurs. The ROL is the embodiment of total learning, measuring the degree of retention under standard instructional conditions.

The Rate of Learning Model

Kindergarten is the first exposure to the group instructional process for most children. Each child reacts personally and individually to the group process. Therefore, the primary effect, that of group instruction, must be assessed. The Rate of Learning is the measurable effect of that instruction on the developing sensory processes of the child.

The preschool child is predominantly a receiver of stimuli. Learning is initially based upon the reception, recognition and discrimination of stimuli, not on the emission of complex responses. The child is asked to respond to stimuli presented by the teacher. The teacher may present a stimulus, hoping to elicit a single, correct response. Exposing the picture of a sailboat, she asks for the name. The stimulus is carefully controlled in an effort to reduce chances for error in the response. This may be called stimulus-response or associative learning.

However, the kindergarten is a highly stimulating environment. It may be conservatively estimated that 20,000 to 30,000 stimuli are produced every hour by a class of twenty-five children.

Shuffling feet, noises from desks and chairs, laughter, talking and coughing are merely a few of the numerous, repetitive "distractor" stimuli. The frequency and intensity of distractor stimuli is so great that learning can be seriously impaired. Broadbent (1958) has found that children attend to intense, novel stimuli which meet inner biological needs.

Learning depends upon the ability to attend voluntarily to a relatively few controlled stimuli presented by the teacher and to inhibit responses to the numerous irrelevant, distractor stimuli. It has been reported that better learners attend to distractor stimuli *after* the learning task has been completed (Turnure, 1968). Learning will take place only if distractor stimuli can be intentionally "tuned out" and ignored. The child incapable of response inhibition will attend to many of the nonessential, distractor stimuli, which are ever present in all classrooms.

At various times during a lesson, teachers redirect attention to the appropriate stimuli to be learned. However, having no control over the child's nervous system, the teacher cannot force attention without help from the child. The child who is stimulus bound responds to the last stimulus, regardless of its source. A child incapable of response inhibition may therefore learn at a slower rate.

Although the classroom is the place in which learning germinates, learning is an individual process, not a group phenomenon. The classroom setting acts differentially upon children, enhancing learning for most, but creating impedences for others. Educators are obliged to determine which children learn slowly in the typical classroom and provide educational alternatives which will compensate for this inherent weakness of individuals in the educational system.

The rate of learning has many constitutional and environmental components. However, the act of learning (in the school setting) may be conveniently divided into several basic elements for analysis: (1) learning style, (2) task orientation, (3) self-confidence, (4) understanding directions, (5) retaining direction, (6) span of concentration, (7) independent learning activity, (8) task completion, (9) retention.

Learning Style

Each child utilizes an individual approach to learning which can be called a primary learning style. The child's initial response tendency is related to personality and behavioral factors. A cautious, reckless or timid approach is basically a manifestation and extension of personality. Response time, which Kagan (1965) calls reflection-impulsivity, is the consistent tendency to make a fast or slow decision in a problem setting. This tendency is found to be relatively stable, but children can be trained to delay their response after tutoring. Individual differences in response time were found to influence the quality of cognitive performance in reading, serial learning and inductive reasoning.

The first role of the teacher is to introduce novel but constructive response strategies. Guiding the child to analyze his approach is much more important than providing the correct answer. Suggesting a new approach may be helpful for a lifetime; the correct answer is only momentarily useful. Therefore, the child's modus operandi should be studied very carefully because of its impact upon ultimate performance. The initial response tendency may be a serious impediment to learning. Clues to success or failure may be provided by careful observation of pupil response. The teacher should attempt to remedy noticeable weaknesses in learning style. The child who guesses haphazardly should be instructed to scan the entire problem before answering. The child who responds before instructions are complete must be taught to wait. The overly anxious child who fears committing errors should be encouraged to try and praised for the effort. The child who uses a perseverative response to several learning tasks should be taught to seek alternative solutions. The frequency with which perseveration occurs can be reduced or eliminated by an alert teacher. Variations in response style are typical of normal children (Goulet and Barclay, 1967). A slow rate of task performance is indicative of children who may eventually develop learning disabilities (McGrady and Olson, 1967).

Each child should be instructed regarding any inherent weaknesses of approach. The teacher should remind the child who hurries to proceed slowly, as occasions arise. However, the teacher should instruct the child to say aloud, "I must go slowly." The child should verbalize and be given an opportunity to interiorize the new direction his behavior must take before a change can be expected. The teacher is judge of whether a response style accelerates or impedes the learning process. It would appear that the lack of skill in the approach or tactics appears to be a significant handicap to learning.

Task Orientation

Each learning activity has certain distinct characteristics. If components of the task are familiar to the learner, orientation is expedited. Familiarity facilitates a positive orientation, enabling the child to draw upon previous experience to guide the present response. Disorganized, diffuse or inappropriate responses are often produced to unfamiliar tasks. The act of reading is incomprehensible to a child who has rarely noticed books or never been read to. Without experiential cues upon which to base a response, the child may hold the book incorrectly, may read from right to left, may begin at the end, or may throw the book away. The teacher should provide orienting cues through demonstration, which are imitated. The child must be capable of imitation, a simple form of learning, as this inability will result in poor orientation skills.

Self-Confidence

Learning is built upon initial failures and erroneous trials (Travers, 1964). The desire to continue the pursuit of learning, after initial setbacks, depends largely upon the degree of self-confidence. If self-confidence is absent, the child's reaction to an erroneous trial is to stop trying. Initial defeats discourage many learners who refuse to try again.

Ego strength, need achievement (McClelland, 1961) and the self-concept (Combs and Snygg, 1959) are personality and motivational variables which influence the degree of self-confidence a child feels. Subtle remarks by parents or teacher, self comparisons with brothers or sisters, negative criticism, and personal sensitivity can undermine self-assurance. Parents who did poorly in school sometimes hold limited scholastic expectations for their offspring. The numerous, complex factors which influence persistence in learning tasks are not well understood and therefore not amenable to change.

Understanding Directions

To proceed through a learning activity smoothly, directions must be clearly grasped. Those able to begin with limited assistance often have little difficulty. However, a child failing to understand the essence of a task will talk to neighbors, gaze out the window, or otherwise occupy himself to avoid what may now be an anxiety-producing task. Any youngster requiring the teacher's personal attention more than once in an activity will quite likely have difficulty completing the assignment. Repeated opportunities for individual attention do not arise because of the teacher's instructional obligation to other pupils.

Retaining Directions

A child may initiate the learning assignment appropriately but gradually experience a loss of self-direction as the lesson progresses. The child who fails to interiorize the requirements of the task is unable to proceed independently. Teachers spend considerable time repeating directions. The child who cannot retain the basic elements of the assignment (unless directions are repeated two or three times) will likely learn at a slower rate. During a busy school day teachers do not always have the time to be so accommodating. The child may be left to do his best as the teacher helps those who are proceeding with some degree of success.

Span of Concentration

The physiological maturity of the nervous system limits the attention of the child. Numerous personality and environmental variables, i.e. anxiety, tension, excitability, fatigue and the nature of the learning task, account for variations in concentration. Inhibition of bodily movements, especially the eyes, are associated with attention and concentration. The need for teachers to provide and maintain a modicum of order to all classroom activities enhances the potential for concentration. Excesses in activity may not be conducive to academic learning. Periods of physical activity and inactivity should be alternated so that both preferences can be accommodated.

Independent Learning Activity

The teacher can guide, demonstrate and help children individually to a large degree, but the child must carry on independently when the teacher is busy with other children. Herein lies a critical aspect of learning. Learning depends upon the constructive use of time, by the child, between teacher contacts. In large classes the interval is lengthy and the number of teacher contacts per pupil diminishes greatly.

The greater part of the school day is non-pupil-teacher contact. A child incapable of independent, self-directed learning activity is certain to learn at a slower rate and may develop learning deficiencies. The child who is able to help himself learn will not likely become a slow learner. The difference between fast and slow learners is the use made of the interval between teacher contacts. Independent work habits should be taught to those who have not developed that ability. Self-application should become an integral part of the child's primary learning style.

Task Completion

There are many detours along the road of learning. The road is long and the obstacles many. Intervening events, a lack of interest or stimulating diversions distract from the learning process. The importance of completion is self-evident. Pupils should also feel the satisfaction associated with completing a task. Successful completion is the embodiment of many components of learning.

Retention

In the final analysis skills and activities which are practiced should be retained over time. Retention is the ultimate criterion. The rate of learning assesses the effects of instruction and the degree to which retention occurs.

DIAGNOSTIC GROUPING

The developmental pretest is primarily a diagnostic device which reveals certain strengths and weaknesses in the basic skills. Raw scores which convert to the first, second, third or fourth stanine (unweighted) suggest skill weaknesses which require instructional remediation. The child is guided into a personalized instructional program suited to his particular needs. Children with similar deficiencies can be diagnostically grouped for instruction. For example, the children who perform poorly on the differences subtest should be given a variety of exercises to develop visual discrimination. Optical illusions, figure-ground discrimination, puzzles and games which exercise precise visual attention are recommended activities.

Instructional materials should be carefully selected by the teacher to meet pupil needs. To avoid pupil boredom a variety of materials should be rotated to preserve interest. Diagnostic instruction should never be limited to one method or one procedure. A variety of activities and materials is almost always preferable; a variegated instructional approach is recommended. Instruction in each of the basic skills should be undertaken daily throughout the school year to provide continuity and reinforce the learning process. Unless the teacher is willing to persevere with a daily instructional strategy, little measurable gain will result.

The pretest — instruction — posttest design of the Developmental Kindergarten fulfills the requirements for measuring the Rate of Learning. Developmental factors are measured by the pretest upon admission to kindergarten. A year of kindergarten instruction is followed by an identical posttest which measures the learning gain, over and above the initial developmental level. By utilization of the pretest — instruction — posttest design, a reliable determination of the rate at which a child learns in kindergarten, is made.

THE RATE OF LEARNING TEST

INTRODUCTION

IN a preliminary investigation a variety of measures were initially administered to 352 kindergarten children. The Metropolitan and California Achievement Tests given at the end of first grade served as validity criteria. Final selection was based upon prediction of criteria and ease of administration. A brief description of the five subtests which constitute the Rate of Learning Test follows.

Picture Vocabulary

The picture test is composed of common objects, action verbs and animals. Nouns and verbs in the child's speaking vocabulary are assessed. The picture test measures the ability to label. Deprived children of average ability do poorly on the pretest but improve their scores on the posttest. The test is a verbal measure influenced by environmental exposure.

Preliminary experimentation began with seventy-eight pictures, administered to 600 children. Through item analysis (Davis, 1949) the number of items was reduced to forty-one, then thirty-five. Product moment correlations with achievement test criteria ranged from .49 to .56, thus validating predictability.

Sentence Memory

Learning and auditory memory functions are related phenomena. Bradway (1962) reported that preschool measures of memory

---

The Rate of Learning Test may be purchased from Educational Consultation Services, 921 Academy Lane, Bryn Mawr, Pa. 19010.

remained stable in a twenty-five-year follow-up study of intelligence. Auditory discrimination and retention are prerequisites for appropriate classroom behavior. Retaining the verbal directions of the teacher is basic to successful group participation. Multiple regression analysis revealed that the ability to repeat sentences was an important predictor of first grade reading achievement. Ease of administration and scoring also favored inclusion.

Counting Blocks

Rote counting should not be mistaken as knowledge of number concepts. Many children can parrot the numbers from one to ten without awareness of number values. A preliminary study of 483 children revealed the test did not discriminate sufficiently at the upper difficulty levels. To extend the scale, addition and subtraction problems were included. Counting blocks is the best single predictor of first grade reading and arithmetic, as measured by the achievement test. A grasp of simple number values appears to be a necessary prerequisite for learning. Overall maturity to undertake formal learning is measured by this test.

Differences

Acute visual discrimination is an essential prerequisite skill for reading. A child unable to discern fine differences between letters and words will encounter insurmountable reading difficulties. Twenty-one items were initially developed. Two items of doubtful value were eliminated by item analysis. Success depends upon the child's ability to notice minute differences among the figures and shapes.

Drawings

Copying figures is a test frequently used with preschool children. Simple to administer and score, the test measures fine eye-hand coordination. The development of perceptual-motor skills is basic to many scholastic tasks, such as writing, coloring and copying. The more difficult drawings require integration of two figures.

STANDARDIZATION AND STATISTICAL ANALYSIS

Sample

The urban and rural samples were obtained in Northeastern Pennsylvania and Southern New York State. The suburban sample was taken from the environs of Philadelphia.

The schools, at which the children were evaluated, were selected on the basis of heterogeneity. In all communities the elementary supervisor was asked to suggest those elementary schools which represented a cross-section of the population rather than that which sampled predominately one social strata. All children were examined by the author (see Table III).

TABLE III

STANDARDIZATION SAMPLE

| | Number Examined | | |
	Male	Female	Total
Urban:			
Southern New York	299	243	542
Rural:			
Northeastern Pennsylvania	255	296	551
Suburban:			
Southeastern Pennsylvania	55	62	117
Total	609	601	1,210

Occupational Comparison

A comparison with the 1970 census reveals the sample included a greater number of children whose fathers are in a somewhat lower occupational category (see Table IV). The sample included fewer children whose fathers were craftsmen, foremen and laborers. The large number of rural children sampled undoubtedly accounted for the discrepancy. It is probably safe to assume that children from environments of greater affluence should perform somewhat better than the standardization group.

TABLE IV

FATHER'S OCCUPATION

N= 1,093

	%ROL Sample	% 1970 Population*
Professional & Technical	19	14
Managers & Proprietors	14	27
Craftsmen & Foremen	14	23
Operatives & Service workers	39	30
Laborers	14	6

*Department of Commerce, 1970 Census.

Intercorrelation

The Rate of Learning Test samples five distinct verbal-developmental functions. Picture vocabulary measures labeling ability. Sentence memory taps auditory discrimination and retention. These measures demonstrate a considerable degree of correspondence because both tasks require a verbal response based upon immediate recall (see Table V).

Although counting blocks correlates higher with the verbal factors and is typically considered a verbal skill, correlation with the perceptual-motor factors is considerable. It would appear that knowledge of number concepts is a complex verbal-developmental function which may be maturationally based.

The differences and drawings measure visual and perceptual-motor skills. The differences subtest is a measure of visual discrimination; the drawings tap perceptual-motor processes, including eye-hand coordination. The product-moment correlations on Table V were based on raw scores and are significant beyond the .01 level.

TABLE V

INTERCORRELATION

N= 100

Subtest	Sentence Memory	Picture Vocabulary	Counting Blocks	Differences
Picture Vocabulary	.71			
Counting Blocks	.53	.57		
Differences	.46	.34	.48	
Drawings	.30	.33	.43	.45

Reliability of the Developmental Pretest

The reliability estimate was determined by the Rulon (1939) split-half method for each subtest. Reliability for the developmental pretest as a whole is the mean of the five coefficients, after conversion to Fisher's z. Although the split half method may have slightly overestimated true reliability, a statistical comparison between pretest and posttest administrations was not significant. A test of significance for the difference between coefficients of correlation for an independent sample did not reach the .05 level for any of the five subtests. It may be safe to conclude that the pretest has good reliability. The average age of the children taking the pretest was five years, one month.

TABLE VI

RELIABILITY COEFFICIENTS AND STANDARD ERROR

OF MEASUREMENT OF THE DEVELOPMENTAL PRETEST

N=50

(September Administration)

Subtest	r	SE_m
Picture Vocabulary	.75	2.63
Sentence Memory	.85	1.05
Counting Blocks	.95	.58
Differences	.89	1.02
Drawings	.90	1.25
Developmental Pretest	.87	1.25

Reliability of the Posttest

The reliability estimate of the posttest was determined by the test-retest method. The retest was administered not less than three weeks and not more than four weeks after the first administration. An interval of approximately one month was deemed sufficient for the children to forget specific items and yet minimize maturational gains (see Table VII).

The nonsignificant differences between the reliabilities of the pretest and posttest administration can be attributed to differences in statistical technique. The split half method usually generates higher reliabilities than the test-retest method.

Differences in the standard error of measurement are due to variations in the standard deviation of the five subtests. The picture vocabulary and drawings subtests have larger standard deviations which account for the increased error of measurement.

TABLE VII

RELIABILITY COEFFICIENTS AND STANDARD ERROR

OF MEASUREMENT FOR THE RATE

OF LEARNING POSTTEST

N=100

(June Administration)

Subtest	r	SE_m
Picture Vocabulary	.83	2.54
Sentence Memory	.71	1.45
Counting Blocks	.82	1.47
Differences	.63	2.37
Drawings	.73	2.24
Rate of Learning	.91	1.22

Chronological Age Range

The Rate of Learning Test is specifically designed for the kindergarten age child. The age range has been intentionally limited to increase precision of measurement. The Rate of Learning Test can be individually administered to children between the ages of four-and-one-half and six-and-one-half. See Table VIII for the age distribution of children in the standardization group.

TABLE VIII

CHRONOLOGICAL AGE DISTRIBUTION

Age Yr. Mo.	*Frequency*
4-4 to 4-6	4
4-7 4-9	42
4-10 5-0	69
5-1 5-3	91
5-4 5-6	138
5-7 5-9	299
5-10 6-0	296
6-1 6-3	208
6-4 6-6	53
6-7 6-9	10
	1,210

Predictive Validity Studies

The Rate of Learning Test is of little value unless accurate assessment of academic performance occurs. Two validity criteria of pupil performance were selected for the study: Metropolitan Achievement Test, Primary Battery, Form B, and teacher judgment. In the spring, first grade teachers were asked to rate each child in reading and arithmetic on a nine-point scale. After the evaluations were gathered, the achievement test was administered. Of 1,093 children examined in kindergarten, 728 were available for follow-up in first grade.

The coefficients of correlation obtained between the total score on the Rate of Learning Test, administered in June, are reported in Table IX. The results suggest that the Rate of Learning Test can be relied upon to indicate the degree to which a child is or is not ready to undertake formal instruction in a typical first grade. The test predicts teacher judgment as well as achievement test performance with equal accuracy.

TABLE IX

PRODUCT MOMENT CORRELATIONS

OF RATE OF LEARNING TEST

WITH SELECTED VALIDITY CRITERIA

N=728

(1) Metropolitan Achievement Test, Primary Battery, Form B:	
Word Knowledge	.65
Word Discrimination	.64
Reading	.66
Arithmetic	.70
(2) Teacher Judgments:	
Arithmetic	.70
Reading	.71

Multiple Regression Analysis

In order to reduce the influence of measures in the battery which contributed minimally to predictive validity, the iterative procedure for computing beta weights was utilized (Guilford, 1950). Coefficients of correlation for each subtest with the Reading Test of the Metropolitan Achievement Test resulted in the following beta weights (rounded):

	Beta Wt.
Picture Vocabulary	1
Sentence Memory	2
Counting Blocks	3
Differences	1
Drawings	1

Follow-up Study

To validate the effectiveness of the beta weights and especially the pretest-posttest design, a second study was conducted. In Montgomery County (suburban Philadelphia), 117 children from the Norristown and Upper Merion School Districts were examined. Thirty children were selected from a kindergarten located in a lower socioeconomic area and thirty from an upper socioeconomic locale. The remaining fifty-seven were selected from a kindergarten in a middle-class neighborhood. The Developmental Pretest was individually administered in late September, and the Rate of Learning Posttest was administered in June of the kindergarten year. The primary purpose of the pretest is to identify slow, average and fast developing children so that diagnostic grouping can be arranged and individualized instruction provided. The instructional interval between administrations was ten months.

The mean and standard deviations for the Developmental Pretest and the Rate of Learning Posttest appear on Table X. The raw scores were converted into stanine scores, weighted (beta), then totaled. The weighted pretest and posttest stanines were combined for a total score. The Metropolitan Achievement Test, Primary Battery, Form B, administered at the conclusion of first grade, was the criterion measure of pupil achievement.

A change in the statistical treatment was undertaken. The achievement test scores can be conveniently divided into three stanine groupings: high (stanines 9, 8, 7); average (stanines 6, 5, 4); and low (stanines 3, 2, 1). Therefore, a trichotomized prediction was made and Jaspen's formula (Peatman, 1947) for tri-serial correlation was used. The combined total of the Developmental Pretest and the Rate of Learning Posttest scores was the continu-

TABLE X

MEAN AND STANDARD DEVIATION OF PRETEST

AND POSTTEST IN FOLLOW-UP STUDY

RAW SCORE DATA

N=117

Subtest	Developmental Pretest September		Rate of Learning Posttest June	
	Mean	S. D.	Mean	S. D.
Picture Vocabulary	14.13	5.25	20.50	6.05
Sentence Memory	8.84	2.70	11.26	2.69
Counting Blocks	5.01	2.50	9.63	3.41
Differences	5.07	3.00	11.22	3.88
Drawings	5.97	3.90	12.38	4.30

ous variable. A tri-serial correlation of +.75 was obtained between the combined total score and the Metropolitan Achievement, Reading Test. This increase in predictive validity from +.66 to +.75 is significant at the .05 level. The accuracy demonstrated by the pretest and posttest design warrants its use in effectively identifying the instructional needs of children in an effort to improve their academic performance.

RATE OF LEARNING TEST
DIRECTIONS FOR ADMINISTRATION AND SCORING

General Instructions* — A Note of Caution

An individual examination is necessary to provide an in-depth understanding of each child's approach but also to minimize testing error. Misunderstood directions, guessing, and inappropriate test set tend to invalidate test scores. Individual examination minimizes these potential errors of measurement at the preschool level. However, the test must also be practical. The Rate of Learning Test was designed for ease of administration and scoring. Testing time is four or five minutes per child.

The instrument is designed for administration by kindergarten teachers possessing some sophistication regarding standardized testing procedures. Therefore, the teacher should not administer the test without preliminary preparation. Five or ten practice examinations should be conducted by every teacher under the supervision of an experienced psychologist. A standardized administrative style should be developed by each teacher.

In-service workshops and clinical demonstrations will prepare teachers for its use. Administrators unwilling to provide the necessary in-service workshops to train kindergarten teachers may engage an educational diagnostician or psychologist to administer the Rate of Learning Test and evaluate its results. However, such a procedure creates a problem of rapport with the five-year-old. The diagnostician should spend a day in the classroom becoming acquainted with the children. A stranger should not begin examining without a period of familiarization. Rapport is critical at this age level, and the performance of sensitive or wary children may suffer.

Kindergarten teachers may find it convenient to team up in pairs. As one teacher is examining, the other teacher can supervise both classes. The procedure is then reversed as each teacher examines the children in her own class. All examinations can be com-

---

*The Developmental Pretest (September) and the Rate of Learning Posttest (June) are administered in identical fashion both times.

pleted in a few days. If teacher aides are available, the aides can supervise classes as the children are being examined.

Administration by the Teacher

Whenever possible, the kindergarten teacher should administer the Rate of Learning Test to every pupil in her class. Testing should not begin until the second or third week of school. Familiarity with the teacher and classroom routine enables the child to perform comfortably and optimally. The individual examinations should be administered in a room as close to the kindergarten classroom as possible. Familiar surroundings should be used at all times. The entire procedure should retain the informality of the kindergarten program. The Rate of Learning Test should always be administered according to the standardized instructions. The examiner should not supply the child with additional clues.

The Rate of Learning Test also assesses the child's personal learning style. As the teacher administers the test, she should carefully record all spontaneous remarks, many of which reveal attitudes. The re-mark, "I know all of them. Don't I?" is sometimes a defensive, overconfident posture taken by children who experience difficulty with portions of the test.

Rapport Establishment

The teacher must establish a good relationship with the children before attempting to administer the test. Two weeks of school attendance is usually sufficient to provide an opportunity for acclimatization. Familiarity with the school routine and the personality of the teacher enables the child to proceed comfortably with the examination.

The teacher can begin by explaining that she plans to show them some pictures. She should then ask, "Who would like to be first?" Most children enthusiastically volunteer. A shy, retiring child should not be examined first. These children prefer to observe the situation before developing sufficient courage to step forward.

Children who refuse should not be examined, unless or until they are willing to cooperate. Test results obtained from children pressed to comply are not valid. If a child breaks into tears at any time during the examination, discontinue administration at once. Tell the child that the pictures can be completed at another time. Reexamination is necessary.

1. PICTURE VOCABULARY
Materials: Booklet with 35 pictures.
Directions
As you expose the picture of the dog ask, "What is that?" If after presentation of any item, the child remains silent, the examiner should say, "Take a guess." or "What do you think it is?" For items 9, 10, 11, 12 and 13, ask, "What is he/she doing?"

Discontinue
After five consecutive failures.

Scoring
Score one point for each correct answer. Maximum score is 35.

PICTURE	PASSING CRITERIA	PICTURE	PASSING CRITERIA
1. Dog	Dog, puppy, any breed name.	18. Turkey	Turkey, gobbler.
		19. Giraffe	Giraffe.
2. Cow	Cow.	20. Tiger	Tiger.
3. Saw	Saw.	21. Scooter	Scooter.
4. Star	Star.	22. Goat	Goat, Billy, Nanny.
5. Snake	Snake, rattler, any type.	23. Grapes	Grapes.
6. Elephant	Elephant.	24. Twins	Twins.
7. Glass	Glass.	25. G. Washington	Washington, Father of Country.
8. Wagon	Wagon, cart.	26. Zebra	Zebra.
9. Smiling	Smiling, laughing, grinning.	27. Windmill	Windmill, mill.
10. Praying	Praying, saying grace, clapping, patty cake.	28. Thermometer	Thermometer, mometer.
		29. Statue	Statue.
11. Sitting	Sitting, resting.	30. Teepee	Teepee, Indian tent, wigwam.
12. Jumping	Jumping, dancing, hopping, stamping.	31. Violin	Violin, fiddle.
		32. Penguin	Penguin.
		33. Thimble	Thimble.
13. Pointing	Pointing.	34. A. Lincoln	Abe or Lincoln.
14. Clouds	Clouds.	35. Dinosaur	Dinosaur, prehistoric monster.
15. Stamp	Stamp.		
16. Camel	Camel.		
17. Cross	Cross, Red Cross, Blue Cross.		

2. SENTENCE MEMORY

Directions

The child must repeat the sentences verbatim as read to him. After eliciting the child's attention, read the sentences, slowly, enunciating each word clearly. It may be necessary to get close to the child as the sentences are read.

Say, "I am going to say something and you say it. Say it just like I say it."

"I am a big boy/girl."

Even if the child fails to say it correctly, read sentence 1. Read each sentence only once; repetition is not permitted.

Discontinue

Discontinue whenever two consecutive sentences are failed. Failure includes two errors in any one sentence, i.e. plurals, omissions, word reversals, additions, or improper word endings.

Scoring

An error is an omission, transposition or substitution of any word. Sentences correctly stated are scored 2 points. Sentence A is scored only one point. One error in a sentence, score one point; two errors, no points. Maximum score is 17.

SCORE	SENTENCES
0 1	A. I am a big boy/girl.
0 1 2	1. School is lots of fun for me.
0 1 2	2. Only big boys/girls go to school.
0 1 2	3. I have a pet and his name is Rover.
0 1 2	4. Brothers and sisters should have a good time when they play.
0 1 2	5. When it rains, my friends and I play inside.
0 1 2	6. Both my mother and father told me to study very hard in school.
0 1 2	7. Fred and Betty like ice cream, cake and candy very much.
0 1 2	8. Almost every Sunday, father takes the family for a ride along the countryside.

———

Total

3. COUNTING BLOCKS

Materials: 16 one-inch or half-inch cubes, same color.

Directions

Place the blocks in front of the child and ask, "Can you give me three blocks?" "Count them."

If three blocks are counted accurately, ask for five, seven, nine, eleven and fifteen. If fifteen blocks are counted accurately, administer the problems. "How much is three plus two?"

If three blocks are failed, ask for two, then one. Only one trial is permitted for each amount asked for.

Discontinue

Cease administration when any two consecutive attempts are failed. Stop administration of problems when any one is failed.

Score

One point for each correct count. One point for each correct problem. If three blocks are counted correctly, give credit for one and two. Maximum score is 17.

BLOCKS COUNTED	SCORE
1	0 1
2	0 1
3	0 1
4	0 1
5	0 1
6	0 1
7	0 1
9	0 1
11	0 1
15	0 1
3+2 = 5	0 1
4+3 = 7	0 1
7+5 = 12	0 1
8+7 = 15	0 1
5-2 = 3	0 1
9-4 = 5	0 1
12-7 = 5	0 1
	Total

4. DIFFERENCES
Materials: Nineteen cards with various figures, bound in a booklet.
Directions
   Exposing the first card, say:
   "Point to the one that is not the same, that doesn't match, the one that's different."
   If the child points to an incorrect figure, indicate the correct one. Explain which figures are similar and which are different.
   If any of the first three cards is failed, the child is shown the correct figure and helped to see why it is dissimilar. No further help is permitted. On each item the child's first response is scored.
Discontinue
   Cease administration after four consecutive failures.
Scoring
   One point for each correct answer. Maximum score is 19.

5. DRAWINGS
Special Note: The drawings may be administered in small groups of ten to twelve children.
Directions
   Copy the cross and circle on the board. Then provide each child with a pencil and the figures to be copied.
   Say: "We are going to draw. Here is a cross. Watch me make one under it. Then see if you can make one like it. Watch me make a circle, now make one yourself. Now do the rest of the drawings."
   The teacher should go around to each child to see that each drawing is at least attempted. The teacher can only point to the drawings to be copied. No further help is permitted. The children should be encouraged to try every one but not forced.
Scoring
   Score two points for each drawing correctly copied. One point is subtracted for either rotation or partial distortion. If a figure is both rotated and distorted, no credit is given. Maximum score is 22. See Appendix A for examples of scoring.

CHAPTER 11 _____

INTERPRETATION

_____

ADMISSION to kindergarten is usually based on a legal chronological age. Children are accepted at all stages of developmental learning. Therefore, it becomes especially important that the developmental learning functions of every child be assessed upon admission. With the availability of specific diagnostic information, instruction can be precisely formulated for individual programming. A new direction is posed for the kindergarten. The kindergarten is utilized as a diagnostic-instructional-evaluative program of learning.

DEVELOPMENTAL PRETEST — SEPTEMBER

The developmental pretest measures the present status of certain verbal, numerical, listening and perceptual-motor skills which developed in the preschool years. The primary purpose of the pretest is to direct the teacher's attention to those areas of weakness which require special instruction. The pretest identifies areas of strength and weakness, thus enabling the teacher to initiate grouping immediately. The instructional process can begin immediately with diagnostic precision. A month or two of familiarization is no longer necessary and instructional time is not wasted. Haphazard or repetitive instruction is prevented by the administration of the pretest.

Late Admission

Children admitted to kindergarten after October should be administered the Rate of Learning posttest in June. The posttest alone will not reveal a rate of learning.

Converting Raw Scores

To convert raw scores for each subtest into stanines see Figure

189

18, "September Pretest." Scoring and interpretation may be aided by the example of Mary, shown in Table XI.

TABLE XI

MARY'S PRETEST SCORE

Pretest	Raw Score	Stanine	Beta Weight	Weighted Stanine
Picture Vocabulary	14	5		5
Sentence Memory	10	6	x 2	= 12
Counting Blocks	4	4	x 3	= 12
Differences	9	6		6
Drawings	3	3		3
Total	40			
			Weighted Stanine Total =	38

The weighted stanine total represents a general level of development attained in skills known to be related to academic achievement. A weighted stanine total of 38 (Table XII) indicates that Mary has developed at an average rate. However, to categorize Mary as a child who is developmentally average does not provide any information regarding strategies for instruction.

Instructional direction can be drawn from the stanine profile. Mary's stanine profile indicates that the drawing subtest score is at the 3rd stanine. We can assume that she is experiencing minor difficulty with fine perceptual motor coordination skills like copying and coloring. Exercises using crayons, scissors, chalk, pencils and paint brushes should improve the development of this skill.

A poor developmental pretest score may be due to numerous complex causes, but perhaps the most frequent is simply the lack of environmental opportunity. Teachers should not assume that children with low development scores will not learn. On the contrary, many children entering kindergarten with poor initial scores are able to utilize kindergarten effectively and demonstrate significant learning gains.

RATE OF LEARNING — JUNE POSTTEST

Administration of the posttest is identical to the pretest. The

SEPTEMBER PRETEST

(Developmental)

Stanine Score	Vocabulary	Sentences	Counting Blocks	Differences	Drawings	Stanine Score
9	30+	15+	12+	17+	20+	9
8	25 - 29	14	10-11	15 - 16	17 - 19	8
7	20 - 24	12 - 13	9	10 - 14	12 - 16	7
6	16 - 19	10 - 11	7 - 8	7 - 9	8 - 11	6
5	13 - 15	9	5 - 6	4 - 6	6 - 7	5
4	10 - 12	7 - 8	4	3	4 - 5	4
3	8 - 9	5 - 6	3	2	3	3
2	6 - 7	3 - 4	2	1	2	2
1	0 - 5	0 - 2	0 - 1	0	0 - 1	1

| Beta Weight* | 5 | + | 6 x 2* | + | 4 x 3* | + | 6 | + | 3 | = | 38 |

Pretest Total

JUNE POSTTEST

(Rate of Learning)

Stanine Score	Vocabulary	Sentences	Counting Blocks	Differences	Drawings	Stanine Score
9	30 - 35	15 - 19	15 - 17	18 - 19	20 - 22	9
8	28 - 29	14	12 - 14	17	18 - 19	8
7	25 - 27	13	11	16	16 - 17	7
6	23 - 24	12	10	14 - 15	14 - 15	6
5	19 - 22	10 - 11	9	12 - 13	11 - 13	5
4	16 - 18	9	7 - 8	10 - 11	9 - 10	4
3	13 - 15	8	4 - 6	7 - 9	7 - 8	3
2	11 - 12	6 - 7	3	4 - 6	5 - 6	2
1	0 - 10	0 - 5	1 - 2	0 - 3	0 - 4	1

| Beta Weight* | 6 | + | 6 x 2* | + | 5 x 3* | + | 6 | + | 5 | = | 44 |

Posttest Total

| 82 |

Combined Total

Figure 18. Profile for Mary. Stanine equivalents of raw scores.

TABLE XII

SEPTEMBER PRETEST

(Developmental)

N=117

Beta Weighted Stanine Total	Developmental Rating
63 +	*Superior
51 - 62	*Advanced
45 - 50	High Average
36 - 44	Average
27 - 35	Low Average
15 - 26	Slow
8 - 14	Very Slow

*Instruction in reading may begin.

posttest assesses the learning gain resulting from kindergarten instruction. The posttest records the degree of measurable learning which has occurred. The effectiveness of the instructional process on the developing capabilities of the child can be analyzed. A comparison of pretest and posttest scores reveal those skill areas of measurable gain.

High Absenteeism

If a child is absent more than 25 percent, the posttest should be interpreted with caution. Without the opportunity for continued daily instruction, the rate of learning may be slowed. Kindergarten children are often absent due to illness. The absenteeism for all children should be carefully checked.

To convert raw scores for each subtest into stanines see "June

Posttest." Scoring may be aided by continuing the example of Mary, Figure 18, and Table XIII.

TABLE XIII

MARY'S POSTTEST SCORES

Posttest	Raw Score	Stanine	Beta Weight	Weighted Stanine
Picture Vocabulary	23	6		6
Sentence Memory	12	6	x 2	=12
Counting Blocks	9	5	x 3	=15
Differences	14	6		6
Drawings	12	5		5
Total	70	Weighted Stanine Total		44

The posttest reveals the raw score gain which is primarily the result of kindergarten instruction. Mary's gain of thirty points (the difference between the pretest and the posttest raw score totals) is average (see Table XIV).

An additional comparison is also available. The raw score gains of high, average and low first grade achievers (on the Metropolitan Achievement Test) were obtained on the Rate of Learning Test (see Table XV). Mary's raw score gain of thirty points is similar to children who are average achievers in first grade.

The most valid measure of performance combines the weighted stanine from both pretest and posttest. The weighted stanine for the pretest is 38 and 44 for the posttest, for a combined weighted stanine total of 82. Table XVI reveals that Mary has an average rate of learning. Barring unforeseen circumstances, Mary can be expected to achieve within the average range in her first year.

Characteristic Patterns

Aside from the normal learning pattern as represented by Mary, two additional patterns appear with some degree of regularity. A slow learning pattern and a neglected learner pattern are revealed by the Rate of Learning Test.

The Slow Learning Pattern

Two conditions appear to indicate such a pattern. A low pretest

TABLE XIV

RAW SCORE GAIN

N=117

Total Raw Score Gain	Rating
50 +	Very High
40 - 49	High
35 - 39	High Average
20 - 34	Average
15 - 19	Low Average
10 - 14	Low
1 - 9	Very Low

TABLE XV

COMPARISON OF RAW SCORE GAIN AMONG HIGH,

AVERAGE AND LOW FIRST GRADE ACHIEVERS

ON THE RATE OF LEARNING TEST

	N	Mean Pretest Raw Score	Mean Gain	S.D.
High Achievers	38	53.60	26.20	9.15
Average Achievers	30	40.33	30.41	9.31
Low Achievers	49	20.04	21.70	14.84

Metropolitan Achievement Test

TABLE XVI

COMBINED PRETEST AND POSTTEST

WEIGHTED STANINE SCORE

N=117

Weighted Stanine Total	Rate of Learning
130 - 145	Superior
100 - 129	High
90 - 99	High Average
60 - 89	Average
50 - 59	Below Average
10 - 49	*Slow Rate of Learning

*A complete case study is necessary to determine the multiple causation for the slow rate of learning. Psychological, pediatric, psychiatric and neurological examinations may be necessary. Placement in a low pupil-teacher ratio educational setting may be recommended on a part-time or full-time basis.

score is the first indicator. However, a low pretest score alone is never sufficient evidence. Minimal gains on the posttest confirm the slow learning. When kindergarten instruction results in limited learning, unknown impedance factors are undoubtedly at work, slowing the learning rate. Children with a slow learning pattern in kindergarten are very likely to be an extremely poor learning risk in a typical first grade, where reading and writing are generally expected of all.

Figure 19 illustrates the case of John. Three aspects of his performance are at our disposal: the pretest, the raw score gain and the posttest score. A weighted score of 15 on the pretest indicates that John begins kindergarten with low development in all assessed areas.

TABLE XVII

JOHN'S SCORES

Pretest	*Raw Score*	*Stanine*	*Beta Weight*	*Weighted Stanine*
Picture Vocabulary	6	2		2
Sentence Memory	6	3	x 2	6
Counting Blocks	1	1	x 3	3
Differences	2	3		3
Drawings	1	1		1
Total	16			15

Posttest	*Raw Score*	*Stanine*	*Beta Weight*	*Weighted Stanine*
Picture Vocabulary	14	3		3
Sentence Memory	7	2	x 2	4
Counting Blocks	3	2	x 3	6
Differences	3	1		1
Drawings	3	1		1
Total	30			15

Raw Score Gain = 14

Combined Pretest and Posttest Weighted Stanine Score = 30

John's raw score gain of only fourteen points on the Rate of Learning posttest is quite low when compared with other children (see Tables XIV and XV). The posttest reveals that John has profited minimally from kindergarten instruction. Learning gains were obtained on picture vocabulary, but regression resulted on the sentences and differences. A weighted stanine score for pretest and posttest of 30 places John distinctly in the slow rate of learning category (see Table XVI).

The results indicate that John is learning so slowly that he has

SEPTEMBER PRETEST

(Developmental)

Stanine Score	Vocabulary	Sentences	Counting Blocks	Differences	Drawings	Stanine Score
9	30+	15+	12+	17+	20+	9
8	25 - 29	14	10-11	15 - 16	17 - 19	8
7	20 - 24	12 - 13	9	10 - 14	12 - 16	7
6	16 - 19	10 - 11	7 - 8	7 - 9	8 - 11	6
5	13 - 15	9	5 - 6	4 - 6	6 - 7	5
4	10 - 12	7 - 8	4	3	4 - 5	4
3	8 - 9	5 - 6	3	2	3	3
2	6 - 7	3 - 4	2	1	2	2
1	0 - 5	0 - 2	0 - 1	0	0 - 1	1
Beta Weight*	2 +	3 x 2* +	1 x 3* +	3 +	1 =	15

Pretest Total

JUNE POSTTEST

(Rate of Learning)

Stanine Score	Vocabulary	Sentences	Counting Blocks	Differences	Drawings	Stanine Score
9	30 - 35	15 - 19	15 - 17	18 - 19	20 - 22	9
8	28 - 29	14	12 - 14	17	18 - 19	8
7	25 - 27	13	11	16	16 - 17	7
6	23 - 24	12	10	14 - 15	14 - 15	6
5	19 - 22	10 - 11	9	12 - 13	11 - 13	5
4	16 - 18	9	7 - 8	10 - 11	9 - 10	4
3	13 - 15	8	4 - 6	7 - 9	7 - 8	3
2	11 - 12	6 - 7	3	4 - 6	5 - 6	2
1	0 - 10	0 - 5	1 - 2	0 - 3	0 - 4	1
Beta Weight*	3 +	2 x 2* +	2 x 3* +	1 +	1 =	15

Posttest Total

30

Combined Total

Figure 19. Profile for John. Stanine equivalents for raw scores.

been unable to demonstrate significant gains as a result of a year's instruction. It would appear that John will need an intensified instructional environment, greater than that provided by the typical classroom. The absence of learning gains also suggests the presence of impeding factors. The complex elements which contribute to such a condition should be diagnosed and remedied, if possible. Medical, neurological and psychological evaluations are essential to prescribe remedies that may alleviate the learning delay. Unfortunately, John was not referred for a complete evaluation but placed in first grade and subsequently repeated.

The Neglected Learner

In both the slow learning and neglected learner patterns low pretests scores are standard. Pretests scores for both patterns are indistinguishable. However, the pattern for the neglected learner demonstrates a rather dramatic increase in measurable learning on the Rate of Learning, posttest. The posttest reveals significant gains, substantially the result of kindergarten instruction. This pattern suggests the presence of learning potential which has largely been untapped (neglected). The kindergarten year is extremely beneficial for these children but is rarely sufficient to compensate for a lack of environmental stimulation of two, three or more years, which many underprivileged youngsters undergo.

Ann is illustrative of the neglected learner (see Figure 20). The developmental pretest profile is indistinguishable from that of John. Ann's weighted pretest stanine score of 17 is comparable to John's score of 15. However, significant learning gains are registered as a result of instruction. Counting, visual discrimination and visual-motor skills improved. Ann's raw score gain of 35 is rated as high average on Table XIV. Ann's combined pretest and posttest weighted stanine score of 49 places her at the upper level of the slow rate of learning on Table XVI. With appropriate instruction aimed at her performance level, Ann should demonstrate continued academic progress. In first grade Ann was a low achiever but progressed sufficiently to be promoted to second.

Further Research

Additional analysis of the Rate of Learning may reveal the

SEPTEMBER PRETEST

(Developmental)

Stanine Score	Vocabulary	Sentences	Counting Blocks	Differences	Drawings	Stanine Score
9	30+	15+	12+	17+	20+	9
8	25 - 29	14	10-11	15 - 16	17 - 19	8
7	20 - 24	12 - 13	9	10 - 14	12 - 16	7
6	16 - 19	10 - 11	7 - 8	7 - 9	8 - 11	6
5	13 - 15	9	5 - 6	4 - 6	6 - 7	5
4	10 - 12	7 - 8	4	3	4 - 5	4
3	8 - 9	5 - 6	3	2	3	3
2	6 - 7	3 - 4	2	1	2	2
1	0 - 5	0 - 2	0 - 1	0	0 - 1	1

Beta Weight*	2	+	3 x 2*	+	2 x 3*	+	2	+	1	=	17

Pretest Total

JUNE POSTTEST

(Rate of Learning)

Stanine Score	Vocabulary	Sentences	Counting Blocks	Differences	Drawings	Stanine Score
9	30 - 35	15 - 19	15 - 17	18 - 19	20 - 22	9
8	28 - 29	14	12 - 14	17	18 - 19	8
7	25 - 27	13	11	16	16 - 17	7
6	23 - 24	12	10	14 - 15	14 - 15	6
5	19 - 22	10 - 11	9	12 - 13	11 - 13	5
4	16 - 18	9	7 - 8	10 - 11	9 - 10	4
3	13 - 15	8	4 - 6	7 - 9	7 - 8	3
2	11 - 12	6 - 7	3	4 - 6	5 - 6	2
1	0 - 10	0 - 5	1 - 2	0 - 3	0 - 4	1

Beta Weight*	2	+	3 x 2*	+	5 x 3*	+	4	+	5	=	32

Posttest Total

49

Combined Total

Figure 20. Profile for Ann. Stanine equivalents of raw scores.

TABLE XVIII

ANN'S SCORES

Pretest	Raw Score	Stanine	Beta Weight	Weighted Stanine
Picture Vocabulary	6	2		2
Sentence Memory	6	3	x 2 =	6
Counting Blocks	2	2	x 3 =	6
Differences	1	2		2
Drawings	1	1		1
Total	16			17

Posttest	Raw Score	Stanine	Beta Weight	Weighted Stanine
Picture Vocabulary	12	2		2
Sentence Memory	8	3	x 2 =	6
Counting Blocks	9	5	x 3 =	15
Differences	10	4		4
Drawings	12	5		5
Total	51			32

Raw Score Gain = 35

Combined Pretest & Posttest Weighted Stanine Score = 49

existence of varied learning patterns. If separate and distinct profiles exist, the Rate of Learning Test may be sufficiently sensitive to detect their presence. However, the designations "slow learning" or "neglected learner" should not be placed in the child's permanent record. Each child's learning rate may change from year to year, and the harm done children who are so diagnostically labeled is often irreparable.

GAIN SCORES AND REGRESSION

Every child in this study registered a raw score gain over the pretest score, although not all gains were statistically significant. The accurate measurement of gain scores is contaminated by pretest and posttest unreliability (Lord, 1956, 1958). Therefore, to place complete confidence upon gain scores alone is an unwise statistical procedure. Nevertheless, an analysis of the gain score is important to a full understanding of the Rate of Learning.

That the subtests contribute differentially to the raw score increase can be observed on Table XIX. The less reliable subtests, those with larger standard deviations, contribute most to the gain score. However, other factors appear to be operative. Those subtests most sensitive to instruction are also reflected in the gain score. Labeling objects (picture vocabulary), copying-coloring (drawings), and refining visual cues (differences) are daily activities in the kindergarten and develop rapidly in five-year-olds. Counting and verbal expression (sentence memory) are not as subject to instructional influence. The nature of the subtests per se (the number of items, item difficulty and scoring) also influences the raw score increase.

The regression effect (Lord 1963) which typically occurs in pretest and posttest designs was masked by the year of kindergarten instruction. Children with average pretest scores obtained the greatest raw score gains (see Table XX). It would appear that kindergarten tends to be most beneficial for the average child. This can be explained by the well-known fact that teachers typically direct their instruction to the majority (average?) in the class. These learning gains reflect that treatment.

Raw score gains for high and low groups on the pretest were not significantly different. Our findings confirm those of Leiderman (1968) and the University City School District (1967) that marked gain scores do not necessarily occur for those with low pretest scores. Although these findings are contrary to regression theory, one explanation may be that in long-range studies (over six months) regression effects are clearly minimized or reduced.

Lord (1963) recommends the use of partial correlation (corrected for attenuation) to determine the effect of change scores on posttest scores. With pretest scores held constant, the partial correlation was +.33, significant at the .01 level. This finding suggests that the Rate of Learning contributes substantially to ultimate performance, and therefore should not be ignored.

TABLE XIX

MEAN SUBTEST GAIN BETWEEN

PRETEST AND POSTTEST

N = 117

Subtest	Mean Raw Score Gain
Drawings	6.41
Picture Vocabulary	6.37
Differences	6.15
Counting Blocks	4.62
Sentence Memory	2.42
Mean Gain	25.97

TABLE XX

COMPARATIVE GAINS BASED ON

PRETEST RAW SCORES

	Total Raw Score on Pretest	N	Mean Raw Score Gain	S. D.
High	51 - 84	26	22.19	8.16
Average	26 - 50	60	29.02	9.08
Low	0 - 25	31	25.29	10.68

Analysis of Variance $F = 5.06$, d.f. $2/114$, p greater than .01 level

INTERPRETATION — A CONCLUDING STATEMENT

Three aspects of the child's performance are assessed. The pretest measures the developmental level upon admission to kindergarten, and the posttest determines the amount of learning registered as a result of instruction. Interpretation should be based upon an analysis of pretest scores, posttest gains and the combined scores. The total score weighs both developmental and instructional effects into the child's performance.

The raw score gain should not be interpreted in isolation. Children with high pretest scores, already at the top of the scale, may not improve (scores) at all. For these children a low raw score gain has no significance. For those who have low developmental pretest scores and a slow Rate of Learning, serious problems may exist. This slow learning pattern may continue into first grade unless intensified instructional intervention occurs.

A slow Rate of Learning is a concomitant condition of almost all aberrations of development. Therefore, a procedure which measures the learning rate of each child, within the classroom setting, will have greater sensitivity than present methods of readiness testing. The Rate of Learning Test is able to detect, with a high degree of accuracy, those children who will need dramatic and extraordinary instructional intervention to succeed in school.

In conclusion, the Rate of Learning is not a measure of intelligence. The author has scrupulously avoided using the term to prevent confusion. Although intelligence plays a role in the Rate of Learning, by no means is it the only factor, nor necessarily the most important. Recent revelations indicate that motivation, cultural opportunity, mental health and self-actualization contribute heavily to intelligent behavior and learning, but were formerly misinterpreted as intelligence per se. The Rate of Learning is an analysis of the child's ability to retain measurably the educational experiences to which he has been exposed.

A Note of Caution

Too often, oversimplified explanations are offered for slow learning. A complex of many interacting variables can cause learning delays. A depressing home environment, the lack of verbal stimulation, cerebral damage, mental retardation, emotional disturbance, neurological impairment, premature birth, a chronic medical condition, can singly or in combination contribute to a slow learning pattern. The Rate of Learning Test is a sensitive device which detects those children who learn slowly *in kindergarten. IT CANNOT OR SHOULD NOT BE USED TO IDENTIFY THOSE FACTORS CAUSING THE DELAY, NOR TO PLACE DIAGNOSTIC LABELS ON CHILDREN.* For instance, Bower (1969) has found that the inability to learn is perhaps the single most striking characteristic of the emotionally handicapped children. If so, the Rate of Learning Test should very effectively detect this slow learning pattern. However, the slow learning may well be symptomatic of other intellectual, sensory or physical health factors instead. Therefore, a complete diagnostic study (medical, psychological, psychiatric and neurological) is indicated; and the factors causing the delay should be identified and alleviated, if at all possible.

After Kindergarten

The author estimates that approximately 10 to 15 percent of those admitted to the first year will require a specialized instructional program. The typical first grade classroom, as presently constituted, not only fails to provide an adequate learning environment but aggravates those with learning difficulties.

The transitional class (numerous other names denote these readiness groups with a limited enrollment of under twenty pupils) can provide the individualization so necessary for positive learning. Most do not need an all-day program; daily visits to a resource room with a sympathetic tutor may suffice.

The degree and nature of the learning impedances will determine how quickly these children learn to learn independently, without the need for extraordinary instructional support systems. If in the first three years, intensified instructional services are consistently provided, many of the academic problems of the later years may be prevented.

APPENDIX A

1   0

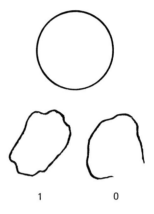

1   0

1   0

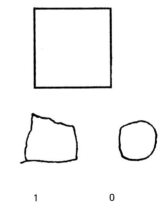

1   0

APPENDIX A (Continued)

1   0

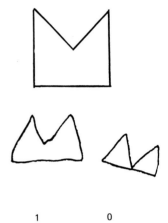

1   0

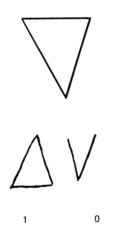

1   0

1   0

APPENDIX A (Continued)

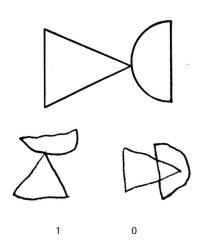

1   0

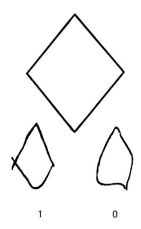

1   0

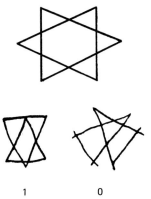

1   0

REFERENCES

Adelman, H. S., and Feshback, S.: Predicting reading failure: Beyond the readiness model. *Except Child,* 5:37, 1971.

Allen, R.M.: Studies in short term retention of educational retardates. In Hellmuth, J. (Ed.): *Educational Therapy.* Seattle, Spec Child, 1969, vol. II.

Almy, M.: Intellectual mastery and mental health. *Teachers Coll Rec, 63:*468-478, 1962.

Ammon, P.R., and Ammon, M.: Effects of training black preschool children in vocabulary versus sentence construction. *J. Educ Psychol, 62:*421-426, 1971.

Anisfeld, M., and Tucker, G.R.: English pluralization rules of six-year-old children. *Child Dev, 38:*1201-1217, 1967.

Appleton, E.: Kindergarteners pace themselves in reading. *Elem Sch J, 64:*248-252, 1964.

Baldwin, A.L.: Changes in parent behavior during pregnancy. *Child Dev, 18:*29-39, 1947.

Balow, B.: Perceptual-motor activities in the treatment of severe reading disability. *Reading Teacher, 24:*513-524, 1974.

Barrett, T.C.: Visual discrimination tasks as predictors of first grade reading achievement. *Reading Teacher, 18:*256-282, 1965.

Beller, E.K.: The concept readiness and several applications. *Reading Teacher, 23:*727-737, 1970.

Bentzen, F.: Sex ratios in learning and behavior disorders. Paper read at the American Orthopsychiatric Association Meeting, New York, 1961.

Bereiter, C., and Engelmann, S.: *Teaching Disadvantaged Children in the Pre-School.* Englewood Cliffs, P-H, 1966.

Berry, M.F., and Eisenson, J.: *Speech Disorders: Principles and Practices of Therapy.* New York, Appleton, 1956.

Bjonerud, C.C.: Arithmetic concepts possessed by the preschool child. *Arith Techer, 7:*347-350, 1960.

Blair, J.R., and Ryckman, D.B.: *Visual Discrimination.* Ann Arbor, U of Mich Pr, 1969.

Blank, M.: Cognitive gains in deprived children through individual teaching of language for abstract thinking. Educational Research Center, 1967.

Blank, M. and Bridger, W.H.: Deficiencies in verbal labeling in retarded readers. Educational Research Information Center, 1966.

Bloom, B.S.: *Stability and Change in Human Characteristics.* New York, Wiley,

1964.

Bloom, B.S.: *Taxonomy of Educational Objectives. Handbook I: Cognitive Domain.* New York, McKay, 1956.

Bolvin, J.O.: Evaluating teacher functions. Educational Research Information Center, 1967.

Bolvin, J.O.: Implications of the individualization of instruction for curriculum and instructional design. Educational Research Information Center, 1968.

Bond, G.L., and Dykstra, R.: The cooperative research program in first grade reading. *Reading Res Q, 2*:5-142, 1967.

Bower, E.M.: *Early Identification of Emotionally Handicapped Children in School.* Springfield, Thomas, 1969.

Bowlby, J.: *Attachment.* New York, Basic, 1969.

Brace, A., and Nelson, L.D.: The preschool child's concept of number. *Arith Teacher, 12*:126-133, 1965.

Bradway, K.P., and Thompson, C.W.: Intelligence at adulthood, a twenty-five year follow-up. *J Educ Psychol, 53*:1-14, 1962.

Braine, M.D.: On learning the grammatical order of words. *Psychol Rev, 70*:323-348, 1963.

Broadbent, D.E.: *Perception and Communication.* London, Pergamon, 1958.

Brown, R.W.: The development of wh questions in child speech. *J Verbal Learning and Behavior, 7*:279-290, 1968.

Brown, R.W.: Linguistic determination and the parts of speech. *J Abnorm Psychol, 55*:1-5, 1957.

Brown, R.W., and Bellugi, U.: Three processes in the child's acquisition of syntax. *Harv Educ Rev, 34*:133-151, 1964.

Bruner, J.S.: *The Process of Education.* Cambridge, Harvard U Pr, 1960.

Carroll, J.B.: A model of school learning. *Teachers Coll Rec, 64*:723-733, 1963.

Caswell, H.L., and Foshay, A.W.: *Education in the Elementary School.* New York, Am Bk, 1957.

Cazden, C.B.: The acquisition of noun and verb inflections. *Child Dev, 39*:433-448, 1968.

Cazden, C.B.: Environmental assistance to the child's acquisition of grammar. Doctoral dissertation, Harvard University, 1965.

Chalfant, J.C., and Flathouse, V.E.; Auditory and visual learning. In Myklebust, H.R. (Ed.): *Progress in Learning Disabilities.* New York, Grune, 1971, vol. II.

Chalfant, J.C., and Scheffelin, M.: *Central Processing Dysfunctions in Children: A Review of Research.* Bethesda, U. S. Dept. of Health, Education and Welfare, 1969.

Chansky, N.: Perceptual training with elementary school underachievers. *J School Psychol, 1*:33-41,1963.

Chelland, O.C.: The effectiveness of taped instruction for select exceptional children. Doctoral dissertation, Heed University, 1973.

Coffman, A.O., and Dunlap, J.M.: The effects of assessment and personalized programming on subsequent intellectual development of pre-kindergarten and kindergarten children. University City School District, Missouri, 1968.

Cohen, S.A.: Studies in visual perception and reading in disadvantaged children. Educational Research Information Center, 1969.

Cohen, T.B.: Diagnostic and predictive methods with young children. *Am J Orthopsychiatry, 33*:330-331, 1963.

Coleman, J.S., et al.: *Equality of Educational Opportunity.* Bethesda, U.S. Dept. of Health, Education and Welfare, 1966.

Combs, A.W., and Snygg, D.: *Individual Behavior.* New York, Har-Row,1959.

Cooper, M.L.: Experimental analysis of effects of teacher attention on preschool children's block building behavior. Paper read at Society of Research in Child Development Meeting, Santa Monica, California, 1969.

Coopersmith, S.: *The Antecedents of Self Esteem.* San Francisco, Freeman C, 1967.

Copeland, R.W.: *How Children Learn Mathematics.* New York, Macmillan, 1970.

Corey, S.M.: The teachers out-talk the pupils. In Duker, S. (Ed.): *Listening: Readings.* New york, Scarecrow, 1966.

Cowe, E.G.: A study of kindergarten activities for language development. Doctoral dissertation, Columbia University, 1967.

Culkin, M.L.: The contemporary kindergarten. *Educ Rec, 24*:345-357, 1943.

Davis, F.B.: *Item Analysis Data.* Cambridge, Harvard U Pr, 1949.

Dawson, M.A., and Newman, G.C.:*Language Teaching in Kindergarten and Early Primary Grades.* New York, HarBrace & World, 1966.

DeHirsch, K., Jansky, J.J., and Langford, W.S.: *Predicting Readinv Failure.* Evanston, Har-Row, 1966.

Dimond, S.E.: Who shall fail? *Natl Sch, 63*:63-65, 1959.

Downing, J.: How children think about reading. *Reading Teacher, 23*:217-230, 1969.

Durkin, D.: Children who read before grade one. *Elem Sch J, 64*:143-148, 1963.

Durkin, D.: An earlier start in reading? *Elem Sch J, 63*:147-151, 1962.

Durkin, D.: Early readers, reflections after six years of research. *Reading Teacher, 18*:3-7, 1964.

Dykman, R., et al.: Specific learning disabilities: Attentional deficit syndrome. In Myklebust, H.R. (Ed.): *Progress in Learning Disabilities.* New York, Grune, 1971, vol. II.

Egland, G.O.: *Speech and Language Problems.* Englewood Cliffs, P-H, 1970.

Eisenberg, L.: *The Epidemology of Reading and a Program for Preventive Intervention in the Disabled Reader.* Baltimore, Johns Hopkins, 1966.

Elkind, D.: An approach to reading instruction. In Hellmuth, J. (Ed.); *Educational Therapy.* Seattle, Spec Child, 1969, vol. II.

Elkind, D., Horn, J., and Schneider, G.: Modified word recognition, reading achievement and perceptual de-centration. *J Genet Psychol, 107*:235-251, 1965.

214   *The Developmental Kindergarten*

Elkind, D., and Weiss, J.: Perceptual activity and concept attainment. *Child Dev, 38*:1153-1161, 1967.

Elliott, F.: An eight year study of shy and unintelligible children. *Childhood Educ, 45*:181-183, 1968.

Erikson, E.: *Childhood and Society.* New York, Norton, 1964.

Ervin, S.M., and Miller, T.: *Language Development.* Thirty-second yearbook of the National Society for the Study of Education. Chicago, U of Chicago Pr, 1963.

Fargo, G.A.: Evaluation of an interdisciplinary approach to prevention of early school failure. Honolulu, 1968.

Fraser, C., Bellugi, U., and Brown, R.W.: Control of grammar in imitation, comprehension and production. *J Verbal Learning and Behavior, 2*:121-135, 1963.

Gans, R., Stendler, C.B., and Almy, M.: *Teaching Young Children.* New York, World Book, 1952.

Getman, G.N., and Kane, E.R.: *The Physiology of Readiness.* Minneapolis, P.A.S.S., 1964.

Gibson, E.J.: The effect of prolonged exposure to visually presented patterns on learning to discriminate them. *J Comp Physiol Psychol, 49*:239-242, 1956.

Glaser, R.: Objectives and evaluation, an indivudalized system. Educational Research Information Center, 1967.

Golden, N., and Steiner, S.: Auditory and visual functions in good and poor readers. *J Learning Dis, 2*:46-51, 1969.

Goodenough, F.: *Anger in Young Children.* Minneapolis, U of Minn Pr, 1931.

Goolsby, T.M., and Lasco, R.: Training non-readers in listening achievement. *J Learning Dis, 3*:467-470, 1970.

Goulet, L.R., and Barclay, A.: Guessing behavior of normal and retarted children under two random reinforcement conditions. *Child Dev, 38*:545-552, 1967.

Gronlund, N.E.: *Sociometry in the Classroom.* New York, Harper Brothers, 1959.

Guilford, J.P.: *Fundamental Statistics in Psychology and Education.* New York, McGraw, 1950.

Gupta, W., and Stern, C.: *Comparative Effectiveness of Speaking Versus Listening in Improving Spoken Language of Disadvantaged Young Children.* Los Angeles, U of Calif Pr, 1969.

Hagen, J.W., and Kingsley, P.R.: Labeling effects in short term memory. *Child Dev, 39*:113-121, 1968.

Harris, A.J.: The craft project: A final report. *Reading Teacher, 22*:335-340, 1969.

Harris, A.J.: The effective teacher of reader. *Reading Teacher, 22*:195-204, 1969.

Harris, I.D.: *Emotional Blocks to Learning.* New York, Free Pr, 1961.

Hartley, R.L., and Goldenson, R.: *Understanding Children's Play.* New York, Columbia U Pr, 1952.

Headley, N.: *The Kindergarten: Its Place in the Program of Education.* New

York, Center for Applied Research, 1965.

Heffernan, H., and Todd, V.E.: *The Kindergarten Teacher*. Boston, Heath, 1960.

Helfenbein, L.: Kindergarten perceptual motor training program. Educational Research Information Center, 1967.

Henig, M.S.: Predictive value of a reading readiness test and of teachers' forecasts. *Elem Sch J, 50*:41-46, 1949.

Herman, K., Goldberg, M.D., and Scheffmore, G.B.: *Dyslexia: Problems of Reading Disability*. New York, Grune, 1972.

Herriot, P.: The comprehension of syntax. *Child Dev, 39*:273-282, 1968.

Herriot, P.: The comprehension of tense by young children. *Child Dev, 40*:103-110, 1969.

Hildreth, G.N.: *Readiness for School Beginners*. New York, World Book, 1950.

Hoggard, J.K.: Readiness is the best prevention. In Harris, A.J. (Ed.): *Readings on Reading Instruction*. New York, McKay, 1967.

Honzik, M.P., MacFarlane, J.W., and Allen, L.: The stability of mental test performance between two and eighteen years. *J Exp Educ, 17*:309-324, 1948.

Hunt, J.M.: *Intelligence and Experience*. New York, Ronald, 1961.

Hurlock. E.B.: *Child Development*, 4th ed. New York, McGraw, 1968.

Ilg, F.L., and Ames, L.B.: *School Readiness*. New York, Har-Row, 1965.

Inhelder, B.: Criteria for the states of mental development. In Tanner, J.M., and Inhelder, B. (Eds.): *Discussions on Child Development*. New York, Intl U Pr, 1953.

Isaacs, S.: *Social Development in Young Children*. London, Routledge & Kegan Paul, 1933.

Jones, M.V.: *Language Development. The Key to Learning*. Springfield, Thomas, 1972.

Kagan, J.: Impulsive and reflective children: Significance of conceptual tempo. In Krumboltz, J.D. (Ed.): *Learning and the Educative Process*. Chicago, Rand, 1965.

Katzman, T.M.: Distribution and produciton in a big city elementary school system. *Yale Econ Essays, 8*:201-256, 1968.

Kellogg, R.: Analyzing children's art. In Jones, M.V. (Ed.): *Language Development. The Key to Learning*. Springfield, Thomas, 1972.

Kendrick, W.M.: *A Comparative Study of Two First Grade Language Arts Programs*. San Diego, Calif Dept Educ, 1966.

Kermoian, S.B.: Teacher appraisal of first grade readiness. *Elem Eng, 39*:196-201, 1962.

King, E.M.: Beginning reading: When and how. *Reading Teacher, 22*:550-553, 1969.

Kinsbourne, M., and Warrington, E.D.: The development of finger differentiation. In Chalfant, J.C., and Scheffelin, M. (Eds.): *Central Processing Dysfunctions in Children: A Review of Research*. Bethesda, U.S. Dept. of Health, Education and Welfare, 1969.

Kohlberg, L., Yaeger, J., and Hjertholm, E.: Private speech: Four studies and a review of theories. *Child Dev, 39*:691-736, 1968.

LaConte, C.: Reading in kingergarten. *Reading Teacher, 23*:116-120, 1969.

Langer, J.H.: Vocabulary and concept development. *J Reading, 10*:448-456, 1967.

Leiderman, F.G., and Rosenthal-Hill, I.: The elementary mathematics study. Educational Research Information Center, 1968.

Lenneberg, E.: *Biological Foundations of Language.* New York, Wiley, 1967.

Lewis, M.M.: *Infant Speech.* New York, Humanities, 1951.

Loban, W.D.: *The Language of Elementary School Children.* Champaign, National Council of Teachers of English, 1963.

Lord, F.M.: Further problems in the measurement of growth. *Educ Psychol Measurement, 18*:437-454, 1958.

Lord, F.M.: The measurement of growth. *Educ Psychol Measurement, 16*:421-437, 1956.

Mager, R.F.: *Preparing Instructional Objectives.* Palo Alto, Fearon, 1962.

Markey, J.F.: *The Symbolic Process.* London, Routledge, Kegan Paul, 1928. Cited by Langer, J.: *Theories of Development.* New York, HR&W, 1969.

Mason, G.E.: Preschoolers' concepts of reading. *Reading Teacher, 21*:130-132, 1967.

McClelland, D.: *The Achieving Society.* Princeton, Van Nostrand, 1961.

McGrady, H.J.: Visual and auditory learning processes in normal children and children with specific learning disabilities. Educational Research Information Center, 1967.

McLaughlin, K.: Kindergarten education. In Monroe, W. (Ed.): *Encyclopedia of Educational Research.* New York, MacMillan, 1960.

McLeod, J.: Some psycholinguistic correlates of reading disability in young children. *Reading Res, 2* (no. 3): 5-31, 1967.

McNeil, J.D., and Coleman, J.C.: *Auditory Discrimination Training in the Development of Word Analysis Skills.* Los Angeles, U of Calif Pr, 1967.

Mecham, M.S.: Shaping adequate speech, hearing and language behavior. In Mecham, M.S., et al. (Eds.); *Communication Training in Childhood Brain Damage.* Springfield, Thomas, 1966.

Menyuk, P.: Children's learning and reproduction of grammatical and non-grammatical phonological sequences. *Child Dev, 39*:849-859, 1968.

Menyuk, P.: A preliminary evaluation of grammatical capacity in children. *J Verbal Learning and Behavior, 2*:429-439, 1963.

Miller, G.A.: *Language and Communication.* New York, McGraw, 1951.

Montessori, M.: *The Absorbent Mind.* New York, HR&W, 1969.

Montessori, M.: *The Montessori Method.* Cambridge, Bentley, 1964.

Morrison, C.A.: A comparison of the reading performance of early and non-early readers from grade one through grade three. City University of New York, Division of Teacher Education, 1968, p. 44.

Muehl, S.: Effects of visual discrimination pretraining with word and letter stimuli on learning to read a word list in kindergarten children. *J Educ,*

53:215-221, 1961.

Mussen, P.M., Conger, J., and Kagan, J.: *Child Development and Personality,* 2nd ed. New York, Har-Row, 1963.

National Education Association: Kindergarten education in the public schools, 1967-68. Washington, D.C., Research Division, 1969.

National Education Association Research Bulletin: Curriculum change is taking place. *48*:103-105, 1970.

National Education Association Research Bulletin: Pupil-staff ratios. *46*:1, 1968.

North A.F.: Research issues in health and nutrition in early childhood. Educational Research Information Center, 1968.

Oakland, T.: *Relationships between Social Class & Phonemic and Nonphonemic Auditory Discrimination Ability.* Los Angeles, American Educational Research Association, 1969.

O'Donnell, C.: A comparison of the reading readiness of kindergarten pupils exposed to conceptual-language and basal reader prereading programs. Augusta, Maine Department of Education, 1968.

Osser, H., Wang, M., Farida, Z.: The young child's ability to imitate and comprehend speech: A comparison of two subcultural groups. *Child Dev, 40*:1063-1075, 1969.

Overstreet, B.W.: *Understanding Fear.* New York, Har-Row, 1951.

Owen, F.W.: The Palo Alto study of educationally handicapped children. Paper read at Society for Research in Child Development Meeting, Santa Monica, Calif., 1969.

Peatman, J.G.: *Descriptive & Sampling Statistics.* New York, Harper Brothers, 1947.

Pendergast, K., et al.: An articulation study of 15,255 Seattle first grade children with and without kindergarten. Seattle Public Schools, 1966.

Perry, H.W.: A perceptual training program for children with learning disorders. Educational Research Information Center, 1968.

Piaget, J.: *Judgment and Reasoning in the Child.* London, Routledge and Kegan Paul, 1951.

Piaget, J.: *The Language and Thought of the Child.* New York, Meridian Bks, 1957.

Piaget, J.: *Psychology and Intelligence.* Patterson, Littlefield, 1963.

Piaget, J.: *Six Psychological Studies.* New York, Random, 1967.

Pringle-Kellner, M.L.: *Deprivation and Education.* London, Longmans Green, 1965.

Rankin, P.D.: The similarity of lower case letters of the English alphabet. *J Verbal Learning and Behavior,* 7:990-995, 1968.

Redalia, B.: The psychological reality of the apparent perceptual dimensions of the alphabet. Educational Research Information Center, 1969.

Redl, F., and Wineman, D.: *The Aggressive Child.* Glencoe, Free Pr, 1957.

Reid, J.F.: Learning to think about reading. *Educ. Res,* 9:56-62, 1966.

Rieber, M.: Mediational aids and motor skill learning in children. *Child Dev, 39*:559-567, 1968.

Robison, H.F., and Spodek, B.: *New Directions in the Kindergarten.* New York, Tchrs Coll, 1965.

Rohr, A.M.: A multi-district use of visual training as an instructional approach in elementary education. Educational Research Information Center, 1968.

Rosen, C.L.: Visual deficiencies and reading disability. *J Reading, 9:*57-61, 1965.

Rosenhan, D.: The kindnesses of children. *Young Children, 25:*30-44, 1969.

Rosner, J.: Perceptual skills — a concern of the classroom teacher. *Reading Teacher, 24:*544-549, 1971.

Ruddell, R.B., and Graves, B.W.: Socio-ethnic status and the language achievement of first grade children. *Elem Eng, 46:*635-642, 1968.

Rudolph, M., and Cohen, D.H.: *Kindergarten, a Year of Learning.* New York, Appleton, 1964.

Rulon, P.J.: A simplified procedure for determining the reliability of a test by split halves. *Harv Educ Rev, 9:*99-103, 1939.

Samuels, S.J.: Letter-name versus letter-sound knowledge in learning to read. *Reading Teacher, 24:*604-608, 1971.

Scandura, J.M., and McGhee, R.: An exploratory investigation of basic mathemtical abilities of kindergarten children. *Educ Studies Math, 4:*331-345, 1972.

Schoephoerster, H., Barnhart, R., and Loomer, W.M.: The teaching of prereading skills in kindergarten. *Reading Teacher, 19:*352-357, 1966.

Scholes, R.J.: The role of grammaticality in the imitation of word strings by children and adults. *J Verbal Learning and Behavior, 8:*225-228, 1969.

Sears, R.R., Maccoby, E.E., and Levin, H.: *Patterns of Child Rearing.* Evanston, Row, Peterson, 1957.

Sheldon, W.D., Stinson, F., and Peebles, J.D.: Comparison of three methods of reading: A continuation study in the third grade. *Reading Teacher, 22:*539-546, 1969.

Sigel, I.E., and McBane, B.: Cognitive competence and level of symbolism among 5-year-old children. Paper read at the American Psychological Association Meeting, New York, 1966.

Sloane, H.N., and MacAulay, B.D.: *Operant Procedures in Remedial Speech and Language Training.* Boston, HM, 1968.

Slobin, D.I., and Welsh, C.A.: Elicited imitation as a research tool in developmental linguistics. Educational Research Information Center, 1967.

Sonenberg, C., and Glass, G.G.: Reading and speech: An incidence and treatment study. *Reading Teacher, 19:*197-201, 1965.

Stanchfield, J.M.: Development of prereading skills in an experimental kindergarten program. *Reading Teacher, 24:*699-707, 1971.

Steinberg, I.S.: *Educational Myths and Realities.* Boston, A-W, 1968.

Stephens, B.: *Training the Developmentally Young.* New York, McKay, 1972.

Strang, R.: *An Introduction to Child Study.* 4th ed. New York, Macmillan, 1959.

Sullivan, H.S.: *The Interpersonal Theory of Psychiatry.* New York, Norton,

1953.

Sutphin, F.E.: *Perceptual Testing-Training Handbook for First Grade Teachers.* Winter Haven, Boyd Brothers, 1966.

Sutton, M.H.: Children who learned to read in kindergarten. *Reading Teacher,* 22:595-602, 1969.

Sutton-Smith, B.: Novel signifiers in play. Unpublished manuscript, Bowling Green University, 1967.

Templin, M.C.: The identification of kindergarten children least likely to show spontaneous improvement in speech sound articulation. University of Minnesota, Minneapolis Institute of Child Development, 1967.

Thompson. B.: A longitudinal study of auditory discrimination. *J Educ Res,* 56:376-378, 1963.

Torrance, E.P.: Explorations in creative thinking in the early school years: Talkativeness and creative thinking. University of Minnesota, Research Memorandum, 1959.

Torrance, E.P.: Peer influences on preschool children's willingness to try difficult tasks. *J Psychol,* 72:189-194, 1969.

Travers, J.F.: *Fundamentals of Educational Psychology.* Scranton, Intext, 1970.

Travers, R.N.: Reinforcement in classroom learning. Educational Research Information Center, 1964.

Turnure, J.E.: Children's reactions to distractors in a learning situation. Educational Research Information Center, 1968.

University City School District, Missouri: Kindergarten research study. U. S. Office of Education, 1967.

Utley, J.: *What's Its Name: A Guide to Speech and Hearing Development.* Urbana, U of Ill Pr, 1950.

Vygotsky, L.S.: *Thought and Language.* New York, Wiley, 1962.

Wang, M.: An investigation of selected procedures for measuring and predicting rate of learning in classrooms operating under a program of individualized instruction. Educational Research Information Center, 1968.

Washburne, C., and Morphett, M.W.: When should elementary children begin to read? *Elem Sch J, 31:*496-503, 1931.

Wattenburg, W.W., and Clare, C.: Relation of self concepts to beginning achievement in reading. *Child Dev, 35:*461-467, 1964.

Weber, E.: *The Kindergarten.* New York, Tchrs Coll, 1969.

Weiner, M., and Feldmann, S.: Validation studies of a reading prognosis test for children of lower and middle socio-economic status. *Educ Psychol Measurement, 23:*807-814, 1963.

Wellman, B.L.: IQ changes of preschool and non-preschool groups during the preschool years: A summary of the literature. *J Psychol, 20:*347-368, 1945.

Wepman, J.M.: Auditory discrimination, speech and reading. *Elem Sch J,* 60:325-333, 1960.

Westman, J.C., et al.: Nursery school behavior and later school adjustment. *Am J Orthopsychiatry, 37:*725-731, 1967.

Weintge, K., and Dubois, P.: Criteria in learning research, report on a conference. St. Louis, Washington University, 1966.

Wilt, M.E.: A study of teacher awareness of listening as a factor in elementary education. *J Educ Res, 43*:626-636, 1950.

INDEX

gross motor, 126
Muehl, S., 214
Multiple regression analysis, 179
Music, 114
  creative movement and, 116
  language and, 114
Mussen, P. M., 215

N

National Education Association, 5, 7, 8, 10-11, 18, 83
Non-adjustment, 50
North, A. F., 19
Numerical skills, 139
  exercises, 156
  one-to-one correspondence, 144
Nurturance, 36

O

Oakland, T., 215
O'Donnell, C., 215
Oral expression, 75
  grammar, 70
  language program, 72
Osser, H., 215
Overstreet, B. W., 36
Owen, F. W., 17

P

Parental, conflict, 39
  involvement, 8
Partners, 46, 139
Patterns, 147
Peatman, J. G., 180
Peer relationships, 48
Pendergast, K., 80
Perceptual-motor, 125-138
  activities, 133
  fine motor, 130
  gross motor, 126
  skills, 125
Perry, H. W., 215
Picture interpretation, 74
Piaget, J., 23, 66, 139
Play, creative, 44
Positive contact, 49

Pluralization, 76
Pringle-Kellner, M. L., 215

Q

Questions, 78

R

Rankin, P. D., 103
Rapport, 183
Rate of learning, 161-170
  components, 165
    independent learning activity, 169
    learning style, 166
    retaining directions, 168
    retention, 163
    self confidence, 167
    span of concentration, 168
    task completion, 169
    task orientation, 167
  influences on, 161
  model, 162
Rate of Learning Test, 171-187
  administration, 182
  converting raw scores, 188
  counting blocks, 172
  differences, 172
  drawings, 172
  follow-up study, 180
  intercorrelation, 174
  interpretation, 188-204
    concluding statement, 203
    gain scores, 199
    pretest, 200
    posttest, 200
  introduction, 171
  occupational comparison, 174
  picture vocabulary, 171
  reliability
    of pretest, 175
    of posttest, 176
  scoring, 184
  sentence memory, 171
  standardization sample, 173
  stanine equivalents of raw scores, 190
  statistical analysis, 173
Rationale, 28